GW01374406

THE BOMBAY PLAN

Praise for the book

This important book draws attention to the historic and patriotic role of Indian business leaders in the building of Independent India.

—Ratan Tata, Chairman Emeritus,
Tata Sons and Chairman, Tata Trusts

Prominent journalist Sanjaya Baru and the eminent economist Meghnad Desai must be congratulated for rescuing from oblivion the Bombay Plan, whose publication was a landmark event in India's developmental efforts.

—Jagdish Bhagwati,
Author of *In Defense of Globalization*, and
co-author of *India's Tryst with Destiny*

A re-reading of the Bombay Plan after 74 years creates a sense of deja vu. The top industrialist and technocrats were struggling with the same issues of today—'how much of government and how much of private', 'how much of self-reliance and how much of openness (globalisation)'. The wrenching renditions and pungent critiques in this book, edited by Dr Sanjay Baru and Lord Meghnad Desai, make exciting reading, adding great value to the contemporary debates on the political economy of India. This book is a must read for a 360 degree view of India's unfolding saga of radical change with inherent continuity.

—Dr Amit Mitra, Finance Minister,
Government of West Bengal, and
Former Secretary-General, FICCI.

Edited by
SANJAYA BARU
MEGHNAD DESAI

THE BOMBAY PLAN
Blueprint for Economic Resurgence

RUPA

Published by
Rupa Publications India Pvt. Ltd 2018
7/16, Ansari Road, Daryaganj
New Delhi 110002

Sales Centres:
Allahabad Bengaluru Chennai
Hyderabad Jaipur Kathmandu
Kolkata Mumbai

Copyright © Sanjaya Baru & Meghnad Desai 2018

The views and opinions expressed in this book are the authors' own and the facts are as reported by them which have been verified to the extent possible, and the publishers are not in any way liable for the same.

While every effort has been made to trace copyright holders and obtain permission, this has not been possible in all cases; any omissions brought to our attention will be remedied in future editions.

All rights reserved.

No part of this publication may be reproduced, transmitted, or stored in a retrieval system, in any form or by any means, electronic, mechanical, photocopying, recording or otherwise, without the prior permission of the publisher.

ISBN: 978-93-5304-937-9

First impression 2018

10 9 8 7 6 5 4 3 2 1

The moral right of the authors has been asserted.

Printed at Parksons Graphics Pvt. Ltd., Mumbai

This book is sold subject to the condition that it shall not,
by way of trade or otherwise, be lent, resold, hired out,
or otherwise circulated, without the publisher's prior consent,
in any form of binding or cover other than that in which it is published.

CONTENTS

Introduction: A Unique Document that Merits Attention / vii
Sanjaya Baru and Meghnad Desai

A Plan for India's Economic Transformation / 1
P.S. Lokanathan

The Making of a Mythical Forerunner / 19
Amal Sanyal

The Bombay Plan and the Frustrations of Sir Ardeshir Dalal / 64
Gita Piramal

A Vision Derailed / 94
Omkar Goswami

Business, Government and Politics: From Plan to Plea / 124
Sanjaya Baru

Created by Business, For Business / 148
Tulsi Jayakumar and R. Gopalakrishnan

Whatever Happened to the Indian Bourgeoisie? / 173
Meghnad Desai

The Surprising Genesis of our State Albatross / 197
Ajay Chhibber

APPENDICES / 225
Appendix I: The Viceroy's Executive Council / 225
Appendix II: Council of Scientific and Industrial Research (CSIR) Constituted: September 26, 1942 / 227
Appendix III: Indian Civil Service Application and Results, 1870-1914 / 229
Appendix IV: Ardeshir Dalal Lifeline / 229
Appendix V: The Bombay Plan Document / 233

Acknowledgements / 333

Index / 335

INTRODUCTION

A UNIQUE DOCUMENT THAT MERITS ATTENTION

Sanjaya Baru and Meghnad Desai

A document of a little over a hundred pages called 'A Plan of Economic Development for India', written in two parts and published in 1944–45, generated widespread interest in India and abroad at the time of its publication. The influential American journal *Foreign Affairs* carried an extensive review written by P.S. Lokanathan—a distinguished economist, United Nations (UN) official and Editor, *Hindustan Times*. There was every reason why the document deserved the attention it got. Its authors were none other than J.R.D. Tata, G.D. Birla, Purushottamdas Thakurdas, Kasturbhai Lalbhai, Ardeshir Dalal, Lala Shri Ram, John Mathai and A.D. Shroff—all business leaders and economic policymakers of repute.

The document's importance derived not only from its impressive list of authors, but also from the fact that it was a unique document in the history of postcolonial development. Nowhere in the developing world had a group of business leaders come together to articulate such a comprehensive vision for national development that simultaneously promoted their own class interests. In doing so, the Indian capitalist class, led by its business leaders, played a vanguard role in the consolidation of India's bourgeois revolution, so to speak. By demanding the creation of a single national economic space and seeking social development and agrarian change, a nascent capitalist class played a historic role in national development. It is worth remarking that these business leaders had built up their businesses against considerable odds. They needed the British rulers even though they constantly challenged them with the charge that Indian industry was being neglected to the benefit of their British counterparts. They also befriended the nationalists, fully cognizant of the risks of alienating the foreign rulers.

J.R.D. Tata was head of an industrial house which dealt in many different sectors, but most famously in steel. G.D. Birla was a traditional Marwari family business head, and a friend of Mahatma Gandhi. Kasturbhai Lalbhai was a textile industrialist from Ahmedabad, sympathetic to the nationalist cause. Sir Purushottamdas Thakurdas was the senior leader in this group. He had been drafted

A UNIQUE DOCUMENT THAT MERITS ATTENTION

into the official committee for a report on the Indian currency problem, and was a liberal leader loyal to the British government. Even so, his experience was considered valuable for drafting the Bombay Plan. The three remaining members—Dalal, Shroff and Mathai—were not industrialists themselves, but managers and administrators in business houses.

The group had a grip on the larger organized sector of Indian industries. All of them wanted the country, when independent, to do well. This is why they formulated the document popularly known as The Bombay Plan. This document has disappeared not just from public memory, but also from undergraduate textbooks of Indian economics.

It is something of a puzzle we need to explore at the outset. The elite of the somewhat small business class, which had grown under a colonial regime, felt that it should take the lead to set out an ambitious programme for economic development (itself a novel idea in the 1940s) as a gesture of helpful partnership with the nationalist leadership, which would be new to the task of governance. The business elite had maintained a friendship with the nationalists while taking care not to antagonise the colonial powers they had to deal with in their daily operations. The new leadership, having to learn on the job, would be heading a new State that would be fragile, and, no doubt, in need of help. The business elite was the Older Brother, knowledgeable in the task of running an economy. It is pertinent to note that it could have used the transition to Independence to establish its hegemony. But far from advocating extensive freedom for business to get on with the job of growth while the State could play the role of a Night Watchman, it gave pride of place to the forthcoming State. In its turn, when the nationalist political leadership did come to power, it spurned the offer of help extended by the business elite and embarked not only on a Statist policy (as advocated by the Bombay Plan) but also on a business-unfriendly strategy. As time passed, the political leadership moved to reverse the power equation between politics and business. Business became subordinate to politics even as it expanded.

This collection of essays is aimed at bringing current policy and academic attention to a document that was not only prescient in its approach to development but was also influential in shaping economic planning and public policy in the first decade of India's Independence. The Bombay Plan shaped the thinking underlying India's first and second Five Year Plans (1952–62). This volume puts together seminal papers published on the Bombay Plan and essays written more recently on it.

According to P.S. Lokanathan, the extraordinarily favourable reception that was accorded to the Plan can be explained in terms of 'an unusual conjunction of circumstances'. First was its timing, coming as it did at the end of the Second World War, and in the aftermath of the Bengal famine. It defined the hope for post-War reconstruction. Its brevity and simple language made it highly accessible to a wide cross-section of people.

Amal Sanyal shows why India's first three Five Year Plans owe a significant amount of intellectual debt to the Bombay Plan—a fact that has not been acknowledged officially. He then moves on to ask why the Plan got so completely wiped off public memory and why, in particular, Indian political parties including the Indian National Congress (INC), the Government of India, and the authors of the Plan let it sink unceremoniously into oblivion.

Sanyal believes that the Plan had faded out of public memory as completely as it had occupied centrestage soon after publication. This is curious because the Plan's strategy and methods foreshadowed the official Five Year Plans of independent India launched just a few years later. Hence it would have been educative to use the Bombay Plan to discuss the evolution of the methods and strategies of official planning in India. Yet it has not been used for this purpose. Secondly, the Bombay Plan's targets were overwhelmingly more ambitious than anything the Planning Commission of the government ever attempted. It had envisaged the doubling of per capita income over fifteen years and proposed appropriate sources of finance for that ambitious target. The Planning Commission never addressed why a target close to the Bombay Plan's was never aimed by it.

Gita Piramal's essay is a tribute to the man she believes was not just the principal author of the Bombay Plan, but also someone who got a shot at implementing it under the aegis of the Imperial government. Ardeshir Dalal, the first Indian Resident Director on the board of Tata Iron & Steel Company, served three Tata chairmen: Sir Dorab Tata, who made Dalal a Director and Partner in Tata Sons; Sir Nowroji Saklatwala (1932–1938) and J.R.D. Tata (1938–1991). He also had had the privilege of being the one to second the proposal, in 1938, that J.R.D. Tata be appointed Group Chairman.

As part of the inner circle, Dalal graduated to the directorships of Andhra Valley Power Supply Company, Associated Cement Companies, Tata Oil Mills, the Taj Mahal Hotel and Tata Chemicals until 1944, when he resigned from all Tata positions to join the Viceroy's Executive Council. The British Imperial government's decision to induct a couple of architects of the Bombay Plan into the government appeared to have the merit of combining damage control with political advantage. While John Mathai was appointed finance minister, Dalal was inducted into the Viceroy's Executive Council as Member-in-Charge of Post-War Reconstruction. Both accepted their positions and resigned from the Tata Group.

A UNIQUE DOCUMENT THAT MERITS ATTENTION

Given the historic importance of the Bombay Plan and the distinguished status of its authors, many have wondered why the Plan has been long forgotten. It was never kept in public memory by its authors, all public men of great standing for decades after its publication, or by the Federation of Indian Chambers of Commerce and Industry (FICCI), the organization that played an important role in its publication. Professional economists hardly bothered to write about it or include it in their teaching of Indian economics. The government of the day never acknowledged that its own Plans were inspired by it. Omkar Goswami blames all of them for the Plan's disappearance from public memory. While the Plan was in fact drafted as a 'nationalist' rather than a 'capitalist' document, says Goswami, Nehru did not wish to own it because of his 'Left Wing' leaning. Nehru would rather credit Mahalanobis and the Soviets for inspiring Indian Plans rather than acknowledge that he was walking the path defined by India's leading industrialists.

Jayakumar and Gopalakrishnan argue that the Bombay Plan was woefully inadequate in defining how the political and administrative leadership at the time could in fact manage the change suggested. The Plan ignored 'the human vector of change management'. They raise the larger question of whether, on an ongoing basis in national public policy, there is sufficient attention paid to the learning derived from cultural experiences in change management. Within companies, the awareness is high, and the attempt to incorporate behavioural techniques is expanding rapidly. It is, of course, far more difficult to do this in a country with as large and diverse a population as India. However, recognizing the cultural vector of change management is exceedingly important in planning and execution of change and must feature more prominently in national planning initiatives. The Bombay Plan's irrelevance may have been due to the absence of an operational strategy.

Meghnad Desai's essay draws attention to an interesting aspect of the political economy of Independent India. The Bombay Plan, he argues, validates the view that the Indian capitalist class ought to be defined as a 'National Bourgeoisie'—as indeed the Communist Party of India (CPI) did in the 1960s. Those among the communists who saw the bourgeoisie as comprador were off-track. Why then did Jawaharlal Nehru not embrace the national bourgeoisie? Desai draws attention to an important fact of contemporary history that is often forgotten— the Congress's principal political adversary in the first decade after Independence were the communists. Nehru had to embrace 'socialism' and distance himself from the business class in order to preserve his own political base. The communist threat to the Congress was real and the parting of ways between the Congress leadership and business leadership was one consequence of that. By the time of Indira Gandhi, especially after she had concentrated power in her hands, the condition of the business elite became much more subservient. The Communist Party was enticed into a subordinate partnership with the Congress and the language of politics became much more Leftist and hostile to business.

Both Goswami and Desai suggest that after the experience of the 1950s, Indian business leadership never again sought an intellectual leadership role for itself. Seventy-four years since the publication of the Bombay Plan, one can confidently say that there is neither the desire nor the courage among the bourgeoisie and their organised bodies like FICCI, Confederation of Indian Industry (CII) and The Associated Chambers of Commerce & Industry of India (Assocham) to repeat such an exercise.

Ajay Chhibber asks an interesting question: could India have followed a different path had the Bombay Plan proposed an alternative approach? He does not rule that out. In his view, one would have expected business groups to look for State support for their own development—much like Zaibatsu in Japan, or the Chaebols in Korea. But India's largest business groups prepared a Plan that ceded key sectors of the economy to State control and ownership, supporting the views of political leaders like Nehru. Perhaps because the Plan paid so much attention to key development priorities such as provision of water and sanitation, primary education and adult literacy, and basic health care, it inevitably ended up giving a larger than expected role to the government in the development process.

Sanjaya Baru argues that the relationship between business and politics has travelled all the way from the vanguard role played by business in the national movement to the ideological divide within the business class between those, like Tata, who believed it was in the interests of the business class to support pro-free market political parties, and others like Birla, who seemed willing to reconcile themselves to operating within the 'cronyism' inherent to the so-called 'Licence-Permit-Control Raj.' In the end, Indian business learnt to adapt itself to the political reality at home rather than seek to change it. Baru credits the Plan for its focus on education, healthcare and agrarian change—all areas neglected by the Mahalanobis plans and areas that have only more recently secured the policy attention they ought to have had immediately after Independence. Baru also wonders why, in more recent years, the leadership of Indian business has acted more as a supplicant for government support seeking concessions, rather than shaping its policy as questions remain about the global competitiveness of Indian industry. Its role remains marginal in shaping the policy discourse.

Has India been a loser because its democratically elected political leadership spurned the friendly help of the business sector, neglected to give it a proper role in economic development and conducted a hostile struggle with it? Was 1991 too late to reverse the balance of power and realise that Statism had cost decades of slow growth?

While academic historians and economists have paid some attention to the Bombay Plan, the fact is that it has disappeared from public memory despite the many valuable ideas it contained and their continued relevance in India's policy discourse. Hopefully, the re-publication of the original Plan and these essays will help revive wider public interest in a unique document in development economics and postcolonial development.

A PLAN FOR INDIA'S ECONOMIC TRANSFORMATION

P.S. Lokanathan[1]

A small group of influential business leaders in Bombay drew up and published in January of 1944, a plan for the economic development of India which may be said to have opened a new chapter in Indian economic history. This Plan was originally intended for private circulation only; and the decision to publish it in pamphlet form with wide consequent publicity, came afterward. The Bombay Plan, as it is now popularly called, did not represent the opinion of the whole business community. But it claimed public attention because it set forth the considered views

---

[1]This is a slightly modified version of the essay that was first published as a book review in *Foreign Affairs*, 1945. Accessed at: https://www.foreignaffairs.com/articles/india/1945-07-01/bombay-plan

of some of the front-rank businessmen and captains of Indian industry.

The signatories were not merely men of business experience, but were inspired by more than a fair measure of public spirit and responsibility. Mr J.R.D. Tata and Mr G.D. Birla were primarily responsible for the initiation of the study. Mr Tata is head of the well-known House of Tata, and is noted in India for his progressive outlook on life and business. Mr Birla, the head of Birla Brothers, who own and manage a variety of industrial enterprises, is interested in educational and social work. Sir P. Thakurdas, the doyen of the business community, has enjoyed a reputation for possessing a wide outlook and for courageous thinking and speaking. Mr Kasturbhai Lalbhai and Sir Shri Ram are leading mill-owners in Ahmedabad and Delhi respectively, and have business activities extending to other fields. The other three signatories—Sir Ardeshir Dalal, Mr A.D. Shroff and Dr John Mathai—are employees and directors of Tata Sons, Ltd., and the fact that they too signed the pamphlet is significant as showing that it was in no sense to be regarded as an industrialist's plan, at least when it was put out.

The reception accorded to the Plan was unique. Within a few days of its publication, the demand for copies was so great that it had to be reprinted for several successive months. Public interest has continued to this day. The Plan has been translated into other languages than English for publication both in India and abroad and has been read by millions of people. Within a few weeks of its publication, Lord Wavell, Viceroy of India, welcomed it in a speech to the Legislature and found in it a new approach to the solution of India's intractable political problems. Sir Jeremy Raisman, Finance Member of the Executive Council, called it a useful contribution in his Budget speech in February 1944, though he doubted the soundness of some of its financial assumptions. The public and the press joined in the discussion and prompted a clarification of the document by the signatories. Towards the end of March, FICCI endorsed the Bombay Plan at its annual meeting, and from then on the Plan came to be regarded as the proposal of India's business community, if not of India's big business.

The extraordinarily favourable reception which was accorded the scheme can be explained only in terms of an unusual conjunction of circumstances. It came out at an opportune moment. The country, disillusioned and disappointed with the slow pace of industrialization, and saddened by the tragic experience of a famine which had exacted a heavy toll of lives in Bengal, was ready for any kind of solution which would bring a ray of hope. And it feared that the talk of post-war reconstruction indulged in by the government was not sincere. Above all, the brevity of the Plan and the remarkably simple and powerful language in which it is set forth contributed to its successful reception.

A BEACON OF HOPE

The Bombay Plan does not provide a complete scheme of economic development; much less does it pretend to be a blueprint for action. All that it does is 'to put forward as a basis of discussion, a statement in as concrete a form as possible, of the objectives to be kept in mind in economic planning in India, the general lines on which development should proceed and the demands which planning is likely to make on the country's resources.' The principal objectives of the Plan are to achieve a balanced economy and to raise the standard of living of the masses of the population rapidly by doubling the present per capita income—i.e. increasing it from $22 to about $45—within a period of fifteen years from the time the Plan goes into operation. A preliminary period of three to five years is to be devoted to preparing the details of the Plan. Unfortunately, however, the per capita income in a country whose population (386,000,000 in 1941) has been increasing at the rate of nearly 1.5 per cent per annum cannot be doubled unless total income increases at a faster rate than the per capita income; hence the planners provide for trebling the total income in order to double the income per person.

Planning in India runs up against a serious difficulty at the outset. There are no reliable figures of national income, and the only reasonably trustworthy estimate is for that of 1931–32, an abnormal year. The Plan had to be framed on the figures of a period of relatively low prices; prices today are 200 to 250 per cent higher than those of 1931–39. The planners warn that 'money is used throughout as a measuring rod only; and in order to keep the measure uniform we have based all money figures on the rupee at the average price level which prevailed during the period 1931-39.' However inescapable and justifiable this method, statistics in the Plan which are expressed in terms of money have no current basis and an element of unreality runs through all of them.

The inadequacy of the present income for even the most essential requirements of the people is vividly apparent in the miserable living conditions of most of India's millions. The planners have laid down minimum living standards on the basis of about 2,800 calories of well-balanced food a day for each person, 30 yards of clothing and 100 square feet of housing; and they also outline the minimum needs for elementary education, sanitation, water supply, village dispensaries and hospitals. The Plan points out that absolutely minimum needs require an annual income of at least $25; and if the income of the country were equally distributed it would give each individual only about $22. The problem is to increase production and to devise a programme for putting the minimum within the reach of all. But this minimum promises only bare subsistence; no one can be satisfied with it. There must be some margin for enjoyment of life and cultural opportunities, and this can be provided only if the total income increases at least to thrice the present level.

This goal, according to the Plan, is to be reached by altering the relative proportions in which agriculture, industry and services contribute to the national income, and increasing the output from agriculture by 130 per cent, from industry by 500 per cent, and from services by 200 per cent. The shares of agriculture, industry and services in the total production are to be changed from 53, 17 and 22 per cent, respectively, to 40, 35 and 20 per cent (neglecting some categories of income not classified). Precisely how these changes in output are to be effected has not been made clear in the report.

The basis of the Indian economy would continue to be agricultural even after this goal was reached. Some critics have said, however, that the Plan lays undue stress on industrialization and sets its sights too low in regard to agriculture. But the Plan explains that India's industrial potentialities are now largely unexploited and that there is much greater leeway for expansion in this field. And agricultural experts have pointed out that even to double the agricultural output in fifteen years would not be an easy task, and that the scheduled increase of 130 per cent is perhaps more than can be managed. Indeed, the most optimistic estimate of the Department of Agriculture dares hope for no more than a 50 per cent increase in 10 years and perhaps a 100 per cent increase in fifteen years. It is unlikely; in fact, that an increase of more than 130 per cent would be required for all purposes, and the more important question is whether the methods suggested for carrying out the agricultural programme are reasonably efficient. The Plan pins its faith on technical methods of improving agriculture—irrigation, model farms, improved implements, etc.—and on bringing fresh land under cultivation. It recommends the consolidation of holdings and cooperative farming, but proposes no further agricultural reorganization. Whether these methods of solving the enormous problem will be adequate is doubtful. It seems to the writer that little improvement can be expected unless the system of land tenure is reorganized and the dead hand of landlordism is removed.

The Plan is highly realistic in its approach to industry. It emphasizes the importance of basic industries but also calls for the development of consumption goods industries in the early years of the Plan. Power heads the list of basic industries which are to be developed, followed by mining and metallurgy, engineering, chemicals, armaments, transport, cement and others.

The goal for expansion in each industry is not made clear. An important place is assigned to small-scale and cottage industries, and transport and communications are also to be developed. Here the objective is quite definite. The Plan proposes doubling the present total of 300,000 miles of roads, increasing railway mileage by 50 per cent from its present 41,000 miles, expanding coastal shipping and investing $150 million on improvement of harbours.

But the attention paid to the social services is the feature that has appealed most to the public. The Plan offers a comprehensive programme of mass education, including primary, secondary and vocational and university schooling. Provision is also made for adult education and scientific training and research. To finance this programme, a capital expenditure of $700 million and a recurring annual expenditure of nearly as much are recommended. A capital expenditure of $840 million and an annual expenditure of $555 million are provided. The Plan guarantees minimum housing for all. It is perhaps overambitious in this field, contemplating the building of nearly 55 million new houses at a cost of $6.6 billion. The capital expenditure proposed for the whole Plan (omitting the annual recurring expenditure) is $27.6 billion. The planners have added about $3 billion to this sum for the recurring expenditure for one year, which in their view may be provided from out of capital funds. The Bombay

A PLAN FOR INDIA'S ECONOMIC TRANSFORMATION

Plan thus proposes an overall investment of $30 billion in fifteen years.

From what source is this enormous sum of capital to be drawn? The Plan distinguishes between external finance, which would be available for payment to foreign countries for goods and services imported from them, and internal finance, for the mobilization of resources within the country. The Plan assumes that roughly $8 billion of external finance may be required and outlines the following methods of obtaining it. Though hoarded gold has been drawn upon for export since 1931, there are still large untapped amounts of it. The planners believe that 'if suitable means are adopted for attracting hoards from their place of concealment and if a national government comes into power in which people have faith,' about a billion dollars could be obtained. This would be available as foreign exchange. Secondly, as a result of India's new creditor position, the balance of trade will improve sufficiently to enable her to use at least about $120,000,000 annually for getting extra capital goods from abroad. In fifteen years this should come to about $1.8 billion. Thirdly, the Plan relies upon sterling balances accumulated to India's credit in Britain to the tune of about $3 billion. Finally, an external loan (mainly from the United States) of $2 billion or more to fill in the gap is advocated.

But the main reliance is placed on internal capital

resources. At the current rate of saving in India, reckoned at only 6 per cent of the annual income, about $12 billion of capital should be available during the 15-year period. But this is a conservative estimate. There are reasons to believe that the rate of saving is nearer 8 per cent than 6, and, as the annual income increases, a larger per centage may be expected to be saved. But whatever the estimated rate of savings, normal savings will clearly not be adequate to the needs; and here the Plan has resorted to the unorthodox method of raising capital by 'created money'. About $10 billion is expected to be obtained by borrowing against *ad hoc* securities from the Central Bank. The planners admit that new money in this amount can be created 'only if people have full confidence in the resources and bona fides of the government that creates it.' But there is nothing inherently wrong or unsound in this procedure, as in the long run assets equal in value to the created money would have been produced. It is recognized, however, that during the planning period there would be a gap between the volume of purchasing power in the hands of the people and the volume of goods available, leading to an inflationary situation. The planners boldly affirm that during this interval 'in order to prevent the inequitable distribution of the burden between different classes which this method of financing will involve, practically every aspect of economic life will have to be so rigorously controlled by government that individual liberty and freedom of enterprise will suffer a temporary eclipse.'

SHARP ATTACKS

No other feature of the Plan has been subjected to so severe or widespread a criticism as its financial aspect. Some of the criticisms are purely formal. For example, gold is said to be as much a country's internal capital as annual saving and therefore should not be classified as external finance. But the point of the classification is that gold is world money and a never-failing method of obtaining goods from abroad. Formally, it is also wrong to regard balance of trade as external capital. But here again, the planners were right in regarding the balance of trade as available for further import of goods from abroad, on the assumption that export and import controls will continue in the planning period. Another important criticism, not so much from India as from Britain, is that the financial foundation of the Plan is seriously shaky in so far as it relies upon sterling balances which may not be available for a considerable period after the war. The answer to this is that India has a right to expect that the question of unblocking sterling will be solved to her satisfaction, and that even if the balances are funded over a period, repayment will start immediately. If, for any reason, it is found that Britain cannot start the payment until, say, five years after the war, some arrangement should be concluded with the US, which would enable India to draw upon America until Britain is in a position to begin instalment payments. As regards $2 billion foreign loan, India believes that her credit is so strong and the investment opportunities which she can offer the rest of the world are so vast that there would be no difficulty in getting even twice this amount.

The sharpest attacks have been directed against 'created money'. It is said that there is danger in resorting to created money in the period after the war, when the country is still in its inflationary phase. But in the context of economic planning, created money has no perils at all. Indeed, the planners went wrong in treating the subject from the traditional point of view in terms of created money, rather than in terms of planned savings. This defect has since been remedied by Mr G.D. Birla, who pointed out in a clear and competent amplification of the Plan that what is required is annual savings of about 16 per cent, and that what they are called does not matter. He believes that such savings are practicable. Since the Plan gives special attention to the supply of consumption goods in the initial period, savings of 16 per cent may be achieved without imposing excessive or unequal burdens upon the poor, provided price control and rationing are effective. The Plan does not discuss the question of how the savings would be raised, but it obviously expects that several methods will be followed—taxation, direct restrictions on consumption, allocation to reserves in State-owned and controlled businesses, special allowances from taxation in reporting allocations to reserves, etc. The real issues are, first, how much control will be required to put through the financial scheme, and, second, how much control can or should the public stand?

In a final chapter, the Plan sketches in broad outlines the three five-year periods into which the scheme of economic development has been divided. In the first five-year period, the distribution of capital among basic industry, consumption goods industries, communications and services gives equal importance to the first two, and allocates smaller amounts to the latter two. In the second five-year period, basic industry is to receive another and still larger appropriation; in the third stage, the social services are to be allocated the largest amount, and the development of communications also receives special attention.

A POWERFUL APPEAL DESPITE FLAWS

This, then, is the substance of the Bombay Plan. It rests on one or two basic assumptions and does not pretend to be a complete programme. It assumes that details will be elaborated by a National Planning Committee to be set up by a national government enjoying the confidence of the people, and that the Plan will be executed by a supreme economic council. The scheme also postulates the economic unity of India as an essential condition of effective planning.

It has many a gap. It leaves for further examination such important questions as the methods to be used in putting the Plan through, and the principles on which industry is to be organized. Will industry be owned and directed by the State or by private enterprise? Or to what degree will the two principles be blended? And how is income to be distributed among the various sections of the people so as to guarantee to all the basic minimum which is the fundamental idea of the whole Plan? And yet, in spite of all the omissions, the Plan has rightly exerted a powerful appeal. It has made the country planning-conscious. And that the foremost industrialists of the country should go on record as being willing to subject themselves to a certain degree of social and economic control is itself no small gain.

To the outside world, the natural questions are:

1. Is this merely a paper plan, large-sounding but empty of content and unlikely to be adopted?
2. Is it practicable in the sense that the financial, technical and material resources necessary for its success are within reach?
3. If it succeeds, what effect would it have on the economy of the rest of the world? In particular, is so

A PLAN FOR INDIA'S ECONOMIC TRANSFORMATION

rapid an economic development of India advantageous from the American point of view?

These are highly important questions to which some answer should be attempted here.

The Plan is not a mere paper plan. Its influence is already apparent in the various schemes of post-war economic reconstruction prepared by the Government of India, and in the appointment of Sir Ardeshir Dalal, one of the signatories to the Bombay Plan, as head of the Government's Planning and Development Department. Within the framework of the existing constitution, but with the hope of obtaining powers of coordination and central control, the government has prepared a fairly comprehensive plan embracing the development of agriculture, forests, fishery and transport and the provision of education, sanitation, public health and other social services. Unlike the Bombay Plan, these proposals have no overall objective and are perhaps somewhat pedestrian in their methods. But there is no reason to think that the results of government planning would differ very materially from the goals set by the Bombay Plan. Both aim, for example, at doubling agricultural output, doubling transport facilities, liquidating illiteracy, providing sanitary and medical facilities and increasing industrial output. Only in respect of housing is the government scheme pitifully inadequate.

TOWARDS ECONOMIC TRANSFORMATION

Whatever the political conditions of the country are after the war, economic reconstruction of one kind or another will be undertaken. But the speed with which it is done will depend upon whether India is independent and can initiate and execute plans herself, and upon the kind of constitutional setup the country has. Central planning, central coordination and central direction are necessary for successful economic development; but it is impossible to say whether the provinces and states in the future Government of India will agree to subject themselves to so much control. There is no reason to think that the reconstruction scheme prepared by the industrialists is unsound or impracticable. The writer ventures to say that, contrary to general opinion, the financial shortcomings of the Plan are not the most serious ones. India is fortunately placed in this respect. Her internal financial resources are vast and untapped, her foreign balances substantial; loans from abroad may safely be expected. The more serious problem is one of administrative and technical personnel and lack of knowledge, of 'know-how'. It is here that the need for close cooperation between India and the West, particularly the US, is most essential. India must send out at least a few hundred men every year for training of all spheres of economic activity, and she must arrange to bring American engineers, technicians, chemists, businessmen and administrators to India. Another limitation of the Plan is the rate at which capital investment can be absorbed into the Indian economy. Absence of one or two essential factors can hold up any scheme, and India's planning period may have to be extended beyond fifteen years. It is also possible that some goals are set too high—that in agriculture, for example, unless there is to be radical reform of land-tenures and some form of collective farming. But despite all doubts and difficulties, there is no warrant for the view that the Plan is inherently impracticable.

A sudden transformation of India's economy would, of course, have a deep and far-reaching impact, but her economic development will have nothing but a favourable effect on the rest of the world. India does not propose to adopt self-sufficiency as her goal, although her special geographical and strategical position in Southeast Asia will no doubt influence her to become more self-sufficient than in the past. The immediate effect of her economic reconstruction will be a great impetus to imports from abroad, particularly from the US—perhaps the only country that can meet the demand. After she attains a fair degree of industrialization, the nature of her import and export trade will alter, but experience has shown that trade tends to radiate among industrial countries. Industrialized India will foster wider and larger international trade. A mounting standard of living for

India's millions will exert not a little power on the export possibilities of the rest of the world.

There are important reasons why Britain and especially America should encourage India's scheme of post-war economic reconstruction. For a year or so after the war, America may be fully engaged in meeting her own backlog demand, but subsequently India's demand will be a factor strengthening world economy and enabling America and Britain to maintain full employment. The fear that with American machinery India will build up industries which will ultimately damage America's markets or reduce her competitive power is unreal. The character of trade will alter with time, but at every stage there will be cost differences of hundreds of articles which will compel trade to flow from and to both regions. India's economic development will contribute to economic expansion and fuller employment both within her own borders and abroad.

◆

P.S. Lokanathan was Professor of Economics at Madras University and for many years Editor, *Eastern Economist*.

REFERENCES

[i] *The 'Bombay Plan' for India's Economic Development*. Bombay: The Commercial Printing Press, 1944.

THE MAKING OF A MYTHICAL FORERUNNER

Amal Sanyal

'The Bombay Plan' is the nickname of a 15-year economic plan for India proposed by a group of industrialists and technocrats in January 1944. Initially, it was released for private circulation only. Soon afterwards, the Plan was published as a pamphlet in response to the interest generated by it.[1] Demand led to a number of reprints within the first few months; the document was also translated into several languages during this period. Within a few weeks of publication, Lord Wavell, the Viceroy of India, mentioned it as containing a useful and novel approach to the country's economic problems,[2]

---

[1] *The 'Bombay Plan' for India's Economic Development,* Bombay, The Commercial Printing Press, 1944.
[2] He would however revise his opinion soon as British industry reacted adversely to the document. See footnote 25.

and Jeremy Raisman, the Finance Member, welcomed it, though doubting some of its financial assumptions (Lokanathan, 1945). By March of that year the FICCI endorsed the Plan at its annual meeting. Later, the document was edited by Purushottamdas Thakurdas into two tiny pamphlet-sized volumes[3] and published as *A Brief Memorandum Outlining a Plan of Economic Development for India* in 1945.

Looking back at it today, one cannot help feeling that the Plan lives a curious, almost spooky, existence. Books on Indian planning mention it as a mythical forerunner without revealing any more detail. Students generally get to know of the existence of such a document, but very few have had an encounter with it. The Plan has faded out of public memory as completely as it had occupied centrestage soon after publication. This is curious because the Plan's strategy and methods foreshadowed the official Five Year Plans of independent India launched just a few years later. Hence it would have been educative to use the Bombay Plan to discuss the evolution of the methods and strategies of official planning in India. But it has not been used for this purpose. Secondly, the Bombay Plan's targets were overwhelmingly more ambitious than anything the Planning Commission of the Government of India ever attempted. It had envisaged the doubling

---

[3] The two volumes had 55 and 34 pages respectively.

of per capita income over fifteen years and proposed appropriate sources of finance for that ambitious target. The Planning Commission never addressed why a target close to the Bombay Plan's was never aimed for by it. Was the Bombay Plan unrealistic in its technical assumptions or did the proposed finance options become unfeasible afterwards? These questions are of interest to students of economic history and planning, and to economists generally.

I believe that the publication of the Bombay Plan was a significant economic and political event and it is an important document. It, therefore, becomes imperative to describe the making of the Plan and its background, the assumptions, targets, sectoral outlays and the intertemporal strategy. We also need to compare the Plan with the first three Five Year Plans of independent India which spanned fifteen years, like the proposed Bombay Plan. The first three Five Year Plans owe a significant amount of intellectual debt to the Bombay Plan—a fact that has not been acknowledged officially.[4] With these discussions forming the background, we need to understand the reasons for the Plan to get so completely wiped off from public memory. We also need to understand why Indian political parties including the

---

[4]Except when former Prime Minister, Dr Manmohan Singh, made some statements acknowledging the Plan's intellectual heritage.

Indian National Congress (INC or the Congress), the Government of India, and the authors of the Plan let it sink unceremoniously into oblivion.

MAKING OF THE PLAN

The Bombay Plan had as its backdrop, the political developments of the 1930s that began emphasising economic issues. The Congress had adopted an economic programme and an agrarian programme in 1931 and 1936 respectively. The Wardha session of 1937 debated the need for national planning as a means of economic development and closed with a resolution in its favour. Next year, the Haripura session followed it up and set up the National Planning Committee with Jawaharlal Nehru and K.T. Shah as chairman and secretary respectively.[5]

The Bombay Plan was published against this background in January 1944. Though the National Planning Committee had started work, it did not publish anything until 1948.[6] Therefore, the Bombay Plan was not a reaction but an original proposal. The document was signed by the following:

---

[5] This committee was succeeded by the Advisory Planning Board set up by the Interim Government in 1946.
[6] Its report published in 1948, Shah (1948), was reviewed by Vera Anstey in *Pacific Review*, see Anstey (1950).

- J.R.D. Tata, son of a cousin of Jamsedji Tata, one of India's pioneer industrialists. At the time of the Bombay Plan, J.R.D. Tata had business interests in iron and steel and the aviation industry. He would later develop one of the largest industrial conglomerates and be regarded as an industrial leader of modern India.
- G.D. Birla, the leader of the Birla group of industries. At the time he had business interests in textiles, jute and insurance. At least three large business groups originated from the businesses established by G.D. Birla.
- Sir Ardeshir Dalal, a noted administrator and technocrat, had experience of working in government administration in various capacities and was the first Indian appointed as Municipal Commissioner of Bombay in 1928. He joined Tata Iron and Steel Company Ltd. as Resident Director in 1931 and initiated reforms like profit sharing bonus for workers, which were a first at the time. In 1944, the Viceroy of India invited him to join the Executive Council as Member-in-Charge of Planning and Development.
- Lala Shri Ram, a prominent north Indian industrialist who turned the Delhi Cloth Mills (DCM) into an industrial conglomerate later known as the DCM Shri Ram Industrial Group. Lala is reputed for early managerial and workplace reforms like profit sharing with employees and workers' participation

in management. He established, or was a major influence, in a number of institutions: Shri Ram College of Commerce, Lady Shri Ram College for Women, Indraprastha College for Women, and the Shri Ram Institute for Industrial Research.

- Kasturbhai Lalbhai had wide ranging interests in textiles business and shipping. He served as a director of the Reserve Bank of India (RBI) from 1937 to 1949. Active in the education sector, he was a member of the group that started the Ahmedabad Education Society which grew into the Gujarat University. He was also an important influence in establishing and developing the Indian Institute of Management, Ahmedabad.
- D. Shroff was director of a number of prominent industries including a few of the Tata Group. He was an unofficial[7] delegate to the Bretton Woods Conference. He later became the founder-director of the Investment Corporation of India and the chairman of the Bank of India and the New India Assurance Company Limited.
- John Mathai was a professor of economics at Madras University and a political personality as well. He served as the Director-General, Commercial Intelligence and Statistics during 1935-40. He was India's first railway minister and then served as finance minister for two

---

[7] Unofficial because India was still not independent.

years. He was also director of Tata Sons Ltd.
➢ Purushottamdas Thakurdas was a Mumbai-based businessman and business leader. He, along with G.D. Birla, was involved in building business associations like the Indian Chamber of Commerce (ICC) and FICCI. He was an advisor for the Indo-British Trade Agreement and served as member in a wide range of public committees and negotiations.

The purpose of the Bombay Plan, as the signatories discussed among themselves, is recorded in the minutes of the Plan's secretariat meetings. According to the minutes, the following was the purpose behind the effort. The government (they meant the future government of free India) might take populist economic measures in a hurry after the war. Such measures were all the more likely if the government faced organised political demands for redistribution of income and wealth. These measures would harm the prospects of India's economic development in the long run. However, this possibility could be avoided by proceeding in an orderly and more caring path of development before such a contingency arose. The Plan was proposed to initiate the process and make both the government and the public aware of the long run issues of development and income distribution.[8]

---

[8] General Note, J. Mathai to Thakurdas, 8.12.1942, in *PT Papers*, File 291, part 1, Nehru Memorial Museum and Library.

UNDERSTANDING DEEPER MOTIVES

This documented objective notwithstanding, many people have speculated on the deeper motives of the industrial houses. They have pointed to two domestic developments that could have influenced the motives. First, it was clear by then that the Congress would initiate some form of planned industrialization after Independence. This, according to some observers, prompted the biggest industrial houses to push forward their own wishlist in the form of a plan. The second was the Quit India Movement of 1942. Letters written by authors of the Plan to one another, and to the government, record that they had an apprehension of a worst case scenario where the Congress might lose control of mass movements, which might then turn generally against private property.[9] Lala Shri Ram, for example, wrote to P. Thakurdas, 'I am afraid that this sabotage[10] may any day start of private property also. Once the Goondas know this trick, any Government...will find it difficult to control it. Today Mahatma Gandhi may be able to stop it, but later on it may go out of their hands too.'[11]

---

[9]Chibber documents a number of these exchanges and communications in *Locked in Place: State-building and Late Industrialization in India* (2003).
[10]He was referring to events in his mills.
[11]Shri Ram to Thakurdas, *PT Papers*, file 239, part 4, Nehru Memorial Museum and Library.

Left parties in general and a number of Left-oriented scholars emphasised this apprehension to be behind the Plan, which they interpreted as a document for polishing up public image. They reasoned that private business had a robber baron image[12] and its reputation particularly plummeted during the war. In view of the violent events of 1942, a threatened Indian business felt it must improve its public image to survive in the fast changing political environment.[13] This view was common among the various Left parties who stated it with different degrees of force. The most clear statement that I came across is from the Indian Trotskyites who claimed pointedly that the Indian bourgeoisie had been scared by revolutionary movements in the country and elsewhere and wanted the government to escort the process of industrialization after Independence. I quote here from an article in the *Workers' International News* that conveys the characteristic flavour: 'Having been frightened out of their wits by the revolutionary energy of the masses in 1942, now the Indian bourgeoisie attempt to bypass political power through an economic weapon. This is the background of the famous "Bombay Plan" put forward by the Indian industrialists' (Naidu, 1944).

The Quit India Movement and related violence

---

[12]This view is supported by some scholars, e.g. Kochanek (1974), chapter IX, and the references in that chapter.
[13]See Chibber (2003), p. 95.

closely preceded the Plan—the first meeting of the Plan secretariat took place in December 1942. It might have given a disproportionate importance to these events in contemporary analysis. Though the industry was wary of violent events, I did not find any direct indication that it was fearful of losing private property rights to the people of the country around this time.[14] I find it more reasonable to interpret its anxiety as a general concern, which was shared by many others outside industry and business circles as well. Nor was it based on the experience of the Quit India violence alone. Political and economic developments of the time generally shaped this anxiety much like what is reflected in these lines from Birla to Rajagopalachari in 1946:

> 'It is hardly necessary for me to draw your attention to the economic consequences of the disturbed conditions. If I do so, it is only to emphasize the danger and I hope that our Government may be able to take timely steps to prevent the catastrophe which is hanging on our head...In provinces like Bengal, Bihar, UP, production is seriously affected. Today, you can't even build a house...serious labour shortages, coal shortages, no bricks, Muslim *mistris*

---

[14] They were indeed more fearful of losing property to the government for some time after the publication of the report of the Economic Programme Committee in 1948.

don't come in Hindu areas and Hindu labour doesn't enter Muslim areas.'[15]

In spite of the events of 1942, industry leaders like Mr Birla were confident by 1943 that the years of the Raj were over and that they would be soon called upon by the nation to play a critical role in the post-war reconstruction of the country. There is some evidence that they therefore wanted to share each other's views on the future industrialization of the country.[16]

As the agitations of 1942 waned, G.D. Birla took the initiative of producing an appropriate document. The group set up a secretariat. Tata was to pay for half of the expenses and the rest was to be shared by other secretariat members. John Mathai, director of a Tata company at that time, was assigned the secretary's role.[17] The Plan got ready by January 1944. As mentioned in the introduction, it was first released for private circulation, and then published as a pamphlet and saw a number of editions, reprints and translations soon. What was initially

---

[15]Birla to Rajagopalachari, 12 November, 1946. *Birla Papers*, Series II, File No. R–5. In 1946, of course, the religious relations were much more volatile than in 1944.

[16]See Kudaisya's biography of G.D. Birla, Kudaisya (2003), pp.224–225.

[17]Proceedings of the First Meeting of the Committee on Post-War Economic Development, 11.12.1942, *PT Papers*, File 291, part 1, Nehru Memorial Museum and Library.

circulated was later called Volume 1 of the monograph. It contained the Plan targets, the physical and financial plan and the time sequence of investment outlays. The second volume was written later and addressed issues of income distribution and planning machinery. It is worth a mention that the second volume was not an afterthought—i.e. not produced in response to the leftist critique that the Plan was silent on income distribution. It was stated in the introduction to the first volume that the authors were working on income distribution issues, to be published soon. They were anxious to start public discussion and hence the Plan was released into circulation before other parts were ready.[18]

BOMBAY PLAN AND INDEPENDENT INDIA'S FIVE YEAR PLANS

The first three Five Year Plans of the government of free India spanned fifteen years which equals the horizon of the Bombay Plan. So it is instructive to compare the Bombay Plan with the first three plans, particularly their sectoral outlays and the time sequence of priorities. I will describe the essential features of the Bombay Plan first to facilitate comparison.

---

[18]See Bombay Plan, p.1.

The aim of the Bombay Plan was to attain in fifteen years' time, 'a general standard of living which would leave a reasonable margin over the minimum requirements of human life' (Bombay Plan, p.7). This minimum requirement comprised food, clothing, shelter, healthcare and basic education.[19] It was calculated that per capita real income of the time would have to be doubled to attain the targeted consumption.[20] But because population was increasing by 5 million a year,[21] national income had to be trebled in fifteen years to attain the proposed increase of per capita income.

A set of sectoral growth rates was then established from this targeted increase of national income. Together, the rates would ensure the required growth of national income and were taken to be feasible, given the technology of the time. Over the fifteen year horizon, the Plan envisaged 130 per cent increase in agricultural output, 500 per cent in industry and 200 per cent in the services.

---

[19]The authors considered 2,800 calories of well-balanced food per day, 30 yards of clothing per year and 100 square feet of housing as the minimum need for any person.
[20]₹74 per person per year was taken as necessary to attain the minimum at pre-war prices. Target per capita income was calculated using this. V.K.R.V. Rao's national income estimate of 1931–32 was used as the basis to estimate the income in 1943–44. Calculations were at constant prices—the average of 1931–39.
[21]The Plan used the latest Census.

This meant a structural transformation of the economy. According to the Plan's calculation, the contribution of agriculture, industry and services to GDP would change from 53, 17 and 22 per cent[22] respectively at the time, to 40, 35 and 20 per cent at the end of the proposed Plan.[23] Chapter 3 of the Plan explains the logic of the sectoral targets and their interrelations. These discussions show that the secretariat had done extensive research for the Plan. The Plan also developed targets for education, health and housing, based on an informed discussion of requirements.

Sectoral growth targets were then used to work out outlays needed for the respective sectors. The Plan estimated capital and recurring costs separately, which made the assumptions about costs easy to follow. It then combined the two to produce the total outlays as shown in Table 1.

---

[22]The Plan notes that in fact the proportion of agriculture was higher. The figures available to them were based on 1931–32 prices, when agricultural prices were abnormally low due to the Great Depression.
[23]Some small and unclassified incomes were not included in these figures.

Table 1:
Bombay Plan: Sector-wise Capital Outlay

Capital Outlay	Rupees (In Crore)
Industry	4,480
Agriculture	1,240
Transport and Communications	940
Education	490
Health	450
Housing	2,200
Miscellaneous	200
Recurring expenses	–
Total	10,000

The size of the Plan at ₹10,000 crore was equivalent to $30 billion. It discussed a financial strategy and the sources of finance for both rupee resources and foreign currency in chapter 4. First I want to compare the sectoral allocation of the Bombay Plan with that of the Five Year Plans of independent India to highlight the extent of similarity. Table 2 provides this comparison.

Table 2:
Bombay Plan and the first three Five Year Plans

Sectoral Outlay in per centage.

	First Plan	Second Plan	Third Plan	Bombay Plan
Agriculture and Community Development	15.1	11.0	14.0	8.3
Irrigation, and Multipurpose Irrigation and Power	28.0	19.0	22.0	45.0
Industry, including Small Industries	7.6	24.0	24.0	
Transport and Communication	23.6	28.0	20.0	9.0
Social Services	22.6	18.0	17.0	27.6
Miscellaneous	3.0	-	3.0	10.0

Let me point out the differences now. Allocation for 'Transport and Communication' (row 4) in Bombay Plan is significantly smaller. What is itemised under this heading in Bombay Plan is also different. Spending itemised and discussed in the Bombay Plan is for transport alone, which included rail, roads, waterways, harbours and reconstruction. There is no separate discussion of non-transport communication items like Post and Telegraph. It appears that those items were to be funded from the miscellaneous category and some might have been also included in investment for engineering goods.

Even if we make reasonable assumptions for these outlays, the Bombay Plan's allocation ratio for Transport and Communication would fall short of the Five Year Plans'. On the other hand, the size of the Bombay Plan was much larger. So the absolute amount of spending on Transport and Communication would not be much smaller, and the amount of spending on Transport alone would be no smaller at all.

The second difference is in social services (row 5). The Plan discussed the requirements of Housing, Education and Health to sketch a thoughtful, though very brief, outline of policy for each of them. The discussion led to a well-researched proposal with breakdown for various aspects. For example, it allocated the education budget over primary, secondary, tertiary, adult education, vocational and scientific education as well as research, providing reasons for the corresponding allocations. The government's Five Year Plans provided for a smaller allocation on Social Services. Arguably, they also show a lack of vision compared to that of the Bombay Plan.

STRIKING SIMILARITIES

Leaving these two sectors, the rest of the allocations are strikingly similar. It is important to appreciate the extent of similarity:

- Items classified as 'Irrigation, and Multipurpose Irrigation and Power' (row 2) and 'Industry, including Small Industries' (row 3) in the Five Year Plans were clubbed together in the Bombay Plan's presentation. Together, they form a very similar per centage of overall outlay both in the Bombay Plan and the Five Year Plans.
- The difference in agricultural spending (row 1) between the Five Year Plans and the Bombay Plan is only apparent. The amount in the Bombay Plan presents only direct spending on Agriculture, while for the Five Year Plans it includes spending on Community Development. When Community Development items are taken out from Five Year Plan outlays, the proportions are almost equal.

Therefore, the allocation ratios for Industry and Agriculture were almost the same and the proposed spending on Transport not very different.

Time sequence of investment outlays is also similar between the two sets of plans. The Bombay Plan had laid out how sectoral outlays were to be sequenced over the fifteen year horizon. It explained the rationale and importance of the sequence in chapter 5 of volume 1. The fifteen year period was broken into three five-year terms. Investment strategies were formulated for the three terms in a way that the transitional costs like inflation could be minimised. The first five-year period was to give significant emphasis on agriculture and consumption goods while investment in basic industries was to be started off, and a relatively modest beginning would be made for transport.[24] The second five-year term was to increase the allocation for heavy and core industries by reducing that for consumption-oriented industries. The assumption was that economic growth of the first five years would spur private initiative in food and consumption goods production in later years. In the final five years, transport and social services came in for special attention even as industrial investment was to continue. The Indian government's first three Five Year Plans chalked out an identical intertemporal path. It stressed agriculture and consumption goods in the first plan, and then heavily invested in basic industry and transport from the second plan onwards.

These similarities are not coincidental but follow from common assumptions and identical strategic vision, of which the following are the most important.

(i) Both assumed a central role of the government. This is well known for the official Five Year Plans both

---

[24] I am using 'Transport' where the text of the Bombay Plan uses 'Transport and Communication' or simply 'Communication'. This is because the Plan's spending on transport and communication was mostly in transport as I pointed out earlier.

from actual experience and from proclamations like the Industrial Policy Resolution. But the extent of emphasis on the government's role in the Bombay Plan is not known widely. It was indeed the central institutional assumption for the Bombay Plan document. At the very beginning the document states '...we think that no development of the kind we have proposed will be feasible except on the basis of a central directing authority which...possesses the requisite powers and jurisdiction' (Bombay Plan, p.2). The amount of power the authors wanted for the central mechanism can be judged from the following statement, '...in order to prevent the inequitable distribution of the burden between different classes which this method of financing will involve, practically every aspect of economic life will have to be so rigorously controlled by government that individual liberty and freedom of enterprise will suffer a temporary eclipse' (p.48). This view, uncharacteristic of private industry as it is, surprised observers. On the other hand, it means that there was no difference between the Bombay Plan's vision of the implementing mechanism and that of the Government of India.

(ii) Both plans emphasised rapid development of the basic and core industries as part of overall strategy. Official Five Year Plan documents mention it again and again. Perhaps it is most summarily stated in the second plan

THE MAKING OF A MYTHICAL FORERUNNER

document when describing its objectives as 'rapid industrialization with particular emphasis on the development of basic and heavy industries' (2nd Plan, chapter 2, section 6). The Bombay Plan, on the other hand, states the idea this way: 'Basic industries, which will get priority over the other type of industries... would include among others the following groups: Power..., Mining and metallurgy..., Engineering..., Chemicals..., Armaments, Transport..., Cement... These industries are the basis on which the economic superstructure envisaged in the plan will have to be erected' (Bombay Plan, p.25).

(iii) Both denied any role to foreign direct investment (FDI). Bombay Plan made it clear in chapter 4, titled 'Sources of Finance'. Discussion of the finances made it obvious that foreign investment had no place in the scheme, though the Plan carefully avoided stating it explicitly anywhere.[25] Government of India documents were however explicit from a fairly early

---

[25]Bombay Plan's insistence on no foreign investment became a sore point with the British. As an alternative, Lord Wavell proposed a portfolio of ideas for 'reconstruction' which L.S. Amery, an influential British conservative politician, described to be 'bold and...methods more practical than those of the Birla scheme'. 'Birla scheme' here refers to the Bombay Plan. British industry suggested cooperation between British and Indian business using the framework of wartime cooperation as a model. See Wainwright (1994), p.39 and footnote 28 on that page.

date. The Advisory Planning Board of the interim government of 1946-47 wrote, 'Foreign capital should not be allowed to enter or where it already existed, to expand—even in non-basic industries such as consumer goods. If necessary, the country should rely on imports. In due course of time it will be possible to restrict or discontinue foreign imports; but foreign vested interests once created would be difficult to dislodge.'[26] This position was carried over into the government of India's Five Year Plans and would not change until the liberalization of 1991.

(iv) Both wanted to increase agricultural output by managing technology and inputs—i.e. through irrigation, modern inputs and by bringing more land into cultivation. Land reform was not considered as part of the plans. Bombay Plan discussed land reform as a social and distributive measure in volume 2 and not as an output augmenting measure in volume 1. The government of India too did not propose change in land relations as part of the plans.

These four common features form the basis of the Bombay Plan as much as of the Government of India's Five Year Plans. To stress the idea of similarity even further, I would draw special attention to the official second Five Year Plan. This plan is considered unique and original,

---

[26]Quoted in Chaudhury (1984), p.9.

bearing the hallmark of Nehru era planning and vision. However, the strategy on which the plan was based was already proposed by the Bombay Plan. The official second plan had two distinguishing features: (i) large amount of public investment to be concentrated in the heavy and basic sectors of industry; and (ii) resources for investment were to be raised by forced saving. Forced saving was justified on the premise that large amounts of core sector investment would increase productivity in the long run sufficiently to justify the welfare loss of involuntary saving in the short run.[27] We have already noted the emphasis on heavy and basic industries in the Bombay Plan. I also mentioned that the Plan proposed the emphasis to be heightened in the second of its five-year periods and that overall allocation ratio for heavy industries was in fact more in the Bombay Plan than in the Five Year Plans.

While proposing large outlay on core investment, the Bombay Plan was aware that investment of the proposed magnitude could not be supported by voluntary saving alone. The Plan, and later a pamphlet by G.D. Birla,[28] argued for forced saving in this context very succinctly. Observing that wars were able to mobilise resources by

---

[27] Mahalanobis' paper (1953) illustrated a path where sufficiently large investment allocation results in a long run growth rate that compensates the short run consumption loss from the large investment.
[28] G.D. Birla, *The Plan Explained*, (pamphlet), speech at FICCI.

aggressively forcing down consumption, the Plan asked why this could not be done for economic development in peace time (Bombay Plan, p.5). It later mentions, '...a large part of the capital required, about ₹3,400 crores, would have to be created by borrowing against *ad hoc* securities from the Reserve Bank... There is nothing unsound in creating this money because it is meant to increase the productive capacity of the nation and in the long run is of a self-liquidating character' (Bombay Plan, p.47). Thus the Plan justified involuntary saving on the ground that the long run increase of output will automatically liquidate the loans for raising investment. Therefore, the idea of industrialization by pre-empting consumption with higher allocation to investment was not an original idea of the official second Five Year Plan. There is no doubt, however, that to adopt this strategy in a newborn State outside the communist bloc was certainly novel. The Bombay Plan had dared to propose this novelty and Nehru's government had taken it up for implementation.[29]

---

[29] For this reason the belief that the second plan was 'based on' the Mahalanobis model is misleading. The paper by Mahalanobis (1953) did not discover any growth strategy but was merely illustrative of an existing idea.

BETTER UNDERSTANDING OF MACROECONOMIC IMPLICATIONS

Bombay Plan was, however, ahead of the official plans in its awareness of the macroeconomic implications of the plan strategy. It had realised that the large magnitude of forced saving would stoke serious inflation. To quote the Plan, '…financing of economic development by means of "created money" on this scale is likely to lead to a gap between the volume of purchasing power…and the volume of goods available. How to bridge this gap and to keep prices within limits will be a constant problem which the planning authority will have to tackle' (Bombay Plan, p.48). The Plan had proposed two precautionary measures. First, it emphasised the production of consumer goods in the early years, specifically discussing the production of textiles, leather goods, oil, glass, paper and tobacco.[30] The suggestion was that while in later years private supply would increase in response to demand, the Plan itself had to make provisions for the early years. This was built into the Plan's temporal outlay sequence. Second, the authors believed that investment in consumption goods production alone would not suffice given the scale of the Plan. They therefore suggested curbs on consumption

---

[30] See *Bombay Plan*, pp.27-28. It was noted that though initially these industries were in focus, the course of consumption goods industry would evolve with consumer choice and market demand.

with some form of rationing.

Arguably, the Planning Commission did not understand the economics of its own plan as clearly as the Bombay Plan authors. The Commission approached the plan somewhat mechanically—as if it consisted only of deciding about investment allocations and raising finance. This led to non-fulfilment of targets, inflation and disappointingly small increase in the number of jobs. G.D. Birla criticised the second Five Year Plan document extensively, bringing out the lack of clarity in the official vision. He pointed out that in order to succeed, the Mahalanobis strategy must leave room for all sorts of industry—small, medium and big, even as it emphasised the heavy and core sectors. He noted that the restriction on the factory sector accompanying the plan would create massive shortage of consumption goods and jobs, and would get in the way of the public sector investment.[31] An article in the *Eastern Economist*, owned by Birla, described Mahalanobis as a 'statistician completely devoid of a sense of economic organisation', and the second plan framework as 'a theoretical shibboleth which if enforced, would in one sweep endanger India's future industrialization.'[32] Taking a look in retrospect, it is difficult to accord credit to the official second Five Year Plan for either originality or clarity of thinking.

---

[31] Letter by Birla to Morarji Desai, referred to by Kudaisya (2003), p.327, notes.
[32] Quoted by Kudaisya (2003), p.315.

THE DIFFERENCE IN SCALE AND AMBITION

There was however significant difference between the scale and ambition of the Bombay Plan and the official plans. The former had a target of trebling the real GDP in fifteen years—which translates into an annual compound growth rate of 7.6 per cent.[33] Five Year Plans were substantially less ambitious, target growth rates being 2.1 per cent, 4.5 per cent and 5.4 per cent per year in the first, second and the third plan respectively.[34] This is reflected in the plan outlay as a ratio of GDP. Average annual outlay of the first three Five Year Plans was ₹945 crore,[35] which was 10.3 per cent of the national income at the starting year of the plans in 1951-52.[36] A comparable ratio for the Bombay Plan is more than 25 per cent.[37]

---

[33] Some scholars have suggested that the target was too high. 'In particular the growth rate recommended seems too high in view of the fact that there is no detailed policy outline for agriculture.' Markovits (1985, p.27, footnote 70).

[34] Five Year Plans, Government of India.

[35] Outlays for the three Five Year Plans were respectively ₹2,069 crore, ₹4,600 crore and ₹7,500 crore. Source: Five Year Plans, Government of India.

[36] GDP in 1951-52 at 1952–53 prices was ₹9,110 crore.

[37] Bombay Plan estimated India's per capita income as $22 in 1944-45. Taking the population to be 340 million (interpolation using Census data), GDP would be $7.48 billion in that year. With the Plan's average annual outlay of $2 billion, the ratio of the first year's income to annual outlay was more than 25%.

The difference of ambition arose from the inability of the government to raise resources on the scale proposed by the Bombay Plan. It was partly due to the changed circumstances resulting from the partition of the country, partly because some assumptions about trade surplus and exchange rates of the Bombay Plan did not hold in the post-war era, and partly because the Nehru government did not want to go for market borrowing as aggressively as the Bombay Plan had proposed.

Given the similarity discussed earlier and the difference of scale noted now, it is difficult to escape the suggestion that the first three official Five Year Plans constituted a scaled down version of the Bombay plan.

A number of observers have more recently commented on the similarity discussed above. They include Krishna who writes without any qualification or caveat that the Nehru era implemented the Bombay Plan (Krishna, 2005, p.59). In a very similar tone Kudaisya (2003) writes '...as things eventuated the Plan became the basis of independent India's first Five Year National Plan' (p.236). Also notably, India's former prime minister, Dr Manmohan Singh, said in a speech at the centenary celebration of J.R.D. Tata: 'As a student of economics in 1950s and later as a practitioner in government, I was greatly impressed by the "Bombay Plan" of 1944. In many ways, it encapsulated what all subsequent plans

THE MAKING OF A MYTHICAL FORERUNNER

have tried to achieve...'[38]

WHY WAS THE PLAN FORGOTTEN?

Given the continuity of policy from the Bombay Plan to the official plans and their remarkable similarities, it is surprising that references to the Plan started thinning out in the late forties and then stopped entirely by the early period of official planning. By the time the fourth Five Year Plan was launched, the Bombay Plan was already thought of as a part of the prehistory of Indian planning. So why didn't the government of India, India's political parties, and Indian business itself show any keenness to refer to the Plan after Independence?

Communist Party of India and the Left: We may start with the political parties and first consider the Communist Party of India (CPI). Immediately after the publication of the Bombay Plan, CPI's criticism was directed at the question of income and wealth distribution, which were not addressed in the first volume. CPI claimed that the Plan was irrelevant to the people of India because it had not addressed income distribution. To quote B.T.

---

[38] It was reported in all major Indian newspapers on 24 August, 2004. The speech can be found at the website of the prime minister's office, government of India. The URL is http://pmindia.nic.in/speech/content.asp?id=12.

Ranadive, at the time a member of the central committee of the CPI, 'Without an equitable distribution of wealth through minimum living wages, social security, etc., an all-round increase in the standard of living is not possible...a plan which defers distribution or ignores it... cannot be called a "plan" for economic development...'[39] The overall assessment of the CPI was that the Plan was a blueprint for building capitalism with the help of the State. A related feature with which the CPI and other Left parties joined issue is that the Plan did not propose change of land owning pattern. According to them, the Plan's attention to agriculture was not for the benefit of farmers but for developing capitalism in an agrarian country.[40] The CPI did not revise this opinion even after the publication of the second volume of Bombay Plan where the question of income distribution was central. This volume also discussed land tenure (p.14), explained the merits of ryotwari and reasoned for replacing zamindari settlements with ryotwari (p.16). But the CPI

---

[39] Ranadive (1944), p.11.

[40] To quote an article written later by a Marxist scholar, 'The leading sections of the Indian bourgeoisie, who were responsible for drawing up the Bombay Plan, were not interested in developing agriculture *per se*, their interest in agricultural development derived from their overall objective which was the promotion of capitalism, notably industrial capitalism in India' (Patnaik, 1993, p.121).

and other Left parties were not impressed. They did not respond to these discussions either by welcoming them or rejecting them with reasoning.

The CPI never revised its assessment of the intentions of Indian business for proposing the Plan and soon distinguished between the Bombay Plan and the National Planning Committee's proposals, which were published in 1948. It theorised that the former was a blueprint for capitalism, while the latter promised a 'non-capitalist' path of development.[41] In a pamphlet published on behalf of the party, the position was later summarised in these words: '...basic difference between the approach of the national bourgeoisie and the Left democratic movement regarding the public sector...while the latter wanted gradual curtailment of the role of big private capital and socialisation of major means of production in order to take to the path of non-capitalist development, the former wanted the State to enable it to develop the economy by taking to an independent capitalist path' (Mishra, 1975, p.6).

Even as it dismissed the Bombay Plan so thoroughly, the CPI became a supporter of Nehru era economic planning as a sequel to its support for the National Planning Committee's proposals. Its criticism of Nehru

---

[41]See Mukherjee (1978) for a discussion of the position of the Indian Left on the question of Indian capitalists' intentions.

era economic planning was based on the lapses and opportunism of implementation rather than its principles. It theorised that the Industrial Policy Resolution, central planning, and import substitution together provided a preferred alternative to capitalism until socialism could be established.

This led the CPI into a seriously contradictory position. Institutions, policies and strategies that CPI came to support now had been proposed by and justified in the Bombay Plan. In these circumstances, it was not possible to continue to cry down the Bombay Plan. Yet, acclaiming the Plan would amount to an admission of previous mistakes which the party was not prepared to do. The troubling question the party had to face was this: Nehru era planning could not presumably be expected to move India away from capitalism if its institutions and strategies were the same as those proposed by India's big business. Further, as planning progressed, the similarity of vision and allocations of the Bombay Plan's five-year blocks and the official Five Year Plans was to become more and more apparent. The contradiction remained a source of serious discomfort.

Thus, the CPI had got itself into a position where it could neither laud the Bombay Plan nor cry it down. I would speculate that the leaders of CPI avoided all references to the Bombay Plan to escape this difficulty. Given that in a communist party what is avoided by the leadership is avoided by the rank and file, including the intellectuals who sympathise with the party, the silence of the leaders became an unofficial gag. Indeed by the middle of the fifties, there was hardly any mention of the Plan from their side.

Congress and the Government*:* The Congress and the government led by it also went silent on the Plan. It appears that like the CPI, the Congress too was in a position where they could neither praise the Plan nor reject it.

After Independence, the Congress-led government projected itself as the champion of an alternative path of development and a socialist pattern of society. This idea was exploited in its foreign policy too; for instance, in building and leading a group of import-substituting countries—the Non-Alignment Movement (NAM). The idea was also used to rationalise the government's relations with China and the Union of Soviet Socialist Republics (USSR). At home, the Congress-led government used the Industrial Policy Resolution and the Five Year Plans to project a seriously left-of-centre image in the political spectrum. To be seen as implementing or following the suggestions of big industrial houses at this point would seriously damage its stance at home and abroad.

Further, the Bombay Plan had been favourably mentioned by several members of the Congress soon after its publication, and the Opposition used this to paint the party as pro-business.[42] Similarly, the closeness of Mr Birla to Mahatma Gandhi and to a group within the Congress remained a point of embarrassment and a reminder that the party was close to industry and business. The Congress as a party would have liked to shake off these sources of embarrassment and distance itself from the Plan and its authors.

But it did not have convincing or credible excuses to dismiss the Plan. Ideas and strands of the Bombay Plan were writ all over the official plans. The National Planning Committee had copiously interacted and exchanged notes with the Plan authors and *vice-versa*, and that was public knowledge.[43] Also, some of the Plan authors played

---

[42]Here is an example: 'Any possible doubt about the attitude of the older parties towards the Bombay Plan, which frankly postulates a dictatorship of big business, has been dispelled by what happened in the autumn session of the central assembly. One Muslim League member had tabled a resolution calling upon the Government not to entertain the capitalist plan... During the debate the Leader of the Congress Party did not have one word to say against the Big Business Plan. On the contrary he went out of his way to shower eulogies on the Member in charge of the Department of Planning and Development of the Government, who is one of the authors of the Bombay Plan. If that is not supporting the Big Business Plan, then human behaviour has no logic, and words have no meaning' (from the Presidential address at the Conference of the Radical Democratic Party, 1945). See p.899, Ralhan (1997).
[43]See Chattopadhyay (1989) and Mukherjee (1976), and Mukherjee (1978).

important roles in technical and economic committees of the Congress. Some had been nominated for important government positions by the party. For example, Sir Ardeshir Dalal was appointed Member for Planning and Development of the government of India in August 1944, just a few months after he had co-authored the Bombay Plan. A.D. Shroff served as India's delegate to the Bretton Woods Conference on post-war monetary and financial systems, and in 1948, Tata was India's delegate to the United Nation's General Assembly (UNGA).

Thus, much like the CPI, the Congress too could neither cry down the Bombay Plan nor praise it. This possibly was the reason for the Congress to go silent on the Plan and let it move out of attention and interest. This silence was presumably understood by the upper echelons of the government bureaucracy. Hence, official plans and other documents of the Planning Commission carried no references to the Plan, as much as Congress as a party never mentioned it.[44]

Parties of the Right: We do not have enough material to speculate about the parties right of the Congress. The only party on the right of Congress in 1944, the Akhil Bharatiya

---

[44]Tarlok Singh of the erstwhile Indian Civil Service who oversaw the mechanism and working of the Planning Commission and the plans in Nehru's time wrote his article on the Bombay Plan (Singh, 1963) only after he retired from the government.

Hindu Mahasabha, had a different set of preoccupations at the time and I could not find it commenting or referring to Bombay Plan. Some personalities who later founded or joined the Bharatiya Jana Sangh (est. 1951), the Forum of Free Enterprise (est. 1956) and the Swatantra Party (est. 1959) were in the Hindu Mahasabha or inside Congress in 1944. Many of them took public positions on India's economic plans during their career in Jana Sangh or the Swatantra Party, but I did not come across anything on the Bombay Plan itself.

Swatantra Party's election manifesto of 1962 opposed 'the policy of Statism' and announced, 'the business of the State is not business but Government.'[45] But its opposition was not against economic planning *per se*. It was against the curb on economic freedom for which it held the economic and political strategies of the Nehru era responsible. The distinction between economic planning in general and that of the Indian government of the time, was commented on not only by the Swatantra Party, but also other parties and forums of its kind. To take an example, Forum of Free Enterprise, founded by A.D. Shroff, was vocal against the growing marginalisation of private business during the first Five Year Plan and the proposed nationalization measures looming at the time.

---

[45]From the Swatantra Party manifesto, *To Prosperity Through Freedom*.

Shroff, an author of the Bombay Plan, clearly cannot be counted as against economic planning. The resistance of these parties and organisations was directed against the restrictions on economic freedom and was located in the context of the on-going political process. Hence they did not, nor did they need to, refer to the Bombay Plan which in any case was fading from public memory.[46]

Authors of the Bombay Plan: We may finally ask why the authors of Bombay Plan themselves did not dwell on it subsequently. The Plan was based on extensive research, economic calculations, reasoning and foresight. Hence, it is expected that even if the authors lost political interest, they would retain an intellectual interest in it. For some time after its publication, secretariat members did actively promote the Plan in various constituencies and forums.[47] But after a period of activism, they seemed

---

[46]That the left-right co-ordinate determines the position on economic planning does not hold in all cases, at least not apparently. Mr Shyama Prasad Mukhopadhyay who was a founder of Bharatiya Jana Sangh was the union minister of industry and supply when the Constituent Assembly adopted the Industrial Policy Resolution. Later on Mr Mukhopadhyay had resigned from Nehru's government protesting against certain policies but not against its industrial policy.

[47]G.D. Birla was particularly active in promoting the Plan. He wrote a pamphlet (referred to earlier) and spoke at a number of forums. Like Birla, Dalal also wrote a pamphlet in 1944 to promote

(cont)

to have withdrawn from the campaign and even stopped referring to it. They did not try to revise, edit or reprint the document any time later. The probability that this happened by default is very small given the involvement of a group of serious-minded industrialists and technocrats. It is more likely that the authors consciously decided to allow the document to fade from public memory.

We could speculate on a number of reasons for this. The first is that the leaders of Indian business who authored the Plan realised that business in general was not too happy with the document. FICCI's endorsement of the Plan was not spontaneous but came after serious efforts from Mr Birla[48] and others. Even after endorsing the Plan, FICCI had not shown any interest in it. As Tripathi writes in *The Oxford History of Indian Business*, '...the federation (i.e. FICCI) refused to contribute even a paltry sum of ₹1,000 to its (Bombay Plan's) funds, citing budgetary constraints.'[49] Dislike was even more pronounced among businesses outside the organised part that FICCI represented.[50] Apart from this dislike,

---

the Plan. See the role of Birla generally in the Plan endeavour as recollected by Tata and reported in Lala (1988).

[48]Birla's pamphlet (referred to earlier) was written for persuading FICCI.

[49]Quoted by P. Guha Thakurta in 'Bombay Plan and Mixed-up Economy', in *Business Line*, 7 September, 2004.

[50]Kochanek (1974) discusses the attitude of small and medium

some business personalities had apprehensions about possible abuse of the Plan by the British. Sir Padampat Singhania, for example, feared that if India did not get freedom soon, then the Bombay Plan's proposals could be used by the British in controlling the Indian economy to their own advantage. He wrote about his fears to the authors of Bombay Plan.[51] The fear turned out to be true to an extent with the announcement of the government of India's plan of 1945, which proposed to place twenty-odd key industries under government control. While business, political parties and Indian newspapers protested and opposed that plan,[52] it certainly would have made the Bombay Plan even less popular among industry and business.

The authors wanted the government to play an active role in building infrastructure and core industries after Independence. It is likely that when they understood that the government led by the Congress would move in that direction anyway, they were happy to de-emphasise the Plan. This would have helped arresting the alienation of business leaders from business at large. Further, the leaders might have realised that if the official plan effort

---

business of different sizes and different regions on the question of central planning, and their political dilemma in the late forties and early fifties.
[51]See Mukherjee (1978), p.1517.
[52]See Mukherjee (1978).

was seen as emerging from the suggestion of big business houses, it would lose a significant bloc of support, not just from the communists and socialists but also from within the Congress party itself. This probably was another reason for their pushing Bombay Plan into the background.

A likely third factor is that even though the Plan itself had proposed central planning, business leaders were surprised by the extent and form of control generated by Nehru era planning. Business and industry were seriously concerned about growing curbs on economic freedom by the end of the first plan. This concern was a major factor in the changeover of Hindu Mahasabha to Jana Sangh with more economic issues on its agenda. The same concern led to the emergence of the Swatantra Party and led Shroff to establish the Forum of Free Enterprise. This concern continued through the period as is reflected in the statements of business leaders. After the end of the sixties, Tata in his annual statement as chairman of TISCO, said, 'In the past twenty years, the freedom of action and the scope of operation of the private sector have been subjected to a gradual but continuous process of erosion in the course of which the government has achieved a measure of control and ownership of the means of production and distribution, which would have been inconceivable to any of us if introduced all at once at the start and which is unprecedented in any country other than those under totalitarian rule...'[53]

Leaders like Birla and Tata probably sensed the rising culture of control much earlier. It could even be as early as in 1948 when the report of the Economic Programme Committee of the Congress was published and Indian business was shocked by the proposal of nationalization and other measures mooted in the document. Kudaisya (2003) refers to a letter by Homi Mody to Birla written in 1948, which shows the concern quite clearly.[54] G.D. Birla was so perturbed that he, with Mody, drafted a strong refutation of the Economic Programme Committee's proposals on behalf of FICCI soon after. Around this time Birla wrote to G.B. Pant, 'The British have gone and the princes and the *zamindars* are in the background. The Congress accustomed to a target for its hatred, is now finding only one target, that is the capitalist.'[55] I believe that the Plan authors realised almost as soon as Congress started the warm up for Five Year Plans that they had not anticipated the extent and form of control that centralised planning would generate. If this assessment is correct, then it would be another reason for the Plan authors to move away from making any reference to the Plan.

---

[53]Tata (1971)
[54]Homi Mody to Birla, 28 January, 1948, in *Birla Papers*, Series I, File No. M-19, Mody, Sir Homi and Russi.
[55]Birla to G.B. Pant, 15 October, 1948, in *Birla Papers*, Series 1, File No. P-10, Pant G. B.

In his review of the first Five Year Plan, V.K.R.V. Rao noted that the Bombay Plan and the first Five Year Plan both provided for significant government control, but did not propose that the government should take over the economy like the Soviet plans (Rao, 1952). Rao possibly implied that in this sense Indian planning was a novel institution, not an emulation of anything of the past. I would add that this novel idea was the most important contribution of the Bombay Plan.

The Plan was forgotten not because it was worthless or faulty or lacked vision. It was pushed out of memory for strategic reasons. Feigning selective amnesia happened to be the best strategy in the fifties for all the important players in the game.

I would suggest that it is worthwhile to bring Bombay Plan back into academic discussions and classrooms. It will help in understanding the beginning of planning in India as also a part of the economic and political history of the 1940s.

◆

Amal Sanyal taught economics and retired as Associate Professor from Lincoln University, New Zealand. The author gratefully acknowledges research assistance from Rajiv Jha.

REFERENCES:

Anstey, Vera (1945), 'Review: A Brief Memorandum Outlining a Plan of Economic Development for India', *International Affairs* 21 (4): 555–557.

Anstey, Vera (1950), 'Indian Economic Planning', *Pacific Affairs*, Vol. 23, No 1 (Mar., 1950), pp.83-86.

Birla Papers: Birla to G.B. Pant, 15 October, 1948, Series 1, File No. P-10, Pant G.B.

Birla Papers: Homi Mody to Birla, 28 January,1948, in Series I, File No. M-19, Mody, Sir Homi and Russi.

Birla Papers: Birla to Morarji Desai, 27 June 1955, Series I, File No. D-4, Desai, Morarji.

Birla Papers: Birla to Rajagopalachari, 12 November, 1946. Series II, File No. R-5.

Birla, G.D. (1944), *The Plan Explained* (pamphlet), FICCI, speech delivered at the Annual Meeting of the FICCI, March 1944.

Chattopadhyaya, R. (1989), 'Attitude of Indian Business Towards Economic Planning, 1930–1956' (mimeo), presented at the IIM Ahmedabad seminar on '*Business and Politics in India: A Historical Perspective*', 29–31 March 1989.

Chaudhury, Saumitra (1984), 'Indian Bourgeoisie and Foreign Capital, 1931–1961', *Social Scientist*, May 1984.

Chibber, Vivek (2003), *Locked in Place: State-building and Late Industrialization in India*, Princeton: Princeton University Press, 2003.

Government of India, Planning Commission website, first, second and third Five Year plans, http://www.planningcommission.nic.in/plans/planrel/fiveyr/index9.html

Kochanek, S.A. (1974), *Business and Politics in India*, University of California Press, Berkeley, 1974.

Krishna, Ananth V. (2005), 'Globalization and Communalism: Locating Contemporary Political Discourse in the Context of Liberalization', in Ram Puniyani (ed) *Religion, Power and Violence: Expression of Politics in Contemporary Times*, New Delhi: SAGE, pp.44–67.

Kudaisya, Medha M. (2003), *The Life and Times of G.D. Birla*, Oxford University Press, New Delhi, 2003.

Lala, R.M. (1988), *Beyond the Last Blue Mountain, A Life of J.R.D Tata*, New York, Viking, 1988.

Lokanathan, P.S. (1945), 'The Bombay Plan', *Foreign Affairs*; July 1945; 23.

Mahalanobis, P. (1953). 'Some Observations on the Process of Growth of National Income', *Sankhya*, September, 307–12.

Markovits, Claude (1985), *Indian Business and National Politics, 1931-39: The Indigenous Capitalist Class and the Rise of the Congress Party*, Cambridge University Press, Cambridge, UK, 1985.

Mishra, G. (1975), *Public Sector in Indian Economy*, Communist Party of India Publications, February 1975.

Mukherjee, A. (1976), 'Indian Capitalist Class and the Public Sector', *Economic and Political Weekly*, Vol. II, No. 3, 17 January, 1976, pp.67–73.

Mukherjee, A. (1978), 'Indian Capitalist Class and Congress on National Planning and Public Sector, 1930–47', *Economic and Political Weekly*, Vol. 13, No. 35, 2 September, 1978, pp.1516–1528.

Naidu, M. (1944), 'The Bombay Plan', *Workers' International News*, Vol.5 No.7, December, 1944.

Patnaik, Prabhat (1993), 'Critical Reflections on Some Aspects of Structural Change in the Indian Economy' in T.J. Byres (ed) *The State and Development Planning in India*, Oxford University Press, Oxford, 1993.

Prime Minister's Office, Government of India, http://pmindia.nic.in/speech/content.asp?id=12

Prasad, P.S.N. (1945), 'Some Arguments in the Bombay Plan', *Indian Journal of Economics*, 1945, pp.25–40.

Purushottamdas Thakurdas Papers, Nehru Memorial Museum and Library, New Delhi.

Ralhan, O.P. (1997), (ed), *Encyclopaedia of Political Parties*, Anmol Publications, New Delhi, 1997.

Ranadive, B. T.(1944), *The Tata-Birla Plan*, The People's Publishing House, Bombay, 1944.

Rao, V.K.R.V (1952), 'India's First Five-Year Plan-A Descriptive Analysis', *Pacific Affairs*, Vol. 25, No. 1, March, 1952, pp.3–23

Shah, K.T. (1948), *National Planning: Principles and Administration*, National Planning Committee Series, Bombay, Vora and Company, 1948.

Singh, Tarlok (1963), 'The Bombay Plan Recalled', *Eastern Economist*, XL, No. 22, 7 June, 1963.

Swatantra Party, *To Prosperity Through Freedom*, Bombay, 1962.

Tata, J.R.D, 'The Future of the Private Sector', *Journal of the Indian Merchants' Chamber* 65 (1971): 43.

Thakurdas, Purushottamdas (1945) (ed.) *A Brief Memorandum Outlining a Plan of Economic Development for India* (2 vols.), London: Penguin.

Tripathi, D. *The Oxford History of Indian Business*, Oxford University Press, New Delhi, 2004.

Wainwright, Martin A. (1994), *Inheritance of Empire, Britain, India and the Balance of Power in Asia 1938–55*, Praeger Publishers, Westport, USA, 1994.

THE BOMBAY PLAN AND THE FRUSTRATIONS OF SIR ARDESHIR DALAL[1]

Gita Piramal

When the Bombay Plan was introduced, it generated tremendous interest. At the same time, it produced an army of doubters and naysayers. At one end of this spectrum was M K Gandhi. At the other end was the colonial regime, led by Lord Archibald Wavell, the Viceroy of India (Oct 1, 1943–Feb 21, 1947), and Lord Leo Amery, the Secretary of State for India in Britain (May 13, 1940–Jul 26, 1945).

In August 1944, Wavell invited Ardeshir Dalal to the Viceroy's Executive Council as Member, Post-War

---

[1] In his PhD thesis, *The Idea of Planning in India, 1930-1951*, Raghabendra Chattopadhyay named a chapter 'The Frustration of Ardeshir Dalal'. The chapter title is tweaked here with thanks.

THE BOMBAY PLAN AND THE FRUSTRATIONS OF SIR ARDESHIR DALAL

Reconstruction. Working under trying circumstances, Dalal embedded several core ideas of the Bombay Plan into the Industrial Policy Resolution of 1945. Post-Independence, several of these ideas went into the Industrial Policy Resolution of 1948, and subsequently into the early Five Year Plans. Simultaneously, Dalal used his position to strengthen India's scientific research base through the Council for Scientific and Industrial Research (CSIR) and the creation of the Indian Institute of Technology (IIT), Kharagpur.

His was the last signature on the Bombay Plan. But who was Sir Ardeshir Rustomji Dalal (24 Apr, 1884– 8 Oct, 1949)?[2]

THE BRIGHT BOMBAY BOY

Not much is known about Ardeshir's early life. What is confirmed is that Ardeshir was born in Bombay to Aimai Dorabji Bomanberam and Rustomji Dalal, a Parsi share-broker after whom is named a tiny but formidable alley, Dalal Street. Its name is often used as a metonym for the entire Indian financial establishment, similar to Wall Street in New York. In 1912, Ardeshir married Manebai,

---

[2]Not to be confused with Maneck Ardeshir Sohrab Dalal. Born 24 December 1918; son of Ardeshir Dalal, OBE and Amy Dalal; married 1947, Kathleen Gertrude Richardson; two daughters (one died).

daughter of Jamsetji Ardeshir Wadia. They had three children: a son and two daughters.[3]

The son grew to be 'rather tall and sparsely built' and was always well groomed. 'His heavy lidded eyes and gentle mouth may suggest the dreamer but there is an indefinable atmosphere of preciseness about him. Even his cheroot seems trained only to scatter its ashes in the ashtray,' is how Michael Brown, an editor of the *Illustrated Weekly of India*, described Dalal.[4]

SWIFT PROGRESS IN THE INDIAN CIVIL SERVICE

These traits served Dalal well. In 1905, twenty-one year old Dalal, with his eyes on the Indian Civil Service (ICS), applied for a scholarship to the JN Tata Endowment.[5] The loan scholarship, established in 1892[6] by Jamsetji Nusserwanji Tata (3 Mar 1839–19 May 1904), aimed at enabling Indian students aspiring to go abroad for post-

---

[3] Who's Who & Who Was Who. 'Dalal, Sir Ardeshir Rustomji'. https://doi.org/10.1093/ww/9780199540884.013.U224399 Published online: 1 December, 2007.

[4] Russi M Lala. *The Creation of Wealth: The Tatas From The 19th To The 21st Century*. Penguin: Delhi, 26 April, 2007 edition. Chapter 12: Dreamers and Performers.

[5] ibid.

[6] Jai Wadia. 'Enabling a dream education'. tata.com: December 2009. Online at http://www.tata.com/sustainability/articlesinside/ReI18gUGuYU=/TLYVr3YPkMU=. Retrieved on 19 March, 2018.

graduate studies, and mid-career professionals wanting to pursue a specialised course of study unavailable in India. Having stood first both in school and in Bombay University's Elphinstone College[7] besides being a Parsi, it was no surprise that Sir Dorab Tata, group chairman from 1904–1932, approved Dalal's application.

'It was one evening early in 1905 when I was summoned to the Library on the ground floor of the house at Waudby Road and told I was selected as one of the J.N. Tata scholars to proceed to England for higher studies,' wrote Dalal.[8] He took the Tripos in Natural Science at St John's College, Cambridge,[9] and successfully passed the ICS exam.[10]

---

[7] Tata Central Archives (TCA). 'Reminiscences of Sir Ardeshir Dalal'. Online at http://www.tatacentralarchives.com/documents/VOL-02-ISSUE-2-2003.pdf. Retrieved on 19 March, 2018, and TCA 'Sir Ardeshir Dalal'. VOL XI Issue 1, 2014. Pg5. Online at http://www.tatacentralarchives.com/documents/Vol-XI.Issue-1-2014.pdf. Retrieved on 19 March, 2018.
[8] TCA 'Sir Ardeshir Dalal'. Vol XI Issue 1, 2014. Pg5. Online at http://www.tatacentralarchives.com/documents/Vol-XI.Issue-1-2014.pdf. Retrieved on 19 March, 2018.
[9] ibid.
[10] The only Indian to top the ICS examination in 88 years was Kumar Padmanabha Sankara Menon who stood first in the 1921 batch. RK Kaushik. 'The men who ran the Raj'. Hindustan Times: Chandigarh, 17 April, 2012. Online at https://www.hindustantimes.com/chandigarh/the-men-who-ran-the-raj/

(cont)

The ICS was a tiny administrative elite, never more than twelve hundred in number and, until the twentieth century, overwhelmingly British in composition.[11] Its strength was restricted to the number 'absolutely necessary to fill the supervising and controlling offices' of the governing structure.[12]

The lower ranks of the administration were peopled by a vast army of subordinate clerks and provincial staff, recruited in India to do the more humdrum tasks. But the hierarchy was headed and guided by the well-controlled hands of carefully selected ICS officers. 'These officers held all the key posts: they surrounded the Viceroy, dominated the provincial governments and were ultimately responsible for overseeing all government activity in the two hundred and fifty districts that comprised British India,' describes Ann Ewing.[13]

That Dalal managed to graduate in 1907 is remarkable.[14] Competition was intense for English

---

story-S6yQeWGkqIw7xzgRhH5wIO.html. Retrieved on 19 March, 2018.

[11] Ann Ewing. 'The Indian Civil Service'. Posted online at http://www.britishempire.co.uk/maproom/india/ics.htm. Retrieved on 19 March, 2018.

[12] ibid.

[13] ibid.

[14] TCA. 'Reminiscences of Sir Ardeshir Dalal'. Online at http://www.tatacentralarchives.com/documents/VOL-02-ISSUE-2-2003.pdf. Retrieved on 19 March, 2018.

candidates, more so for Indians. The syllabus was designed such that European Classics had a predominant share of marks. The maximum age was 23 years and minimum age was 18 years. Examinations were conducted in London. Travel and lodging was expensive. It was only in 1922, after World War I and the Montagu Chelmsford reforms that the British agreed to hold the ICS examination in India, first in Allahabad and later in Delhi.[15]

On his return to India, Dalal joined the ICS in 1908. Describing the classic civil servant under the Raj, a current IAS officer maintains, 'During colonial times, the Collector was trained to be a despot. Power is essential if your job requires you to maximize revenue generation, and maintain law and order. Under the British, the Collector was policeman, judge and jailor as well as the tax man.'[16]

Dalal's swift progress up the slippery civil service ladder was assisted by a severe shortage of European ICS officers after World War I (28 Jul 1914–11 Nov 1918).[17]

---

[15]Union Public Service Commission. 'Historical Perspective'. Online at http://www.upsc.gov.in/sites/default/files/History%20of%20the%20Commission%20final%20%281%29_0.pdf. Retrieved on 19 March, 2018.
[16]Interview with Ashish Kumar Singh, 2 March, 2018. Mumbai.
[17]Ewing. 'The Indian Civil Service'. Posted online at http://www.britishempire.co.uk/maproom/india/ics.htm. Retrieved on 19 March, 2018.

As the war dragged on, ICS vacancies mounted until, by 1918, the ICS was short of two hundred men, a serious matter in so small an organization.[18] Moreover, after the war, it was difficult to interest young English men in a career in India. The India Office had to abandon its efforts to maintain a set ratio of Indian and European candidates, admitting a 'disproportionate' number of the former.[19]

Dalal was initially posted to the Bombay Presidency, but moved around for the next thirteen years as Assistant Collector and later Collector in various districts.[20] Starting out as Deputy Secretary to the Government of Bombay in the finance department, he was soon upgraded to Acting Secretary, Government of Bombay.[21] After a short stint in Delhi as Acting Secretary to the Government of India in the Department of Education, Health and Lands, Dalal returned to Bombay as the first Indian to be appointed the port city's Municipal Commissioner (1928–31).[22] During his term, he gained the reputation of being 'one of the ablest commissioners' and was 'well regarded for his grasp

---

[18]ibid.
[19]ibid.
[20]TCA. 'Sir Ardeshir Dalal'. Vol XI Issue 1, 2014. p.5. Online at http://www.tatacentralarchives.com/documents/Vol-XI.Issue-1-2014.pdf. Retrieved on 19 March, 2018.
[21]TCA. 'Reminiscences of Sir Ardeshir Dalal'. Online at http://www.tatacentralarchives.com/documents/VOL-02-ISSUE-2-2003.pdf. Retrieved on 19 March, 2018.
[22]ibid.

of financial affairs'.[23] In addition, Dalal was a member the Bombay Legislative Council in 1923 and Member of the Indian Legislative Assembly in 1927 (appendix 4: Ardeshir Dalal Lifeline).

The kudos, learnings and connections he acquired while handling various portfolios during his career would be crucial in shaping Dalal's role in planning.

Towards the close of the 1920s, Dalal would not have failed to notice that his foreign fellow ICS officers had begun finding it difficult to make ends meet as the bottom fell out of the rupee market. ICS salaries and conditions of service no longer compared well with those offered by the business houses, and many European officers began to wonder if they should stay on in India.[24] Dalal nimbly switched from government service to the private sector in 1931.

---

[23]Medha Kudaisya. '"The Promise of Partnership": Indian Business, the State, and the Bombay Plan of 1944'. *Business History Review* 88 (Spring 2014): 97–131. doi:10.1017/S0007680513001426. The President and Fellows of Harvard College. ISSN 0007-6805; 2044-768X (Web). p.103.

[24]Ewing. 'The Indian Civil Service'. Posted online at http://www.britishempire.co.uk/maproom/india/ics.htm. Retrieved on 19 March, 2018.

STRATEGIC AND DECISIVE MAN OF ACTION

At 44, Dalal joined the Tatas as Resident Director at Tata Iron & Steel Company (Tisco), liaising between the Board at Bombay, and the management at Jamshedpur.[25] He moved up swiftly to become Tisco's Director-in-Charge—the first Indian to hold that position. Dalal served three Tata chairmen: Sir Dorab Tata, who made Dalal a Director and Partner in Tata Sons; Sir Nowroji Saklatwala[26] and JRD Tata. At the Tata Sons Board meeting on 26 July, 1938, Dalal seconded the proposal that Tata be appointed group chairman.[27]

As part of the inner circle, Dalal graduated to the directorships of Andhra Valley Power Supply Company,

---

[25] TCA. 'Sir Ardeshir Dalal'. Vol XI Issue 1, 2014. p.5. Online at http://www.tatacentralarchives.com/documents/Vol-XI.Issue-1-2014.pdf. Retrieved on 19 March, 2018.

[26] TCA. 'Reminiscences of Sir Ardeshir Dalal'. Online at http://www.tatacentralarchives.com/documents/VOL-02-ISSUE-2-2003.pdf. Retrieved on 19 March, 2018.

[27] Only four people were present at the 26 July, 1938 meeting of the Board of Directors to appoint JRD Tata as chairman of Tata Sons: JRD, Sorab D Saklatvala, Ardeshir R Dalal and Sir Homi P Mody. Lala. *Beyond The Last Blue Mountain – A Life Of J.R.D. Tata (1904-1993)*. Penguin: Delhi, 1992. p.76. In the same book, p.195, Lala continues, 'J.R.D. was to learn later that the only one sceptical of his abilities to be a suitable Chairman was Ardeshir Dalal, though Dalal had seconded the proposal to appoint him Chairman.'

Associated Cement Companies, Tata Oil Mills, the Taj Mahal Hotel and Tata Chemicals until 1944, when he resigned from all Tata positions to join the Viceroy's Executive Council.

Dalal is often cast in the 'image of an average American's idea of big business'. The descriptor gained him respect among top management but not necessarily among the majority of Tisco's personnel. Unstable labour relations marked this period. Dalal pioneered a profit-sharing and retiring gratuity scheme for labour.[28] An Indianization program for senior managers was gradually introduced.[29]

During World War II, Tisco became a major arsenal. It needed the large orders that only the government could place, while the government needed Tisco's products for the war effort. Dalal's managerial abilities won him a Knighthood in 1939. In 1941, Tata appointed Dalal as Tisco's liaison officer to the Ministry of Supplies.[30]

---

[28]Lala. *The Creation of Wealth: The Tatas From The 19th To The 21st Century.* Penguin: Delhi, April 26, 2007 edition. Chapter 12: Dreamers and Performers.

[29]TCA. 'Sir Ardeshir Dalal'. Vol XI Issue 1, 2014. p.5. Online at http://www.tatacentralarchives.com/documents/Vol-XI.Issue-1-2014.pdf. Retrieved on 19 March, 2018.

[30]Kudaisya. '"The Promise of Partnership": Indian Business, the State, and the Bombay Plan of 1944'. *Business History Review* 88 (Spring 2014): 97–131. doi:10.1017/S0007680513001426. The

(cont)

The August 1942 issue of the in-house publication, *TISCO Review*[31]—another Dalal innovation—proudly asserted that the company was 'rendering the maximum help possible to the Government' in the Allied war effort.[32] A pamphlet on the notice-board aimed at senior-level English-speaking employees encouraged employee donations to pay for a fighter plane with slogans like 'Now is the time to Play Your Part in the Battle for Freedom', and 'No Sacrifice is too Great in the Cause of Freedom.'[33]

The magazine's ink was barely dry when Gandhi made the Quit India call. Jamshedpur began to reverberate with the 'Do or Die' slogan. On 20 August 1942, workers and supervisory personnel at Jamshedpur went on strike, forcing management to hurriedly shut down the plant.[34]

The strike put the Tata management 'in a particularly delicate situation. They wanted to get the plant back up and running, but they wanted to do so with minimum

---

President and Fellows of Harvard College. ISSN 0007-6805; 2044-768X (Web). p.103.

[31] TCA. 'Sir Ardeshir Dalal'. Vol XI Issue 1, 2014. p.5. Online at http://www.tatacentralarchives.com/documents/Vol-XI.Issue-1-2014.pdf. Retrieved on 19 March, 2018.

[32] Ross Bassett. 'The Technological Indian'. Harvard University Press: Cambridge, 2016. p.154.

[33] ibid, pp.154-5.

[34] ibid, p.156.

government involvement.'[35] To achieve this middle path, the Tata management, in meetings with strikers, frequently warned workers of the possibilities of government intervention, while at the same time, urging government officials to let them manage the affair on their own.[36]

Dalal's strategy to break the strike was a suave combination of threats and palliatives, strengthened with divide-and-conquer elements. By 3 September, 1942, 14,000 out of the regular workforce had returned, with more trickling in. 'One sign of how effective the Tata methods had been during the period of labour unrest was that violence was avoided and only eighty five people were arrested during the strike.'[37] Dalal bragged that their approach to the strike had led to a settlement without even 'a pane of glass being broken.'[38]

THE PLANNER

With the Jamshedpur crisis somewhat settling down, Dalal's focus was on a meeting scheduled for 11 December, 1942 at Bombay House to discuss the future of an independent India. The output—*A Brief Memorandum Outlining a Plan of Economic Development for India*, aka

---

[35] ibid, p.157.
[36] ibid.
[37] ibid, p.161.
[38] ibid.

the Bombay Plan—appeared in January 1944.

The year 1944 was big for planning: the UN, the IMF, and the World Bank all had their gestation that year.[39] In India, several plans were published but three stand out: the Gandhian Plan of Shriman Narayan Agarwal with a foreword by Gandhi; the People's Plan of MN Roy, a communist; and, of course, the highly publicized Bombay Plan.

Its eight authors were Sir Purshotamdas Thakurdas (1879–1961), J.R.D Tata (1904–1993), Sir Ardeshir Rustomji Dalal, Ardeshir Darabshaw Shroff (1899–1965), Dr John Mathai (1886–1959), G.D. Birla (1894–1993), Sir Shri Ram (1884–1962) and Kasturbhai Lalbhai (1894–1980). Of all the authors, Dalal was the only one to have formally studied science.

According to Amal Sanyal in *A Forgotten Document*, Mathai was assigned to do the drafting.[40] Sumit K Sarkar in *Crowding out!* suggests that Dalal was the Bombay Plan's principal draftsman.[41] Both Dalal and Mathai

---

[39] Robert S Anderson. *Nucleus and Nation: Scientists, International Networks, and Power in India*. University of Chicago Press: Chicago, 2010. p.114.

[40] Amal Sanyal. 'The Bombay Plan. A Forgotten Document'. Lincoln University: New Zealand, 2012. Online at https://nzsac.files.wordpress.com/2012/05/bombayplanfornzsac.pdf. Retrieved on 13 December, 2017.

[41] Sumit K Majumdar. 'Crowding out! The role of state companies and the dynamics of industrial competitiveness in India'. *Industrial*

worked alongside in a secretariat put together by Tata and Birla. Tata provided for half the expenses, and the rest was shared by the other planners.

The Bombay Plan was initially released in India as a pamphlet and was so popular that it quickly ran out of stock. Part One of The Bombay Plan was published in May 1944. A reprint followed in September 1944. Part Two was first published in India in January 1945. In April 1945, a new edition came out that combined Part One and Part Two. These editions were circulated in Britain as well as in India.

Wavell's invitation to Dalal to join the Viceroy's Executive Council placed Dalal in a bit of a quandary. Dalal left the Tatas in June 1944 and joined the Executive Council a few weeks later in August. As mentioned earlier, Dalal's signature is last on the original document but drops off in the later editions. However, in the April 1945 edition, Dalal is upgraded to third position, below Thakurdas and Tata, but above Shroff, Mathai, Birla, Shri Ram and Lalbhai on the authors page; and fourth position on the title page.

---

and Corporate Change, Volume 18, Number 1, pp.165–207. doi:10.1093/icc/dtn047. p.170.

THE GOVERNMENT CATCH-UP GAME PLAN

The general view is that 'not much came out of the newly established department'.[42] Dalal's resignation in January 1946 and the winding up of the planning department shortly thereafter appear to reinforce that view. A closer look at the government's intentions and Dalal's activities, however, suggest a rethink, beginning with the question: why did the government invite Dalal on the Viceroy's Executive Council? And why did Dalal accept the offer?

Seeing the general enthusiasm produced by the Bombay Plan, Wavell and Amery agreed that 'they must not get left behind' in 'drawing up a more entertaining and interesting picture of India's future' than Birla or anyone else.

Pressure mounted as *The Economist*, an influential London-based journal, began its coverage of the Bombay Plan. On 16 May 1944, Wavell wrote to Amery, 'I see the Bombay Plan has come out... Sir Gregory who takes criticism very much to heart, thought we should at once produce a rival pamphlet and broadcast it through the India Office. I doubt if this would be a success; but we

---

[42]Kudaisya. '"The Promise of Partnership": Indian Business, the State, and the Bombay Plan of 1944'. *Business History Review* 88 (Spring 2014): 97–131. doi:10.1017/S0007680513001426. The President and Fellows of Harvard College. ISSN 0007-6805; 2044-768X (Web). p.126 n103.

are getting Holburn of the *Times* to write a special article about the progress made by the Government of India with planning and development and I do not think we can go beyond something of this kind.'[43]

The option of getting a couple of Bombay Plan planners on board appeared to have the merit of combining damage control with political advantage. Wavell and his advisors zoned in on Dalal and Mathai. Mathai was appointed finance minister.[44] Dalal, given his contribution to the war effort in Tisco and his earlier civil service experiences, joined the Viceroy's Executive Council as Member-in-Charge of Post-War Reconstruction (appendix 1). Both accepted their invitations and resigned from the Tata Group.

From Dalal's point of view, the reason for joining was simple. The war would end soon, and Independence was inevitable. As an insider, there would be opportunities to influence the future of India. As Thakurdas pointed out, Dalal 'felt, and I and others share that view with him, that he might be able to do some good in preparing the

---

[43]Lala. *Beyond the Last Blue Mountain.* Penguin Books: New Delhi, 1992. pp.219-220.

[44]The process of Dalal's selection to the Executive Council is detailed somewhat in Chattopadhyay details. 'The Idea of Planning in India, 1930-1951'. PhD Thesis. Australian National University: Canberra, April 1985. pp.187-188.

ground for a national government.'[45]

However, news of Dalal's appointment received mixed responses. Within the British bureaucracy, 'Dalal's appointment was seen by authorities as being welcomed by the Congress and to that extent leading to an improvement from the administrative angle,' writes Mukherjee. 'However, it was also seen by the loyalist camp as the government capitulating to FICCI and the Congress.'[46]

Within the British industrial elite in India, its upset leader, Sir Edward Charles Benthall (1893–1961) warned Prime Minister Winston Churchill that Dalal's Government Plan would lead to 'the liquidation of the British empire' adding the barb, with Churchill 'presiding.'[47] Benthall seethed at the thought of State aid flowing to 'floundering industries, Congress or FICCI control of key industries, and elimination of British influence in business in India within two or three decades.'[48]

Asked for his opinion, Gandhi was blunt with Tata, Birla and Thakurdas. 'Some little good he [Dalal] will

---

[45] Aditya Mukherjee. *Imperialism, Nationalism and the Making of the Indian Capitalist Class 1920-1947*. Sage Publications: New Delhi, 2002.
[46] ibid.
[47] ibid.
[48] ibid.

certainly be able to do, but it will be at the sacrifice of greater good...Every good man who cooperates with the Government adds to its prestige, and thus prolongs the agony.'[49]

India's scientific community, however, was delighted. Among them was Shanti Swaroop Bhatnagar (1894–1955), a CSIR founder. Writing to Nobel Laureate, Sir Archibald V Hill in August 1944, Bhatnagar described how 'very glad he was that Sir Ardeshir Dalal was appointed Member of the Viceroy's Executive Council.'[50] Bhatnagar was less elated after the government transferred CSIR to Dalal as another portfolio under the Department of Planning and Development. Until that moment, Bhatnagar had endorsed Hill's report which recommended the centralization of all research under a single department. Once he discovered that the director had to work under a bureaucrat, Bhatnagar complained that 'men of science are treated like labourers and the general tendency of the civil service is to grab power', notes V.V. Krishna.[51]

---

[49]Pyarelal. *Mahatma Gandhi, The Last Phase*. Part 1, Volume IX, Book One, First Edition. Navajivan Mudranalaya: Ahmedabad, 1956. p.48.

[50]Anderson. *Nucleus and Nation: Scientists, International Networks, and Power in India*. University of Chicago Press: Chicago, 2010. p.115.

[51]V.V. Krishna. 'Organization of Industrial Research: The Early History of CSIR, 1934-47' in Uma Das Gupta (ed). *Science and*

(cont)

Dalal himself appears to have been driven by the thought that there was no need to 'stand still' until national government was achieved.[52] He not only applied himself with vigour but grew his role substantially. Sir Dalal's brisk activities soon began to worry the government and frustrations set in. What exactly did Dalal do during the sixteen months of his service?

ROADBLOCKS

Dalal was able to join the government in August 1944. The Government of India had been working on its own plans for India and the empire during the war. As soon as he was on board, all the Reconstruction Committees that were set up since 1941 were transferred to Dalal's department.[53] Among them was the Policy Committee on Industries (No. 4, later renumbered as No. 48). Dalal was handed a meaty responsibility—a new Department of

---

Modern India: An Institutional History, c1784-1947. Centre for Studies in Civilization, Pearson Education, Delhi, 2011. p.174.
[52] Aditya Mukherjee. 'Indian Capitalist Class and the Public Sector', *Economic and Political Weekly*, January 17, 1976. p.71 ftn 9, referencing *The Hindu*, 30 May 1944; *Hindustan Times*, 18 December 1944; *The Hindu*, 31 October 1944; *Bombay Chronicle*, 18 September 1944; *Free Press Journal*, 19 September 1944; *Hindustan Times*, 16 May 1945; *Hindustan Standard*, 4 May 1945.
[53] Chattopadhyay. 'The Idea of Planning in India, 1930-1951'. PhD Thesis. Australian National University: Canberra, April 1985. p.215.

Planning and Development created specifically for him.[54] The department's remit was to develop short- and long-term plans for the restoration of normalcy after the war, and for economic reconstruction and development. Over twenty panels of experts were set up.

The Provinces

Dalal's most urgent task was to reduce the impact of the inevitable post-war slump. Writing to the provincial governments, Dalal reminded them of earlier directives from the Centre on this topic; and asked for their collaboration in evolving 'a co-ordinated plan for the whole of India'.[55] The governments of the provinces and Indian states were invited to prepare detailed short-term and long-term plans of fifteen years and send them to the central department.[56]

---

[54]Anderson. *Nucleus and Nation: Scientists, International Networks, and Power in India*. University of Chicago Press: Chicago, 2010. p.114.

[55]Chattopadhyay. 'The Idea of Planning in India, 1930-1951'. PhD Thesis. Australian National University: Canberra, April 1985. pp.211-215.

[56]Kudaisya. '"The Promise of Partnership": Indian Business, the State, and the Bombay Plan of 1944'. *Business History Review* 88 (Spring 2014): 97–131. doi:10.1017/S0007680513001426. The President and Fellows of Harvard College. ISSN 0007-6805; 2044-768X (Web). p.126.

The provincial governments, however, did not show the enthusiasm that was expected of them. Each wanted a firm commitment from the Centre on cost-sharing before drawing up their plans. As Dalal was unable to provide concrete assurances, his only fall-back was to urge them to reconsider their position. Any hesitation to take bold action now would result in a serious slump which would 'give the worst setback to development'.[57]

Dalal kept hammering away with numbers and ideas, thoughtful proposals and fearful predictions. The financial issues kept the Centre and the provinces bogged down in extended correspondence for nearly a year. By that time the war had ended, and a post-war slump was reality.

Policy Committee on Industries No. 48

Another of Dalal's early moves was to refashion one of the Reconstruction Committees, renaming it the Policy Committee on Industries (No. 48).[58] Below it were seventeen panels. Chaired by Dalal, the committee consisted of government representatives from the centre, provinces and Indian states. Experts, and the industrialist elite, both British and Indian, were invited as non-official members.

---

[57]Chattopadhyay. 'The Idea of Planning in India, 1930-1951'. PhD Thesis. Australian National University: Canberra, April 1985. p.211-5.
[58]ibid, p.215.

Most of the Bombay Planners were accommodated, as was the FICCI leadership team. Including Dalal, seven committee members included were Bombay Plan authors: Thakurdas, Tata, Birla, Shri Ram, Mathai and Lalbhai (FICCI president at the time). Five committee members were affiliated to both the Bombay Plan and FICCI: Birla, Shri Ram, Thakurdas, Lalbhai and Dalal himself. Two were non-Bombay Planners but FICCI members: Walchand Hirachand and Sir Padampat Singhania. To add leaven to the dough were old companions with a scientific bent of mind such as Sir Nalini Ranjan Sarkar.[59]

This committee turned out to be an 'empty gesture'.[60] It met only twice in ten months between December 1944 and October 1945. It was not consulted, but merely informed about the Industrial Policy Resolution of April 1945. All that the committee could do was to recommend the control of the concentration of industries in a few provinces and favour economically backward provinces in the allocation of industries; the development of cottage industries to provide employment to the rural unemployed; and the creations of a permanent Tariff Board and a Central Statistical Organisation.[61]

---

[59] Aditya Mukherjee. 'Indian Capitalist Class and the Public Sector', *Economic and Political Weekly*, 17 January 1976. p.71 footnote 9.
[60] Chattopadhyay. 'The Idea of Planning in India, 1930-1951'. PhD Thesis. Australian National University: Canberra, April 1985. p.216.
[61] ibid, p.216.

The Safeguards Rumpus

During the 2nd meeting of the Policy Committee, Dalal reported the failure of his earlier recent visit to Britain.[62] The main agenda of his visit was to find a solution to 'commercial safeguard' clauses in the Government of India Act, 1935[63] favouring the British industrial elite.

Dalal took up the issue with Wavell almost immediately and 'demanded'[64] that the new industrial development should be financed and controlled by Indians as far as possible. The government acquiesced in principle, but as the law stood, it could not discriminate against a British company, Wavell stressed.

Wavell softened the blow by granting Dalal permission to visit Britain and lobby for his case. At the same time, Wavell and Amery quietly agreed that Dalal was pushing

---

[62]In Britain, while WWII was still on, July 1945 saw the Labour Party win a 'land-slide' victory in the general election and Winston Churchill's coalition replaced by Clement Attlee. Attlee and his cabinet colleagues were eager to find a political solution to 'the Indian problem'. Soon after meeting Attlee in London, Wavell announced that general elections would be held in India in December 1945.

[63]Sections 111-121 of Chapter III, Part IV of the Government of India Act, 1935.

[64]Chattopadhyay. 'The Idea of Planning in India, 1930-1951'. PhD Thesis. Australian National University: Canberra, April 1985. p.226.

'the interests of Indian capitalists a bit too hard.'[65]

Recognizing that the challenge was of 'a very difficult political and constitutional character', Dalal reshaped the debate. He began lobbying for 'enacting something like an Unfair Trade Practices Act.'[66]

Industrial Policy Resolution, April 1945

At the top of Dalal's many agendas was to morph an unofficial document penned by a group of Indian businessmen into official government documents. Like all good babus, Dalal recycled and repackaged the Bombay Plan in numerous ways. The Second Report on Reconstruction Planning (1945) is one example of many. Another was the Industrial Policy Resolution, April 1945, often referred to as the Government Plan.

Its objectives were to increase national wealth by the maximum exploitation of the country's resources; to make the country better prepared for defence; and to provide a high and stable level of employment.[67] It

---

[65] Aditya Mukherjee. *Imperialism, Nationalism and the Making of the Indian Capitalist Class 1920-1947*. Sage Publications: New Delhi, 2002.

[66] Chattopadhyay. 'The Idea of Planning in India, 1930-1951.' PhD Thesis. Australian National University: Canberra, April 1985. p.218.

[67] Ajit Roy. *Planning in India*. National Publishers: Calcutta, 1965. p.47.

advocated central government control over twenty key industries. Basic industries of national importance were to be nationalized if adequate private capital for their development was not forthcoming. These industries included aircraft, automobiles, tractors, chemicals, dyes, iron and steel, prime movers, electric machinery, machine tools, electro-chemicals and non-ferrous metals. The statement proposed the use of licensing and other controls to achieve a multiplicity of objectives including prevention of monopolies and regional concentrations, the setting up of a system of targets to determine the direct lines of planned development and thus also to prevent private capital going in the direction of excessive profits. The statement also indicated that these measures were intended to secure fair wages and security for industrial workers among other objectives, eliminate excess profits and ensure improvement of quality of goods.[68] This was old wine in a new bottle but still drew loud objections.

---

[68](1) Information and Library Network Centre. 'Chapter 5: The Formulation of Industrial Policy, 1944-1949'. Online at http://shodhganga.inflibnet.ac.in/bitstream/10603/13974/10/10_chapter%2005.pdf. Retrieved on 21 March, 2018. (2) Information and Library Network Centre. 'Chapter 4: 4.1 Industrial Policy Resolution 1948'. Online at http://shodhganga.inflibnet.ac.in/bitstream/10603/137016/7/07_chapter_04.pdf. Retrieved on 21 March, 2018.

FICCI Protests and Whitehall Objects

Sir Badridas Goenka (1883-1993) who succeeded Lalbhai as the FICCI president, politely described the policy as 'commendable' before lighting into it. Critiquing the policy's silence on 'the important problem of safeguarding Indian industries also from internal competition of non-Indian interests,' he stressed that 'there is no assurance on the part of the Government that they will not permit foreign enterprises from establishing themselves in India behind tariff walls to compete unfairly with or even destroy Indian industries.'[69]

Referring to the policy's objective of 'prevention of concentration of industries in the hands of a few persons or of a special community,' Goenka, a Marwari, and member of the 'special community' argued, 'that while everyone would appreciate Government helping backward communities in participating in the industrial development of the country, the condition stipulated by Government would in effect retard industrialization unless particular communities come forward to undertake the risks of industrial enterprise.'[70]

In any case, Whitehall found the proposals unacceptable and rejected them,[71] tempering the blow by

---

[69]Sir Badridas Goenka. FICCI, Vol.II, 1945. p.126.
[70]ibid.
[71]Sumit K Majundar. *India's Late, Late Industrial Revolution:*

(cont)

awarding Dalal a second and higher ranking Knighthood. The Department of Planning and Development was wound up, 'despite Congress protests' suggests Jivanta Schoettli.[72] To the 'great relief' of the government, Dalal made no 'political capital' out of his resignation.[73]

ARDESHIR GIVES UP

As Mukerjee points out, Dalal's participation in the colonial regime was in the nature of 'short-term collaboration' with the British even though he, like the other authors, was aware of the 'long term contradiction… with British rule'.[74] He resigned from the Executive Council in January 1946 and returned to the Tatas.

But when a new invitation turned up in October 1946, he could not resist. Dalal joined the planning advisory board set up by the Interim Government. After Independence, several ideas developed during Dalal's

---

Democratizing Entrepreneurship. Cambridge University Press: Cambridge UK, 2012. p.158.
[72]Jivanta Schoettli. *Vision and Strategy in Indian Politics: Jawaharlal Nehru's policy choices and the designing of political institutions.* Routledge: Oxford, 2012. p.100.
[73]Chattopadhyay. 'The Idea of Planning in India, 1930-1951'. PhD Thesis. Australian National University: Canberra, April 1985. p.217.
[74]Aditya Mukherjee. 'Indian Capitalist Class and the Public Sector', *Economic and Political Weekly*, 17 January 1976. p.71 footnote 9.

service in the Executive Council—such as the Industrial Finance Corporation, a Central Statistical Organization (CSO), the boards for minerals and coal, Cottage Industries Corporation (CIC)—along with ideas from the 1945 Policy insinuated themselves into the Industrial Policy Resolution of April 1948 and into Nehru's Five Year Plans.

◆

An author, journalist, academic, businesswoman and entrepreneur, **Dr Gita Piramal** is currently Senior Associate Fellow at Somerville College, University of Oxford.

REFERENCES

Aditya Mukherjee.

—*Imperialism, Nationalism and the Making of the Indian Capitalist Class 1920-1947*. Sage Publications: New Delhi, 2002.

—'Indian Capitalist Class and the Public Sector', *Economic and Political Weekly*, January 17, 1976. p.71 ftn 9.

Ajit Roy. *Planning in India*. National Publishers: Calcutta, 1965.

Amal Sanyal. 'The Bombay Plan. A Forgotten Document'. Lincoln University: New Zealand, 2012. Online at https://nzsac.files.wordpress.com/2012/05/bombayplanfornzsac.pdf. Retrieved on 13 December, 2017.

Ann Ewing. 'The Indian Civil Service'. Posted online at http://www.britishempire.co.uk/maproom/india/ics.htm. Retrieved on 19 March, 2017.

David Lockwood. 'Was the Bombay Plan a Capitalist Plot?' in *Studies in History* 28(I) 99-116, Jawaharlal Nehru University/Sage Publications. DOI: 10.1177/0257643013477263. Retrieved on 1 April, 2018.

Jai Wadia. 'Enabling a dream education'. tata.com: December 2009. Online at http://www.tata.com/sustainability/articlesinside/ReI18gUGuYU=/TLYVr3YPkMU=. Retrieved on 19.3.2018.

Jay Weinstein. 'Indian Institutes of Technology' in Arnold P Kaminisky & Roger D Long (eds), *India Today: An Encyclopaedia of Life in the Republic*. Volume 1.

Jivanta Schoettli. *Vision and Strategy in Indian Politics: Jawaharlal Nehru's policy choices and the designing of political institutions*. Routledge: Oxford, 2012.

Medha Kudaisya. '"The Promise of Partnership": Indian Business, the State, and the Bombay Plan of 1944'. *Business History Review* 88 (Spring 2014): 97–131. doi:10.1017/S0007680513001426. The President and Fellows of Harvard College. ISSN 0007-6805; 2044-768X (Web).

Narayana Jayaram. 'IIT System and IIT Bombay', in Philip G Altbach & Jamil Salmi (eds). *The Road to Academic Excellence: The Making of World-Class Research Universities*. World Bank: Washington DC, 2011. Chapter 6.

Pyarelal. *Mahatma Gandhi, The Last Phase*. Part 1, Volume IX, Book-One, First Edition. Navajivan Mudranalaya: Ahmedabad, 1956.

Raghabendra Chattopadhyay. 'The Idea of Planning in India, 1930-1951'. PhD Thesis. Australian National University: Canberra, April 1985.

Robert S Anderson. *Nucleus and Nation: Scientists, International Networks, and Power in India*. University of Chicago Press: Chicago, 2010.

Ross Bassett. *The Technological Indian*. Harvard University Press: Cambridge, 2016.

Russi M Lala.

—— *The Creation of Wealth: The Tatas From The 19th To The 21st Century*. Penguin: Delhi, April 26, 2007 edition.

—— *Beyond The Last Blue Mountain – A Life Of J.R.D. Tata (1904-1993)*. Penguin: New Delhi 1992.

Sumit K Majumdar. *India's Late, Late Industrial Revolution: Democratizing Entrepreneurship*. Cambridge University Press: Cambridge UK, 2012.

Tata Central Archives.

—— 'Reminiscences of Sir Ardeshir Dalal'. Online at http://www.tatacentralarchives.com/documents/VOL-02-ISSUE-2-2003.pdf. Retrieved on 19 March, 2018.

—— 'Sir Ardeshir Dalal'. VOL XI Issue 1, 2014. Pg5. Online at http://www.tatacentralarchives.com/documents/Vol-XI.Issue-1-2014.pdf. Retrieved on 19 March, 2018.

V.V. Krishna. 'Organization of Industrial Research: The Early History of CSIR, 1934-47' in Uma Das Gupta (ed). *Science and Modern India: An Institutional History, c1784-1947*. Centre for Studies in Civilization/ Pearson Education: Delhi, 2011.

A VISION DERAILED

Omkar Goswami

At 7 pm on 12 April 1936 in Lucknow, a dhoti kurta and Gandhi-topi clad man born to a seriously wealthy, westernised and influential Allahabad family, schooled at Harrow and Trinity College, Cambridge, began to deliver his presidential address to the 49th session of the INC. Delivered in Hindi, Jawaharlal Nehru's two-and-a-half-hour long speech was electrifying.

Addressing the Congressmen as 'Comrades', he described India's freedom movement as a part of wider global events encompassing large parts of Asia, a Europe 'struggling for a new equilibrium' and the Soviet Union, where 'a new conception of human freedom and social equality fought desperately against a host of enemies'.[1]

---

[1] *Report of the 49th Session of the Indian National Congress held at Lucknow in April 1936*, henceforth INC Lucknow Report (1936), p.9.

Soon enough, Nehru stated his preferences loud and clear. It was socialism. He said that while conflicts grew everywhere and the Great Depression had overwhelmed the capitalist world, the USSR had made 'astonishing progress...in every direction'. According to him, 'Two rival economic and political systems faced each other in the world... One of them was the capitalist order, which had inevitably developed into vast imperialisms... The other was the new socialist order of the USSR, which went from progress to progress, though often at terrible cost, and where the problems of the capitalist world had ceased to exist.'[2]

About half-way along his speech, Nehru was blunter still. 'I am convinced', he said, '[that] the only key to the solution of...India's problem lies in socialism... I see no way of ending the poverty, the vast unemployment, the degradation and subjection of the Indian people except through socialism. That involves vast and revolutionary changes in our political and social structure, the ending of vested interests in land and industry, as well as the feudal and autocratic Indian states system. That means the ending of private property, except in a restricted sense, and the replacement of the present profit system by a higher ideal of cooperative service... In short, it means a new civilization, radically different from the present

---

[2]ibid., pp.10-11.

capitalist order.'[3] For Nehru, 'Socialism is...[not] merely an economic doctrine which I favour; it is a vital creed which I hold with all my head and heart...I should like the Congress to become a socialist organization.'[4]

SOCIALISM: ANOTHER NAME FOR NEHRU'S IMPATIENCE

For India's capitalists, the alarm bells from Lucknow rang loud and clear. Here was Jawaharlal Nehru, Gandhi's favourite and destined to lead a soon-to-be independent nation, coming out as a firm supporter of socialism and behaving as if he despised the world of business. It mattered little to most industrialists that all the leftist and socialist resolutions proposed in Lucknow were defeated, and that Gandhi had cleverly constrained Nehru's proletarian sympathies by packing the Congress Working Committee with centrists and Right Wingers such as C. Rajagopalachari, Rajendra Prasad and Vallabhbhai Patel,

---

[3] ibid., p.20.
[4] ibid., pp.20-21. Nehru also took swipes at several other things: the failure of the middle-class elements within the Congress to create closer ties with the peasantry, the workers and the poor of the land; the shibboleth of khadi, hand spinning and weaving and village industries which he believed to be 'temporary expedients of a transition stage rather than as solutions of our vital problems'; and the Gandhian emphasis on untouchability and Harijans as one that would disappear under socialism where there would be 'no such differentiation or victimization' [p.22].

and that ten of the fifteen members of the Committee publicly disapproved of Nehru's socialism. Fears of Nehru-led socialism were well and truly sown.

Not surprisingly, barely a month later in May 1936, a group of 21 important Bombay businessmen signed a toughly worded manifesto against the Congress president. Without naming Nehru, the document had 'no hesitation in declaring that we are unequivocally opposed to ideas of this kind being propagated... We are convinced [that] there is a grave risk of the masses of the country being misled by such doctrines into believing that all that is required for the improvement of their well-being is a total destruction of the existing social and economic structure.'[5] The signatories were knighted heavyweights such as Sir Purshottamdas Thakurdas, Sir Chunilal Mehta, Sir Ardeshir Dalal, Sir V.N. Chandavarkar, Sir Homi Mody, Sir Cowasji Jehangir, and Sir Chimanlal Setalvad, among others.[6]

---

[5]Medha M. Kudaisya, *The Life and Times of G.D. Birla*, Oxford University Press, 2003, henceforth Kudaisya (2003), p.169.

[6]In addition, the *Hindustan Times*, controlled by G.D. Birla, editorialized that in a land already 'broken up into diverse creeds and sections...should Pandit Jawaharlal introduce another division into this land of warring sects by propagating the doctrine of class war which forms such a prominent feature of socialism as elaborated by Karl Marx? Secondly, the biggest task before the country today is the attainment of freedom... At such a time, is it wise to drive into the opposite camp vast sections of people like

(cont)

Given his closeness to Gandhi and the people who mattered in the Congress, Ghanshyam Das (G.D.) Birla was disturbed by this Bombay manifesto. He believed that it might unwittingly provide an impetus to the forces working against capitalism, and chided his close friend Purshottamdas Thakurdas for putting his 'name to a document the contents of which...were liable to be seriously misinterpreted.'[7] Birla was tougher still with Walchand Hirachand, an important Bombay-based industrialist and a signatory. Having castigated Hirachand for rendering no service to men of his caste, Birla went on to write, 'It is curious how we businessmen are so short-sighted. It looks very crude for a man of property to say that he is opposed to expropriation in the wider interest of the country.'[8] Privately, Birla was concerned with Nehru's inclinations. Yet he believed that 'Socialism is only another name for the impatience of Jawaharlal', and expected it to be significantly tempered by the necessities of *realpolitik*. Perspicacious on most matters, how wrong he was on this!'[9]

Seven years after the Lucknow session, when the

---

the small businessmen, the petty landlords and the bourgeoisie whose sympathies are sure to be alienated if the Congress... becomes the organ of socialist propaganda?' *Hindustan Times*, 22 May 1936, quoted in Kudaisya (2003), p.182.
[7]ibid, p.170.
[8]ibid, p.170
[9]ibid, pp.169-170.

world was enmeshed in a bloody war, and a year-and-a-half after Gandhi had raised the banner of Quit India in Bombay at the Gowalia Tank Maidan on 8 August 1942, a booklet made its way to the public forum. Titled *A Memorandum Outlining A Plan of Economic Development of India*, and later renamed the 'Bombay Plan', it was truly an amazing document on at least two counts: for what it outlined, and for the fact that some of the seemingly radical positions taken were by its exclusively industrialist and corporate authors.

Given the imminent arrival of political freedom after the war, its aim was 'to put forward...a statement, in as concrete a form as possible, of the objectives to be kept in mind in economic planning in India, the general lines on which development should proceed and the demands which planning is likely to make on the country's resources.'[10] The principal objective of the Plan was to *double* India's per capita income within fifteen years—which, given the rate of population growth at the time, implied a *trebling* of the country's aggregate national income.

That, according to the Plan, would be impossible to achieve without 'a central directing authority which enjoys sufficient popular support and possesses the

---

[10] *A Memorandum Outlining A Plan of Economic Development of India*, henceforth *The Bombay Plan*, part 1, p.7.

requisite powers and jurisdiction.'[11] The authors were also convinced that in addition to a national planning committee akin to a central planning commission for drawing up the plan document, there had to be 'a supreme economic council working alongside the national planning committee' under the authority of the central government for actually executing the Plan.[12]

Much later, J.R.D. Tata gave credit to G.D. Birla for helping create the broad approach to the Bombay Plan. In his words, 'When we were floundering to find a structure in the first few meetings, it was [Birla] who suggested... first estimate [what is needed] to get the people the kind of standard of living that they want... So many calories of food requiring so many million tons of grain, so many metres of cloth...how many cubic feet of housing, so many schools, etc. That concept of quantifying made it easy, and it was on that basis that Dr Mathai wrote the Plan.'[13]

NUTS AND BOLTS: ANTICIPATING MAHALANOBIS AND MUCH MORE

The Plan had an objective of doubling per capita income in fifteen years and, in doing so, ensure that all citizens attain 'a general standard of living which would leave

---

[11] ibid, p.8.
[12] ibid, p.8.
[13] Lala (1993), pp.221-122.

a reasonable margin over the minimum requirements of human life.'[14] With population growing at 5 million per year, this necessitated a trebling of India's aggregate national income over the 15-year period.

The capital outlay needed to finance this over fifteen years was ₹10,000 crore, or $30 billion at the exchange rate of the time. In effect, the Bombay Plan made a case for a structural transformation of the nation's economy.

> **Primacy to Industrialization:** Almost anticipating P.C. Mahalanobis' second Five Year Plan (1956-61), the thrust for industrialization was centred upon rapid development of basic industries. These were: power and electricity; mining and metallurgy, especially iron and steel, aluminium and manganese; engineering, involving machinery of all kind as well as machine tools; chemicals, particularly heavy chemicals, fertilizers, dyes, plastics and pharmaceuticals; armaments; transport and communications, especially railway engines and wagons, shipbuilding, automobiles and aircrafts; and cement. These were, in the Plan's words, 'the basis on which the economic superstructure envisaged in the Plan will have to be erected'—words that Mahalanobis could have copied *in toto* a dozen years later.[15] More specifically, the document wrote:

---

[14]*The Bombay Plan*, part 1, p.12.
[15]ibid, p.31.

'It is obvious that in modern times no industry can be established without power, machinery, chemicals, etc. Similarly, without fertilizers it is difficult to imagine any progress in agriculture. In the absence of adequate shipping and other forms of transport, economic life especially in a country of the dimensions of India will remain stagnant. But for the lack of most of these industries, India would not have been left so far behind other countries of the British Empire such as Canada and Australia in the matter of industrial development... We consider it essential for the success of our economic plan that the basic industries, on which ultimately the whole economic development of the country depends, should be developed as rapidly as possible.'[16]

Although the authors spoke of some consumer goods industries such as textiles, glass, leather goods, paper, tobacco, edible oils as well as small and cottage industries, the document's clear industrial thrust was on rapid electrification and heavy industrialization backed by serious investments in railways and roads. Using a capital-output ratio of 2:4, the Bombay Plan arrived at a 15-year investment and working capital need of ₹4,480 crore to bring about aggregate industrial output in the terminal year to ₹2,240 crore.

---

[16]ibid, pp.31-32.

- **Capital Expenditure Required:** An amazing aspect of the Plan was its attention to detail. In 1944, when hard data was difficult to obtain, it went into specifics to estimate the non-recurring and recurring capital requirements for agriculture including soil conservation and irrigation (₹1,240 crore over fifteen years); for railways, roads and the transport sector (₹940 crore); for education—from primary right up to university and technical training (₹490 crore); on health (₹450 crore); and for housing (₹2,200 crore). The Plan also added capital expenditure for industries of ₹4,480 crore and a miscellaneous rounding-off amount of ₹200 crore.
- **Financing:** The Plan didn't just put forth the necessary capital allocations. It carefully examined various sources of financing. Hoarded wealth could fetch no more than ₹300 crore, if the newly independent national government adopted 'suitable means...for attracting hoards from their place of concealment.' Sterling securities with the RBI were expected to increase to ₹1,000 crore, which could be tapped into after Independence when the Plan was put in motion. India's positive balance of trade was estimated at ₹600 crore, which was also considered as a source of funds. And domestic savings—household as well as corporate—was pegged at ₹4,000 crore. Adding these got the aggregate funding up to ₹5,900 crore.

There was still a gap of ₹4,100 crore.

> Part of that shortfall was to be met through foreign borrowing, which the Plan pegged at ₹700 crore for the 15-year period. Then came the modern masterpiece which one would have scarcely expected from a group that included five noted capitalists: deficit financing. In its own words, 'a large part of the capital required, about ₹3,400 crores...would have to be created by borrowing against *ad hoc* securities from the Reserve Bank.'[17] To assuage conservative concerns, the Plan stated that 'There is nothing unsound in creating this money, because it is meant to increase the productive capacity of the nation and in the long run is of a self-liquidating character. At the end of the period, the general level of prices would in all probability be lower than at the beginning of the Plan.'[18]

---

[17] ibid, p.54.

[18] ibid, p.55. Nevertheless, the Plan issued a cautionary note. 'During the greater part of the planning period, however, financing of economic development by means of 'created money' on this scale is likely to lead to a gap between the volume of purchasing power in the hands of the people and the volume of goods available. How to bridge this gap and to keep prices within limits will be a constant problem which the planning authority will have to tackle. *During this period, in order to prevent the inequitable distribution of the burden between different classes which this method of financing will involve, practically every aspect of economic life will have to be so rigorously controlled by*

> **Sequencing:** Having focused on the sectoral output targets, investment needs and the financing, part 1 of the Plan then outlined a sequencing over three five-year plan periods. The interesting aspect of this was the pronounced 'back-loading'. In the first Plan period, the financial expenditures were more muted than the second, and those of the second Plan were less so than the third. The reasoning was eminently sensible. The first five years would witness the greatest constraints in financial and real resources, which would ease up in the second and even more so in the third. It stated, 'In the initial period the total amount to be spent has been deliberately kept low because the material resources and personnel available at the beginning of the Plan would be comparatively small. With the development of the Plan, both material resources and personnel would become available in rapidly increasing proportions, and the tempo of progress would be accelerated.'[19]

	First Plan	Second Plan	Third Plan	Total
Industry	790	1,530	2,160	4,480
Agriculture	200	400	640	1,240

---

government that individual liberty and freedom of enterprise will suffer a temporary eclipse [emphasis mine]', p.55.
[19] ibid, pp.59-60.

Communications*	110	320	510	940
Education	40	80	370	490
Health	40	80	330	450
Housing	190	420	1,590	2,200
Miscellaneous	30	70	100	200
Total	1,400	2,900	5,700	10,000

*Communications involved railways and road transport. Note that the total financial need doubles between the first, second and third plans.
Source: *The Bombay Plan*, part 1, p.59.

ROLE OF THE STATE

Very few people today have actually read the Bombay Plan; and fewer still have read Part 2. In my opinion, it is truly a classic in terms of how forward thinking its authors were on many issues of production, distribution and the role of the State in a mixed economy. As it stated in the very beginning of Part 2, 'Our first memorandum dealt chiefly with the problem of production. Both logically and as a matter of practical necessity, the question of production must come before that of distribution in a plan of economic development… But it does not follow that increased production will necessarily remedy the problem of poverty if it is not based on a proper system of distribution.'[20]

There were several aspects that called for significantly

---

[20] ibid, p.65.

greater State intervention. The first was the State's role in planning and ensuring that allocations were in line with the Plan. The authors wrote, 'no economic development of the kind proposed by us would be feasible except on the basis of a central directing authority, and further that in the initial stages of the Plan, rigorous measures of State control would be required to prevent an inequitable distribution of the financial burdens involved in it. An enlargement of the positive as well as preventive functions of the State is essential to any large-scale economic planning.'[21] Second, the Plan categorically stated that planning and a wider role of the State was perfectly consistent with a democratic polity. Third—and this is particularly important—the authors believed that with the experience of the Great Depression and developments in some continental countries, 'the distinction between capitalism and socialism has lost much of its significance from a practical standpoint. In many respects, there is now a large ground common to both and the gulf between the two is being steadily narrowed further as each shows signs of modifying itself in the direction of the other.'[22] For the authors, therefore, an expansion in the role of the State in the direction of economic policy and the development of productive resources was both natural and welcome.

---

[21] ibid, pp.90-91.
[22] ibid, p.92.

But what kind of expansion? Was it to be limited to direction setting, fiscal targeting and policing? Or would it also accommodate more direct State intervention in the spheres of production?

The issues were State control, ownership and management. For the authors, State control of key economic enterprises for the common good was perfectly acceptable, especially during the period of the Plan. In their words, 'from the point of view of maximum social welfare, State control appears to be more important than ownership or management... Over a wide field, it is not necessary for the State to secure ownership or management of economic activity for this purpose. Well directed and effective State control should be fully adequate.'[23] The authors were not only comfortable with State controls covering the fixing of prices, limitation of dividends, prescription of work conditions and wages, nomination of government directors on boards as well as licensing, but actually went much further.

In a separate section, the Plan itemized areas where such State interventions and controls could take place. Given the capitalist bent of the authors, the list was truly draconian. The authors outlined controls in:

> ➢ Production, 'to ensure a proper allocation of resources so as to secure better regional

---

[23]ibid, p.94.

distribution of economic enterprises and to reach the targets set for the different branches of industry. The control will operate chiefly through a system of licences for establishing new units and for extending existing ones.'
- Distribution, 'controlled primarily with the object of determining priorities for the release of raw materials, semi-finished materials and capital goods. In the early stages of planning, control will also include rationing and distribution of consumers' goods.'
- Consumption, 'to enforce fair selling prices for essential goods and for goods manufactured by industries receiving State assistance and also to prevent inflation.'
- Investments, where 'new capital issues should be approved by the State so as to secure a proper distribution of available resources, to prevent inflation, to provide for the orderly development of new enterprises, and generally to maintain and promote the interests of Indian nationals.'
- Foreign trade and exchange 'will be subjected to control to such extent as may be required for conserving foreign exchange and for protecting Indian industries.'
- Wages and working conditions, to ensure 'not merely fair conditions for labour, but also

efficiency of management, particularly in public utility concerns and protected industries.'[24]

Seemingly Stalinist in today's context, many of these controls were not as dramatic they seemed in the context of the 1940s. The seeds of widespread State intervention in India's economic and business affairs had been sown with the advent of World War II. Indeed, much of the controls and regulations that India was to groan under in the late 1950s, '60s and '70s emerged out of the Defence of India Act 1939 and its accompanying rules. For instance, Rule 81 of the Defence of India rules created a blanket provision for 'regulating or prohibiting the production, treatment, keeping, storage, movement, transport, distribution, disposal, acquisition, use or consumption of articles or things of any description whatsoever'; and for 'controlling the prices (or rates) at which articles or things of any description whatsoever may be sold.' The same rule allowed the government to set up 'controllers to exercise control over the pricing and distribution of supplies and services essential to the life of the community.' There were other diktats as well, such as giving power to the government to control access to foreign currencies.[25]

---

[24] ibid, pp.99-100.
[25] Rakesh Mohan and Vandana Aggarwal, 'Commands and Control: Planning for Indian Industrial Development, 1951-1990', *Journal of Comparative Economics*, vol.14, 1990, pp.683-684.

The authors were far more circumspect regarding State ownership—or the setting up of public sector enterprises in today's terminology. They believed this ought to be limited to industries involved in security, such as armaments, or those that are 'organizations of vital communications' such as Posts and Telegraphs. Regarding State management of industrial units—even those owned by government—the Plan was even more ambivalent. Yes, there was no *prima facie* reason for the government not to manage what it owned. But it was better in most cases for it neither to own nor to manage.

For the Plan, the role of the State was two-fold: 'It must provide for free enterprise, but...must ensure at the same time that the fruits of enterprise and labour are fairly apportioned among all who contribute to them and not unjustly withheld by a few from the many.'[26] Indeed, it went a step further. In a manner totally different from our modern-day 'captains of industry', the authors clearly stated that trebling of national income in fifteen years *would not be feasible* unless accompanied by significant redistribution of income, greater access of the poor to education, health and housing, and significant reduction in economic and social disparities.

The Plan recognized that while significantly greater employment opportunities could be created with

---

[26]ibid, p.66.

industrial growth—especially in medium and small scale industries—as well as through the expansion of railways and roads, there would be a longer term problem of disguised as well as seasonal unemployment in agriculture. Even so, it believed that by the terminal year, there would be a dramatic shift in occupational distribution. While the number of people dependent on agriculture would increase over the 15-year period, its occupational share would decline from 72 per cent to 58 per cent; that of industries would increase from 15 per cent to 26 per cent; and services would rise from 13 per cent to 16 per cent of total employment.[27] These changes in occupational intensities would translate to changes in income distribution. The authors estimated that in the course of fifteen years, the average income per employed person would rise by 93 per cent in agriculture; by 129 per cent in industry; and by 50 per cent in services.[28]

RADICAL IDEAS

There was no dearth of innovative ideas. Here are three examples.

First, the Plan made a case for power subsidies. The case was elegant and straightforward. India needed

---

[27] ibid, p.75.
[28] ibid, p.84.

significant increases in power supply. However, for even the most efficient generation and distribution entities, the cost per unit would be beyond the reach of much of the population. As a result, no free market system would ever allocate capital for such projects, irrespective of its huge positive externalities. In the Plan's own words,

> 'We have proposed a large increase in the supply of these services and it is an essential part of our plan that their cost to the consumer both for domestic use and for cottage and rural industries should be as low as possible and within the means of the bulk of the population. In order to achieve this object, we propose that these services should be subsidized by the State to such extent as may be necessary and the margin of profits in such services should be subjected to control.'[29]

Second, it suggested setting up of a National Relief Fund, significantly larger in resources and scope than the existing Famine Relief Fund.[30] And third, it not only suggested that a beginning be made with minimum wages in a few key industries such as cotton textiles, jute, sugar, cement and engineering, but also engaging in experiments with social security, beginning with sick

---

[29]ibid, p.85.
[30]Which, incidentally did little to mitigate the horrendous tragedy of the Bengal Famine of 1943.

leave, paid holidays and extension of maternity leave within organized industries.

To prevent gross inequalities in income, the authors suggested a taxation policy that could hardly be imagined, coming from the background that they belonged to. Here is an incredibly radical paragraph from the Plan:

> 'A steeply graduated income tax which would keep personal incomes within limits would obviously be the most important weapon for this purpose in the fiscal armoury of the country. But in any such scheme of taxation…adequate remission should be granted in respect of the depreciation of the assets employed in production, and that incomes ploughed back for increasing industrial or agricultural production should also be granted similar remission. Further, in the taxation of personal incomes, distinction should be made between earned and unearned income, so as to make the latter taxable at a higher rate. As a means of correcting the existing inequalities of wealth, the device of death duties, which has been successfully utilized in other countries, might also be adopted. The advisability of taxing inherited estates more severely at the second and later transfers than at the first would be a further step in the same direction. It is obvious that India's fiscal system will have to place more and more reliance on direct taxation in future if the increase in the cost of

administration which planning will involve is to be met and if provision is to be made for free social services like education, medical treatment, etc., and subsidies for essential utility services.'[31]

WHY AND HOW IT SANK

Seventy-five years later, it still remains a major question as to why five of India's most illustrious capitalists and three of its best known corporate technocrats of the day came up with the Plan that laid so much emphasis on State controls, central planning and an overarching role of the federal government. The technocrats, being what they were, wanted a planned transition to post-Independence growth. But what were the motives of the five industrialists? Was it economic nationalism of men who, while being in industry, were known for their commitment to the public weal? Or was it self-seeking where deficit-financed government investment would lift economic activity to a point after which profit-driven capitalists and business houses could take over? Or was it delusionary, given Nehru's and his followers' vision of a socialist nation?[32]

---

[31] *The Bombay Plan*, part 2, p.87.
[32] Much of this section is from Omkar Goswami, *Goras and Desis: Managing Agencies and the Making of Corporate India*, Portfolio/

(cont)

It certainly wasn't delusionary. Despite a rising tide of socialism within the Congress, one must remember that the Bombay Plan was drafted when the party had quite a few pro-business, right-of-centre leaders with sufficient seniority and gravitas to take on Nehru and the Left Wing—starting with Gandhi, who was anything but a socialist, and buttressed by the likes of Rajagopalachari, Vallabhbhai Patel and Rajendra Prasad. The authors of the Plan were not expected to know that Gandhi would be assassinated in 1948, that Patel was to die in December 1950, that Rajagopalachari would effectively exile himself from the thrust and parry of national politics, or that Prasad would be the first President of the country and so occupy a position of constitutional silence, leaving the field open for Nehru and his socialist young Turks.

Nor was the Plan self-seeking. While none of the eight members could be remotely described as a votary of socialism, each was a nationalist and an advocate of planned industrialization and economic development. Here, it is important to distinguish between capitalists, and to recognize that in terms of their commitment to nationalism and sustainable growth of an independent de-colonised India, people such as Birla, Tata, Thakurdas, Shri Ram and Lalbhai were made of a different material

---

Penguin, 2016, henceforth Goswami (2016), chapter 3, pp.151-156.

than most of their brethren.

Birla, considered a 'son' by Gandhi and very much an 'insider' in the Congress, was by far the strongest champion of India's economic freedom and independence. Having suffered the barbs of being a native from the Scots and English of Calcutta, Birla did everything he could to create various forums to express Indian interests in the country and in Britain. During his presidential address to FICCI in February 1930, long before the advent of the Bombay Plan, Birla had publicly declared before Lord Irwin—the Viceroy of India—that 'the only solution to our present difficulties lies in strengthening the hands of those who are fighting for the freedom of our country'.[33] Thakurdas, a suave, low key, yet hugely well connected cotton trader and merchant, was a behind-the-scenes man who intuitively knew which buttons to press to the get the nationalist agenda going for the benefit of India's capitalists. Lalbhai was a Gandhian to whom nothing mattered more than ridding India of the British. Lala Shri Ram was no less an economic nationalist, though more low key than Birla or Lalbhai. And for all his urbane western sophistication, J.R.D. Tata was a nationalist. In his own words, 'I knew Independence was bound to come;

---

[33]Proceedings of the Annual Meeting FICCI, 16 February 1930, quoted in Kudaisya (2003), p.125. For Birla's trials, tribulations and struggles with British managing agencies in Calcutta, see Goswami (2016), chapter 2.

I knew the country's economy would have to be tackled [and] that economic prosperity needed to reach not only the few but the many' for which 'businessmen and not only the government should play a role.'[34]

A balanced view of why profit-driven capitalists and anti-socialist technocrats drafted such a document must necessarily incorporate the role of such nationalism. Each wanted an independent India and, together, they wanted a mixed economy where the government would not only rationally direct economic activity, but also provide an umbrella under which private enterprise could grow and flourish. In the context of the 1940s, this was neither a radical thought nor a self-seeking stratagem as the communists made it out to be. Instead, it was making the case for a wider nationalist platform where a modern, forward looking newly decolonised State would actively cooperate with the world of business to jointly create the much needed industrial capital of the nation. Instead of creating a politically volatile and unproductive schism between the forces of capitalism and socialism, the Plan was thought of as an attempt to present a 'reasoned' alternative that involved income generation, greater employment and no less importantly, a more just distribution of income and wealth.[35] The authors

---

[34]Lala (1993), p.221.
[35]Amal Sanyal, 'The Curious Case of the Bombay Plan', *Contemporary Issues and Ideas in Social Sciences*, June 2010,

genuinely believed that it would be better for industry to be a trusted partner of government in planned progress.

In a deeper way, the Plan implicitly recognized the limitations of capital available to private enterprise. The authors knew that large scale enterprises would be needed to spur growth led by heavy industrialization and rapid infrastructural development. Until the founding of long term development financial institutions capitalised by subsidized government funds—such as the Industrial Finance Corporation of India (1948) followed by the Industrial Credit and Investment Corporation of India (1955) and the Industrial Development Bank of India (1966)—no business conglomerate in India had access to long term debt. It did not exist. Commercial banks engaged in bill discounting and working capital lending; none had either the capital or the risk taking appetite to offer term loans over a long tenor to help large-scale industrialization. In fairness, the banks did not need to for, barring a few enterprises, there were none that needed substantial chunks of capital for setting up and commissioning huge plants with a large component of machinery.

That had to change if the Bombay Plan was to be followed. In such a scenario—the need for relatively large scale, capital intensive heavy industrial units without the

---

mimeo, henceforth Sanyal (2010), p.6, quoting correspondence between John Mathai and Thakurdas from the Purshotamdas Thakurdas Papers, Nehru Memorial Museum and Library.

presence of institutions offering long term loans available at affordable, even subsidized, rates—the authors realized that private enterprise would largely be unable to make the necessary investments. Hence, the need for a greater role of the State.

Not surprisingly, the Plan was trashed by the Left. The Trotskyites believed that having been alarmed by the revolutionary energy of the Quit India Movement, the Indian bourgeoisie used the Bombay Plan as an attempt to circumvent political power of the masses with an economic weapon.[36] The CPI called the Plan a blueprint for building capitalism with the aid of the State, and nothing would change this stance—even when it later became a firm supporter of the National Planning Committee's proposals and the planning principles of the Nehru era which effected many of the State interventions mooted in the Bombay Plan.

The Plan was also sharply critiqued by the Right. Old-fashioned businessmen thought it to be too radical, and Gandhians criticized it for being too un-Gandhian. Soon enough, someone called Narayan Agarwal came out with *A Gandhian Plan*, while M.N. Roy, the radical humanist, privately published *The People's Plan*.[37]

The Congress was deafeningly silent. At a technocratic

---

[36]ibid, p.7, referring to a 1944 article in *The Workers' International News*.
[37]Lala (1993), p.220.

level, some of the Plan's authors had regularly interacted with the National Planning Committee and exchanged notes. Moreover, some of them served in various technical and economic committees of the Congress, with John Mathai also serving in Nehru's Cabinet up to 1950. Yet, the increasingly important socialist wing of the party led by Nehru nurtured deep antipathy for industrialists and desired a socialistic pattern of development—which necessarily required it to ignore a document prepared by capitalists and their technocrat managers. The growing lobby of socialists and young Turks within the Congress wanted something akin to the Bombay Plan, but would be caught dead acknowledging the parentage.

For a few years after its publication, the Bombay Plan made the rounds, but increasingly in a desultory manner and more often than not in corporate premises, with its ideas yet unaccepted by those that actually mattered. After Independence, with Nehru at the helm, and given his innate dislike for capitalists except perhaps J.R.D. Tata at a personal level, the Plan was effectively buried. In its place came all the edifices of the Plan and an even greater role of the State than what its authors had envisaged: the Industry Policy Resolution of 1948; licensing under the Industries (Development and Regulation) Act, 1951; and public sector reservations enshrined in the Industry Policy Resolution, 1956. This was followed by the second Five Year Plan (1956-61) formulated by Mahalanobis, Nehru's favourite economic advisor which, without a word of reference to the Bombay Plan, accorded 'high priority to industrialization, and especially to the development of basic and heavy industries.'[38]

By then the Bombay Plan was well and truly dead. Which was such a pity. It wasn't brilliant in terms of its exactitude. But it was the first well thought out, well rounded plan for economic development of an independent India. Much of its ideas were taken up by the first two Five Year Plans with nary a word of acknowledgement. And all because its authors were not considered sufficiently worthy by Nehru. It was just that. Capitalists were not to be associated with nationalism, and even less so with the development of a socialistic pattern of society—a sentiment that continued after Nehru, with even greater intensity, under the rule of his daughter, Indira Gandhi.

◆

Omkar Goswami is Chairman, Corporate & Economic Research Group (CERG) Advisory. The author is grateful to Amal Sanyal for some excellent discussions on the Bombay Plan, where he suggested looking at areas that the author had not thought of, and which proved to be very useful in

---

[38]Government of India, *The Second Five Year Plan (1956-61)*, Chapter 2, paragraph 12.

understanding this task of central planning proposed by people who one would have thought should have no truck with it.

REFERENCES

A Memorandum Outlining a Plan of Economic Development of India, parts 1 and 2, Penguin India, 1945.

Omkar Goswami, *Goras and Desis: Managing Agencies and the Making of Corporate India*, Portfolio/Penguin, 2016.

Government of India, *The Second Five Year Plan (1956-61)*.

Medha M. Kudaisya, *The Life and Times of G.D. Birla*, Oxford University Press, 2003.

R.M. Lala, *Beyond the Last Blue Mountain: A Life of J.R.D. Tata*, Portfolio/Penguin, 1993.

Rakesh Mohan and Vandana Aggarwal, 'Commands and Control: Planning for Indian Industrial Development, 1951-1990', *Journal of Comparative Economics*, vol.14, 1990, pp.683-684.

Report of the 49th Session of the Indian National Congress held at Lucknow in April 1936, 1936.

Amal Sanyal, 'The Curious Case of the Bombay Plan', *Contemporary Issues and Ideas in Social Sciences*, June 2010, mimeo.

BUSINESS, GOVERNMENT AND POLITICS: FROM PLAN TO PLEA

Sanjaya Baru

Nowhere in the developing world, in no colonized nation, is there a parallel to the Bombay Plan. Native business leaders were seeking their place in the sun, battling colonial rule from Asia to Africa, from Latin America to Eastern Europe. The inter-war years of the twentieth century witnessed many anti-colonial and anti-imperialist movements. Nationalism was on the rise and was a pervasive sentiment. Patriotic leaders and nation builders were dreaming of a new era of self-reliant economic development. India was not the only country battling for freedom. Yet, it was in India that a group of business leaders, among the most successful business leaders of their time, came together to write a manifesto for development that had no parallels.[1]

In the Soviet Union, the Bolsheviks experimented with economic policy after seizing power. In China, the Communists were staging a revolution with no stated plan as to what they would do once in power. All revolutions and most national liberation struggles focused on overturning the existing order, not on the business of government once a new order was put in place. Governance and public policy became a concern only after the old order had been replaced with a new one.

The Indian national movement was an exception. Even within the Indian National Congress (INC), a National Planning Committee (NPC) came into being in 1938. Inspired by the scientist Meghnad Saha and the engineer M. Vishweshwarayya, Congress President Subhash Chandra Bose created the committee that was then chaired by Jawaharlal Nehru. Ideas about planned national development in a free India sprouted within this body and outside, with much of the discussion inspired by the example of planned industrial development and agrarian change in the Soviet Union. The Bombay Plan

---

[1] It was, of course, helpful for the authors of the Bombay Plan that they had access to independent Indian thinking on economic policy, and were not just dependent on western thinking. See for a review of Indian economic thinking at the time, J Krishnamurthy, *Toward Development Economics: Indian Contributions 1900-1945*, Oxford University Press, New Delhi, 2011.

was one such effort. Indian business leaders showed remarkable understanding of the necessary role of the government in promoting industrial development in a postcolonial situation. More importantly, they understood the importance of public investment in health, education and social development and looked for ways to fund it. In purely Marxian terms, the Bombay Plan could be described as a manifesto of 'State Capitalism'. It was a manifesto of a social class that signalled its evolution from being a 'class in itself' to becoming a 'class for itself'.

STATE CAPITALIST MANIFESTO

What made the 'Bombay Plan' unique in the decolonizing world of the mid-twentieth century was the fact that it was a document written by business leaders but with a focus on national development—both economic and social. It was not a set of demands made by businessmen to a government. It was not merely a statement on industrial policy. It was not a pre-budget memorandum. It was a national plan for long-term economic and social development sought by the leadership of indigenous business in their own interest as well as in the national interest.

The Bombay Plan was written against the background of ongoing discussions on post-war economic policy, including the discussions at the NPC. There was a

Gandhian Plan written by the Mahatma's more dogmatic disciples, there was Jayaprakash Narayan's Sarvodaya Plan, and radical humanist M.N. Roy's Peoples' Plan.[2] Each document presented a perspective on the kind of economic and social policies that independent India ought to pursue.

What set the Bombay Plan apart from all other contemporary exercises was its focus on specifics. In opting to look at numbers and fiscal implications of their proposals, the Bombay Plan went beyond the largely political manifestos of the day, written by Congressmen, communists, Gandhians and an assortment of nationalist groups.

There is one more feature of the Bombay Plan that set it apart from other contending vision statements of the times. Here was a document being written by India's biggest business leaders seeking policies for rapid industrialization and yet it devoted considerable space to a discussion of the foundational role of public investment in education and public health as well as the importance of a progressive tax policy that would address distributional concerns even as the focus remained on rapid enhancement of production.

'The ultimate objective of any planning', asserted

---

[2] See Charles Bettelheim, *India Independent*, Monthly Review Press, New York, 1968.

the authors, 'should be to increase the volume of India's economic production.' Yet, they admitted that this search for growth in output must ensure that enough is provided in terms of food, clothing, housing and healthcare for all. The Plan explained what it defined as the 'the minimum requirements of human life.'[3] These pertained to nutrition, literacy, sanitation and housing. The detailed discussion of the requirements of education and public health was way ahead of its time. An important criticism of economic policymaking in the late 1980s and early 1990s has been the overemphasis on economic growth and relative neglect of social and human development.[4] Clearly, the Bombay Plan authors were more mindful of the distributional dimensions to growth than India's more recent policy planners.

Not surprisingly, therefore, and also reflecting the dominant liberal thinking of the mid-twentieth century, the Bombay Plan authors declared, 'A planned economy must aim at raising the national income to such a level that after meeting the minimum requirements every individual would be left with enough resources for enjoyment of life and for cultural activities.'[5] This

---

[3] Thakurdas, et al (1944), p.12.
[4] See for example, Amartya Sen & Jean Dreze, *India: Economic Development and Social Opportunity*, Clarendon Press, Oxford, 1999.
[5] Thakurdas et al (1944), p.27.

formulation is an early articulation of what more recently has been dubbed by Prime Minister Narendra Modi as the 'Ease of Living'. India remains far from attaining this goal for all its citizens, but the moot point here is that the top rungs of its business leadership at the time of Independence viewed development in much broader terms than a mere increase in gross national product, gross capital formation and economic indicators of such kind. Human and social development was viewed as being integral to national economic development.

If, on the one hand, rapid economic growth, defined in the Plan as a threefold increase in national income within a fifteen year period,[6] was seen to require investment in education and public health—a parallel process of social and human development—the Bombay Plan was also clear that, on the other hand, it would require structural changes in the economy. Such structural changes would include a decline in the share of agriculture in national income and employment, increased urbanization and the growth of modern services.

In the first part of the Plan, published in 1944, there was only a cursory discussion of the role of agriculture and agrarian policy in sustaining growth. The Plan's authors recognized these lacunae and in Part II, published a year later in 1945, they included a detailed

---

[6]Thakurdas et al (1944), p.28.

discussion of the nature of revenue settlements in place in different parts of the country and the need for raising both productivity and revenue from land. Suggesting that a ryotwari settlement was preferable to a zamindari settlement from the viewpoint of revenue generation and security of tenancy, the authors of the Plan went to the extent of recommending to the government that it take over land from zamindars and hand it over to tenants.[7]

Finally, the authors of the Bombay Plan were keen that decolonization should facilitate the integration of a sub-continental market, thereby creating the economic space for the consolidation and growth of a nascent, indigenous capitalist class. In the very opening paragraph of the document the authors state, 'The maintenance of the economic unity of India being, in our view, an essential condition of any economic planning we have assumed for the purpose of our Plan that the future government of India will be constituted on a federal basis and that the jurisdiction of the central government in economic matters will extend over the whole of India.'[8] It took seven decades after that for a nationwide Goods and Services Tax (GST) to be finally introduced, integrating the home market.

The significance of the Bombay Plan does not derive

---

[7]Thakurdas et al, *A Plan of Economic Development for India, Part II*, Penguin Books, London, 1945. p.82.
[8]Thakurdas et al (1944), p.8.

only from its uniqueness as a manifesto of a nascent capitalist class in a postcolonial developing economy, nor merely from the breadth of policy vision of its authors, but from the fact that it became the basis for national economic policy after India attained independence, sidelining all the other contending visions, namely, the Gandhian Plan, the Peoples' Plan and so on. The first Five Year Plan and the second Five Year Plan were constructed on the policy foundations offered by the Bombay Plan.

Not entirely, to be sure. The Indian Planning Commission's first two plans, that defined the so-called Nehruvian vision of industry-led development, fell short of the much wider vision of the Bombay Plan in that the former did not place as much emphasis as the latter on public investment in health and education and agrarian reform. Among all the newly industrialized nations of Asia, India's record on health and education and agrarian reform has been the weakest.

The conception of State Capitalism embedded in the Bombay Plan vision was based on the recognition that without public investment in health and education, free India would not be able to win the war against 'poverty, ignorance and disease' that its founding fathers wished it to. In Part II (1945), the Bombay Plan states, 'In order that every person, whatever his means, should be able to secure the benefits of education and medical relief, we have suggested that primary, middle school and adult education and medical treatment both in rural dispensaries and in hospitals should be provided free of charge.'[9] The authors quote economist A.C. Pigou to say, '...the most important investment of all is investment in the health, intelligence and character of the people.' [10]

The very first substantial chapter, following a brief introductory one, is titled, 'Requirements of a Minimum Standard' and begins with a specification of what constitutes 'balanced diet' for all. Calculating the annual cost of a balanced diet for an adult at ₹65, the document estimates the annual expenditure on this count to be ₹2,100 crores at 'pre-war prices'. Having estimated the cost of providing a basic diet for all, the document then estimates the cost of providing adequate clothing for all. Having entered all the relevant caveats about the clothing requirement being region, culture and wealth specific, and clarifying that the estimate is only for minimum

---

[9] Thakurdas et al (1945), pp.28-29.
[10] It is only after the rise of East Asian economies, including Japan, South Korea, Taiwan and mainland China, that western mainstream economics has come to recognize the foundational role of investment in education for sustained long-term development. Indian planning made a huge mistake not emphasizing the importance of public investment in education. The more recent appreciation of human development as contained in the reports of the UNDP, published in the 1990s, testify to this. See for a recent assessment Surjit Bhalla, *The New Wealth of Nations*, Simon & Schuster, India, 2018.

clothing required and not based on the 'social need' of various classes, the document estimates that the basic requirement of clothing would be 30 yards per person, and that this would cost ₹255 crores.

Having budgeted for food and clothing, the Bombay Plan calculates the cost of providing at least 500 square feet of housing space per family. Separate cost estimates are provided for rural and urban housing. For housing too, the document agrees that the cost would be region specific, depending on weather, availability of land and so on.

The most detailed discussion as far as the 'social sectors' are concerned is focused on healthcare. The 1940s was a period when even in developed market economies, healthcare provisioning was regarded as the responsibility of the State. Mindful of these debates, the Bombay Plan puts forth a detailed case for public investment in public health and general and maternity hospitals. For urban areas, the document recommends the creation of publicly funded general hospitals with at least forty beds for every 10,000 persons. This would cost the exchequer ₹37 crores in fixed costs and an annual recurring cost of ₹1.5 crore. As for maternity care, the document quotes the Indian Medical Review to say, 'it is the right of every woman to have skilled attendance during pregnancy, labour and the puerperium.'[11]

---

[11] Thakurdas et al (1944), p.21.

GENESIS OF A MIXED ECONOMY

The inability of post-Independence governments to ensure the free availability of basic education and primary health, continues to limit India's developmental potential, setting apart the Indian version of State Capitalism from that of the many other variants in East and Southeast Asia, as well as China's post-Deng 'socialism with Chinese characteristics'. Why did India lag on these fronts? Why was India not able to ensure universal literacy and basic education? Why did her public policy fall short of the vision of the leadership of her national movement, when put to practice? The answers are perhaps to be found in the realm of political economy. India's business leaders understood the nature of the challenge but they were either unable or unwilling to influence policy.

While the Bombay Plan was without question the 'manifesto of State Capitalism' at a historically important moment, it should be pointed out that its authors were conscious of the 'transitional and transitory' nature of the policies they were recommending. They were very clear in their minds that with the passage of time the role of the State in the economy would decline, giving greater space for the fuller play of market forces. First, there was as much emphasis on protecting individual freedoms and the development of a free market economy as there was on the immediate need for State support to economic development. While seeking State support for private enterprise development and for public services provisioning, the Bombay Plan reiterated the commitment of its authors to 'the freedom of the individual'. 'If a planned economy involves, as it necessarily must, the restriction of individual freedom in varying degrees, such restriction under a democratic government will be of limited duration and confined to specific purposes.'[12]

Outlining clearly what they regarded as 'basic principles' defining their version of what we have termed 'State Capitalism', the authors of the Bombay Plan conclude: 'Firstly, there should be sufficient scope for the play of individual initiative and enterprise; secondly, the interests of the community should be safeguarded by the institution of adequate sanctions against the abuse of individual freedom; and, thirdly, the State should play a positive role in the direction of economic policy and the development of economic resources.'[13]

The document was very clear that 'public sector' industries created through public investment should, at a later stage in the development process, be disposed off by the State and sold to private investors. Outlining the features of 'State ownership' of enterprises, the document made a distinction between State-owned and

---

[12] Thakurdas et al (1945), p.91.
[13] Thakurdas et al (1945), p.92.

State-managed, on the one hand, and State-owned but privately-managed, on the other.[14] While some industries may remain within State control, for strategic reasons, others can always be privatized. To quote, 'If...private finance is prepared to takeover these industries, State ownership may be replaced by private ownership.'[15]

The Bombay Plan's version of State Capitalism was, therefore, a transitional phase, a way station in India's journey from semi-feudal colonialism to free market capitalism. The idea of a 'Mixed Economy' that came to define the Nehru government's version of planned development found its roots here. However, for the authors of the Bombay Plan, this phase of 'Mixed Economy' was transitional and transient, while Nehru and his planners viewed it as a defining feature of post-Independence economic development.

In that sense, the authors of the Bombay Plan were at least a couple of generations ahead of their time in advocating the eventual privatization of public enterprises. India's policymakers, on the other hand, came to view the public sector as a permanent feature of industrialization in a developing economy and a necessary aspect of socialist development. Not surprisingly, therefore, half a century later, Prime Minister P.V. Narasimha Rao had

---

[14] Thakurdas et al (1945), pp.95-97.
[15] Thakurdas et al (1945), p.95.

to defend his policy of what was euphemistically dubbed 'disinvestment' and the widening of economic space for free market capitalism, as merely marking a new phase in the development of a 'Mixed Economy' rather than a departure from State Capitalism.[16]

BUSINESS AND POLITICS

The Bombay Plan was, so to speak, the last hurrah of the leadership of Indian business as far as crafting public policy was concerned. From the early years of the national movement and certainly during the decades leading up to Independence in 1947, the leadership of Indian business played an active role in public affairs and in shaping public policy. Indian business leaders articulated nationalist views and exposed the downside of colonialism even before the national movement gained momentum. Many were happy to merely seek the benevolence of the imperial government and when protection was granted to a few industries, like cotton, sugar and jute, in the 1920s, they were quite happy.

However, nationalism did motivate many business leaders to get involved in political activity and fund the nationalist cause. Among the earliest patriots from within

---

[16]For a discussion of this proposition, see Sanjaya Baru, *1991: How P.V. Narasimha Rao Made History*, Rupa Publications, New Delhi, 2016.

the business class was Dadabhai Naoroji, who was, of course, not merely a businessman but a man of learning and great public standing. He awakened the consciousness of educated Indians with his landmark book, *Poverty and Un-British Rule in India* (1902), published over a decade before Mahatma Gandhi's historic return to India from South Africa in 1915.

When the demand for protection for Indian industry gained momentum in the 1920s, Indian political leadership supported it. When a group of sugar manufacturers operated a cartel called the Indian Sugar Syndicate in the late 1930s, they secured the support of the INC and in turn, contributed funds to the party. B.M. Birla, who was instrumental in operating the cartel, had no compunction writing a letter to Rajendra Prasad (later the first president of the Indian Republic) that he had made a financial contribution of ₹10,000 as a gesture of appreciation.[17] This is just one example. The intimate link between nascent Indian bourgeoisie and the leadership of the national movement has been well recorded. It was but natural that by 1944, Indian business leaders felt empowered and responsible enough to invest time and effort in the articulation of a long-term plan for economic development of a free India.[18]

---

[17]Sanjaya Baru, *The Political Economy of Indian Sugar*, Oxford University Press, Delhi, 1990. p.65.
[18]See for example Claude Markovits, *Indian Business and*

BUSINESS, GOVERNMENT AND POLITICS: FROM PLAN TO PLEA

The Bombay Plan was, therefore, a natural public policy intervention by business leaders. However, once the government of Jawaharlal Nehru began to settle down to policymaking, it offered little space to business leaders in public policy and the institutions that shaped it. Several reasons have been cited as to why authors of the Plan themselves lost interest in shaping public policy more aggressively, even though their ideas did begin to influence the first and second Five Year plans drafted by Nehru's advisors.

Jawaharlal Nehru's turn to the 'Left', with the INC adopting a resolution in 1956 seeking to establish a 'socialistic pattern of society', was followed by the launch of a pro-free market, anti-State Capitalist political party called the Swatantra Party, in 1959.

While the Swatantra Party's political leader was none other than Chakravarty Rajagopalachari—the last Governor-General of India and the first Indian national to be appointed to that high office—the Party's main ideologue and activist was Minoo Masani, an economist, writer and political activist. While some business leaders, especially those based in Bombay, led by the Tatas, opted to support the Swatantra Party, expressing their disappointment with the Nehruvian variant of

---

Nationalist Politics, 1931-39: Indigenous Capitalist Class and the Rise of the Congress Party, Cambridge University Press, UK. 1985.

State Capitalism, others chose to live with the new Licence-Permit-Control Raj by corrupting the system to their advantage. So their initiative found ready support from J.R.D. Tata and industrialist Dharamsey Khatau, who willingly funded it. On the other hand, the other significant author of the Bombay Plan, G.D. Birla, refused to back the Swatantra Party, opting instead to remain a loyal 'financial' supporter of Nehru's Congress Party. Birla reportedly told a gathering of business leaders that 'Swatantra politics are not good businessman's politics.'[19] Dismayed by the generally poor response of most business leaders to the Swatantra Party initiative, and their willingness to live within the constraints of, and derive the benefits from, Nehru's State Capitalist Raj, Minoo Masani attributed the Swatantra Party's 'distressing finances' to 'the supine and cowardly attitude of the larger part of Big Business.'[20]

India's business leadership, the authors of the Bombay Plan, thus got divided into those who sought to promote a more pro-business political formation and those who were quite happy living within the constraints imposed by the new socialism of an increasingly corrupt bureaucratic system. Perhaps the problem with the Bombay Plan was that it was far too high-minded in its assumptions

---

[19] See H.L. Erdman, *Swatantra Party and Indian Conservatism*, Cambridge University Press, UK. 1967. pp.172-173.
[20] Erdman (1967), p.175.

about the relationship between business and government, assuming both would place national interest above their own class and institutional interests. The fact is that in practice, this idealistic 'State Capitalist' system became a version of 'crony capitalism' in which individual businessmen used their access to public officials to secure benefits for themselves, and politicians and government officials increasingly used their power to operate a system that allowed them to dole out benefits to favoured businessmen.

State Capitalism the world over has run the risk of degenerating into crony capitalism and that is precisely what happened in India. The deployment of the idea of 'planning' and public investment to in fact secure control over financial resources, and the power to grant licences and issue permits to favour specific industries and regions and so on, elicited two sorts of responses from Indian big business. First, some chose to fall in line, curry favour, offer financial support to politicians and public officials and, in turn, win licences and contracts. Not everyone benefited equally from this system as politicians in power played favourites. So, a second response was for some business leaders to openly seek a different regime of policymaking, rejecting the Nehruvian crony capitalist system and advocating a greater play for market forces.

The relationship between business and politics travelled all the way from the vanguard role played by business in the national movement to the ideological divide within the business class between those, like Tata, who believed it was in the interests of the business class to support pro-free market political parties, and others like Birla, who seemed willing to reconcile themselves to operating within the 'cronyism' inherent in the so-called 'Licence-Permit-Control Raj.' Indeed, the origins of 'crony capitalism' go all the way back to the Licence-Permit-Control Raj of the 1960s and is not merely a post-1991 phenomenon as many social scientists have argued.[21]

It is perhaps not mere happenstance that once this *ancien regime* was demolished, in July 1991, Prime Minister Narasimha Rao chose to award the first and, so far, the only Bharat Ratna given to a business leader, to none other than J.R.D. Tata in January 1992.

A PLAN FOR NEW INDIA

If the first and second Five Year Plans set the agenda of development for Free India, the economic reforms and liberalization of 1991 defined a new turn in India's economic policies. The 1991 policy package was widely

---

[21]See for example Chiranjib Sen, *Curbing Crony Capitalism in India*, Working Paper No. 5, Azim Premji University, April 2017. Accessed on 28 May, 2018 at: http://azimpremjiuniversity.edu.in/SitePages/pdf/APU-Working-Paper-Series-5-curbing-crony-capitalism-in-India.pdf

regarded as post-Nehruvian and one that facilitated India's 'reintegration into the world economy' and enabled market forces, rather than the government, to determine investment decisions.[22] One important difference between the Nehruvian policy framework of the first and second Five Year Plan period and the post-Nehruvian policy framework of the post-1991 policies, is that the former were influenced by the Bombay Plan, an agenda defined by the leadership of Indian business, while the latter were almost entirely the product of policy intervention by economists and officials working in the government, the International Monetary Fund (IMF) and the World Bank.

The 1991 policy package came out of the reports of several government committees mostly written in the 1980s and the policy package defined by the IMF and the World Bank when India sought their financial support to avert a balance of payments crisis in 1990-91.[23] There was hardly any articulation of the need for such a policy reset in anything that business leaders

---

[22]For a comprehensive review of the 1991 reforms, see Rakesh Mohan, *India Transformed: Twenty Five Years of Economic Reforms*, Penguin Random House, New Delhi, 2017.

[23]Montek Singh Ahluwalia, 'The 1991 Reforms: How Home-Grown Were They?', *Economic and Political Weekly*, 16 July 2016. Accessed on 29 May, 2018 at: https://www.epw.in/journal/2016/29/1991-reforms.html-0

had said till date. Instead, the initial reaction of most business leaders to the government's decision to liberalize foreign investment and trade policy was one of grave concern. Indian business was not confident that it had adequate competitive advantage to benefit from external liberalization. Even the response to the easing of domestic controls was lukewarm, especially from old and big business groups that had become habituated to working the crony capitalist system.[24]

While the media dubbed the business leaders expressing their concern about the fast-paced external economic liberalization as the 'Bombay Club', individual business leaders like Rahul Bajaj denied that there was in fact any such 'club' mobilizing business support against the government. While both the FICCI and the CII came around to accepting the new economic policies, government officials viewed industry support to reforms as 'touch and go'. The Chief Economic Advisor to the Government of India, Shankar Acharya, told *Outlook* magazine that Indian businessmen actively campaigned against competition from abroad, especially fearing takeovers, 'that things could have turned either way. There may have been no reform if their views had prevailed

---

[24]See, for example, Pragya Singh, 'The Home Alone Boys', *Outlook*, New Delhi, 10 January 2011. Accessed on 29 May, 2018 at: https://www.outlookindia.com/magazine/story/the-home-alone-boys/269748

politically...and they were all politically connected. Fortunately, the government held firm or the outcome would have been different.'[25]

While reconciling themselves to the change in policy, India's national business leadership have failed to invest in intellectual capacity building aimed at furthering India's development process in a manner that would address all national challenges. The Bombay Plan of 1944-45 was a forward looking document that charted a holistic national development plan. Nothing of the kind has since been produced by Indian business. Worse, Indian business has not invested in high quality teaching and research institutions that could in fact then generate such ideas. The ideas often paraded around by organizations like the CII and FICCI are either of western economists or Indian economists trained in the West.

Almost all the Chief Economic Advisors to the Government of India and key economic policymakers have been foreign-trained specialists whose intellectual framework has been shaped by the economics taught in western institutions. True, the Bombay Plan too came out of a generation trained in, or by, the West. But the fact that seven decades after Independence, India still depends on imported modes of thinking on economic policy suggests that the post-Independence generation of

---

[25] Pragya Singh (2011). ibid.

Indian business, who have benefited from this period's growth process, have not invested enough in domestic intellectual capacity building. In fact, almost all business leaders continue to send their offsprings to western institutions for education and training, not recognizing the fact that the most successful economies of the past quarter century have all been to India's east rather than west.

Having acquired qualifications abroad and studying the experience of new enterprise and technology development, the next generation of Indian business leadership seems quite comfortable returning home to operate in a pre-existing business environment, investing little on innovation, research and development, or in creating the intellectual capacity for new thinking.

If the Bombay Plan addressed the challenges of the time and the 1991 policies addressed the challenges of that time, what ideas are associated today with the leadership of Indian business that address the challenges of our time and of the near future? We are constantly borrowing ideas, technology and capital from abroad, generating few indigenously. The foundations of a New India can only be strengthened by investing in our own domestic intellectual and technological capabilities; not always living off the intellectual property of others.

In other words, the challenge to the Indian economy is not merely one of sustaining economic growth, but of discovering new ways to do so, given that the experience of developed industrial economies in the past decade leaves much to be desired in terms of finding new ways of thinking about another leap forward. Will western credit rating agencies continue to decide what is good and what is bad fiscal, monetary and industrial policy? Should India's policies remain captive to external certification?

Prime Minister Narendra Modi has called for a 'New India'. What would be the economics of a New India? Would it continue to be defined by western institutions, western-trained economists and consulting organizations, or would Indian business invest in domestic intellectual capacity building that would enable a new generation of Indians to craft something like a Bombay Plan for the twenty-first century?

CREATED BY BUSINESS, FOR BUSINESS

*Tulsi Jayakumar and
R. Gopalakrishnan*

The year was 1944. A group of eight eminent Indians, from diverse backgrounds, yet related to the world of economics, commerce and industry, came together to chart out a plan for India's economic development whenever Independence would be achieved. They had no way to assess when India would become independent, that it could be partitioned or the inexperience that it would face in managing a diverse, newly independent nation.

Published in pamphlet form in January 1944, the plan, which came to be popularly known as the Bombay Plan, sought 'to put forward as a basis of discussion, a statement in as concrete a form as possible, of the objectives to be kept in mind in economic planning in

India, the general lines on which development should proceed and the demands which planning is likely to make on the country's resources.'[1] The underlying assumption was that on termination of the ongoing World War II or shortly thereafter, a national government would come into existence at the centre which would be vested with full freedom in economic matters.

The doyens involved in charting out the plan—men imbued with a sense of public spirit and responsibility—with their expertise and experience if any, in drawing up corporate level plans, seemed to be well within their right to draw up a plan for India's economic development. For, at one level, although planning for corporates is akin to planning for a nation, national planning is at a totally different level. Both kinds of plans involve goal-setting, resource allocation to areas where advancement is required and inter-temporal allocation. And yet, treating the activities of corporate planning and a government's economic planning as similar may be (at the very least) facetious. For, it ignores the fundamental difference between members of a society (viz. corporates) forecasting and reacting to the future, versus the government of the very same society trying to regulate or control such activities.

---

[1] Thakurdas, P., Tata, J.R.D., Birla, G.D., Dalal, A., Ram, S., Lalbhai, K., Shroff, A.D. and Mathai, J. (1944), *Memorandum Outlining A Plan for Economic Development of India*, Parts One and Two, Penguin Books.

Goal-setting and achievement are different, with the government not only able to set goals for the entire society, but also possessing the sovereign power to achieve such goals with its *externally-oriented influence* and power of taxation, regulation, subsidization, and procurement. In contrast, corporate plans are guided by a corporate purpose, which is in comparison far limited in scope, and which involves implementation activities that are largely *internally-directed*. The consequences of any errors in planning are far severe in the case of national/government plans. Finally, the intellectual dimensions of the planning effort would be very different in the case of these two sets of plans. While a corporate plan, with its details on the factors likely to affect the business is expected to be relatively succinct, a national plan, with its focus on the several economic sectors and their inter-relationships, in the words of Wasily Leontief, 'would look like the statistical abstract of the United States'.[2]

The Bombay Plan caught the imagination of the public, and especially the business at large, and still continues to exercise fascination in the minds of academicians and intellectuals as the earliest known attempt at planned

---

[2] Weidenbaum, M. L. and Rockwood, L (1977), 'Corporate Planning Versus Government Planning', Publication No. 13, 1977, Murray Weidenbaum Publications, https://openscholarship.wustl.edu/cgi/viewcontent.cgi?referer=https://www.google.co.in/&httpsredir=1&article=1043&context=mlw_papers

economic development in India. This is evidenced by important trade bodies endorsing the Plan. As stated in an early essay by noted economist P.S. Lokanathan, 'Towards the end of March (1944), the Federation of Indian Chambers of Commerce representing all business organizations of the country endorsed the Bombay Plan at its annual meeting, and from then on, the Plan came to be regarded as the proposal of India's business community, if not of India's big business.'[3]

THE VISION

The Bombay Plan is an exemplary display of business common sense rather than of economic theory, based on the humanist approach and rising from the well-springs of entrepreneurial energy rather than from the logic of national economic planning. The Plan has no pretence of a formal document laying out the 'Vision' of a national entity in the sense of a blueprint for action; nor, as the architects have clearly stated, does it provide a complete scheme of economic development in terms of 'essential matters as the organization, methods and technique required for carrying out such a plan'.

It contains an *objective*, which is 'to put forward as a

---

[3] Lokanathan, P.S. (1945), 'The Bombay Plan', *Foreign Affairs*, https://www.foreignaffairs.com/articles/india/1945-07-01/bombay-plan.

basis of discussion, a statement in as concrete a form as possible, of the objectives to be kept in mind in economic planning in India, the general lines on which development should proceed and the demands which planning is likely to make on the country's resources.'

It has an objective, and it states it clearly.

The principal objectives of the Plan were to reduce the inequities in the Indian economy, through balanced economic growth of both agriculture and industry, including both large and small industries, and to raise the standard of living of the masses of the population rapidly. The Plan sought to double the per capita income within a period of fifteen years from the time the plan went into operation. This itself would require a trebling of the aggregate national income, given the rate of increase in population. The architects of the Plan envisaged and accorded an important and direct role to the State in this scheme of planned economic development.

Understanding the 'Vision' or the chief aims of the Bombay Plan and its evolution requires a careful examination of prevailing economic thought in the pre-Independence period.

Pre-Independence economic thought can be seen as dominated by Nehruvian socialism on the one hand and Gandhian socialist thought on the other, although these two approaches to socialism differed substantially. In fact Nehru resented the very use of the word 'socialism' by

Gandhi, since, according to him, Gandhi did not use it in the manner in which it was defined in the English language. Gandhi responded to such criticism by stating that the term itself had no clear and unambiguous definition.[4]

In the early years, between 1910-12, Nehru had been attracted to Fabian socialism—a variant of socialism, which unlike the revolutionary Marxian socialism, is largely evolutionary and envisages a complete restructuring of the economic, political and social systems in a society. Nehru's views, expounded in his *Autobiography*, suggest that he held economic factors, especially industrialization and the growth of the capitalist class, responsible for India's political situation.[5]

Nehru's belief in socialism as the panacea to India's problems was strengthened in 1920 when he met the peasantry of Oudh and heard their tales of oppression at the hands of the Taluqdars of Oudh. His trip to Europe and the Soviet Union in 1927 convinced him of the desirability and importance of socialism in India.[6]

---

[4]Sachi, S. (1964), 'Nehru's Conception of Socialism,' *Economic Weekly*, Special number, July, http://www.epw.in/system/files/pdf/1964_16/29-30-31/nehru_s_conception_of_socialism.pdf
[5]Ganguli, B.N. (1964), 'Nehru and Socialism,' *The Economic Weekly*, Special Number, July 1964, pp.1213-1218.
[6]Price, R. B. (1967), 'Ideology and Indian Planning,' *American Journal of Economics and Sociology*, Vol 26, pp.47-64.

Nehru drove the Congress to accept 'democratic socialism'—a variant of the Fabian socialism he was inspired by. The 1931 meeting of the All India Congress Committee (AICC) in Karachi passed a landmark resolution presented by Nehru himself, on 'Fundamental Rights and Economic Policy'—essentially a resolution on adopting socialism. The Congress, driven by Nehru, advocated the nationalization of key industries and services and other measures to reduce the rich-poor divide.[7] Thus, Nehruvian socialism was one of industrialization, albeit a State-led one.

Planning, according to Nehru, was the means of achieving such socialism. The practical formulation of Nehru's socialist ideas before Independence are to be seen in the blueprint that he prepared for the development of Free India under the aegis of the National Planning Committee set up in 1938. The blueprint set out the roadmap for achieving a planned economy by coordinating the various activities—agricultural, industrial, social, economic, and financial—which would contribute towards such an economy.[8]

On the other side was Mohandas K. Gandhi, who also was essentially antagonistic to the idea of private property and personal gain. However, unlike Nehru who

---

[7]Ganguli, B.N. (1964), 'Nehru and Socialism,' *The Economic Weekly*, Special Number, July 1964, pp.1213-1218.
[8]ibid.

believed in a socialism of industrialization, Gandhian socialism was based on the notion of self-sufficient villages 'that would literally drain the modern cities of their populations.'[9]

Thus, the convergence of Nehruvian and Gandhian socialism was in the lack of role they accorded to private enterprise in the development policies of independent India. 'Socialism', thus, came to be seen as the idealistic state, synonymous with progress, and exemplified by either complete nationalization or even a mixed economy with limited public ownership; whereas capitalism, on the other hand, became a dirty word, synonymous with imperialism and monopoly.[10]

Other intellectuals of the time also abhorred the idea of private property. V.K.R.V. Rao, a leading member of the Planning Commission, justified the socialistic position of intellectuals of the era in terms of the moral economy perspective. According to him, when the economy faces unemployment as a chronic problem, capitalism would lead to misallocation of resources, as well as becoming skewed in favour of producing for the rich at the expense of the poor.[11]

The Bombay Plan, against this backdrop of an emergent socialistic pattern of economic thought

---

[9]Price, 1967, p.47
[10]ibid.
[11]Price, 1967, p.51.

which favoured the nationalization of industry, appears to be largely pre-emptive. That this group of Indian businessmen was well aware of the developing thought is clear since the Congress had close connections with the business groups, and in fact relied on the latter to fund the struggle for Independence. As noted by Sanjaya Baru, there was a 'good rapport' between national leaders and native businessmen, with the latter actually funding the former; nor was such a relationship seen as 'unethical'.[12]

LARGER ROLE OF THE STATE

However, it would be naïve to assume that the Bombay Plan was merely a knee-jerk, preemptive action by Indian industrialists to growing socialism. Nor was State planning and State control accepted in the Bombay Plan indicative of a sudden spurt of patriotism, wherein the industrialists were willing to forego or sacrifice their own interests for the larger good. The Indian capitalist class was well aware of the structural weaknesses of pre-Independence Indian economy, which required more than a piecemeal plan for development.

A comprehensive development and modernization

---

[12] Baru, S. (2013, Feb 26), 'From Bombay Plan to Bombay Club,' Business Standard, http://www.business-standard.com/article/specials/from-bombay-plan-to-bombay-club-197081501119_1.html

of the economy required a larger role of the State for multiple reasons.

One, the volume of finance required for financing the large investment requirements in the development of basic industries as also social overheads, given the relative inability of the Indian capitalist class to raise this kind of finance requiring long gestation lags and bulky investments, together with their limited holding power, meant that the role of the State became critical.

Then there arose the question of where such finance would be raised from. The architects of the Bombay Plan could foresee the role of the State in mobilizing and channelizing resources/surpluses in the country of the kind that was required for financing the Plan. In the absence of traditional sources, the need for 'created money' or deficit financing could be undertaken only by the State. These requirements then called for nationalization of the entire system of credit and financial institutions, including the insurance sector. However, the need for the State to provide financial assistance was felt only in the initial stages. 'If later on private finance is prepared to take over these industries, State ownership may be replaced by private ownership, but it is essential in the public interest that the State should retain effective control over them.' The architects of the Bombay Plan visualized no difficulty in the availability of managerial ability, 'an important factor in modern business organization', to render the country self-sufficient 'within a short period'. However, the management of certain institutions such as Posts and Telegraphs would be retained under State ownership.

The architects of the Plan possibly saw the role of the State as important to prevent foreign economic imperialism to continue after the achievement of Independence.[13] They recognized the need for borrowings from foreign credit markets, especially America; they called such external finance 'not unwelcome' provided it came without 'political interference or foreign vested interests'. Yet, at the same time, they felt that it was possible to slowly replace such requirement of external finance through focusing on a program of development of basic industries.

Finally, the architects of the Bombay Plan also envisioned a reduction in 'gross inequalities' in the distribution of income, since such inequalities meant lower purchasing power and would hence constrain production in the economy. State control, together with State ownership, was seen as a means of diminishing inequalities of income. At the same time, however, the Bombay Plan, paradoxically, spoke of the need *not* to abolish inequalities completely. 'Subject to the provision of a basic minimum, it is desirable to leave enough scope

---

[13]Mukherjee, A. (1976), 'Indian Capitalist Class and the Public Sector, 1930-1947', *Economic and Political Weekly*, Vol 11, No. 3, pp.67-73.

for variations in income according to the ability and productivity.' This would provide sufficient motivating factor for improvement in efficiency.

To meet all these objectives, the architects suggested a 'compromise formula', wherein some units of the industry would be owned and managed by the State, while others would be left to private enterprise. The Plan actually recommended a set of controls during the planning period, akin to those present under war conditions (but better coordinated and administered), which would help in the achievement of the objectives. Such controls pertained to those in the spheres of production, distribution, consumption, investment, foreign trade and exchange and wages and working conditions.

That this preemptive plan on the part of the architects of the Bombay Plan was partially successful can be gauged from the 'compromise' built into the Industrial Policy Resolutions of 1948 and 1956 in the form of specifying three groups of industries. Thus, Group 'A' (munitions, atomic energy, iron and steel, heavy engineering and heavy electrical plants, coal, oil, most mining, aircraft, air transport, railways, shipbuilding, communications, and electrical generation and distribution) included those 'the future development of which will be the exclusive responsibility of the State'; Group 'B' (some mining, aluminium, machine tools, ferroalloys and tool steels, heavy chemicals, essential drugs, fertilizers, synthetic rubber, road and sea transport) included those 'which will be progressively State-owned and in which the State will therefore generally take the initiative in establishing new undertakings, but in which private enterprise will also be expected to supplement the effort of the State'; and Group 'C' included the residual, whose 'future development will, in general, be left to the initiative and enterprise of the private sector', but 'it will always be open to the State to undertake any type of industrial production.'[14]

THE WIDTH, DEPTH AND PACE OF CHANGE PROPOSED

As a document of change management, it is important to analyse the Bombay Plan in terms of the width, depth and pace of change proposed.

Width of Change: The width of change proposed in the document was large, comprising not just agriculture and industry, but also public health, education, communication, housing and miscellaneous services.

The Plan proposed industrial development both in the field of capital (basic goods) and consumption goods. The former would mitigate the need for external finance and accelerate the pace of sustainable economic development (financed domestically), while the latter would reduce the hardships faced during planning. It spoke of such

---
[14]Price, 1967, p.49

consumption goods to be produced within small and cottage industries, which would simultaneously generate employment, as also reduce the dependence on expensive plant and machinery.

Agricultural development was given a primary role, since the Plan continued to visualize India as a predominantly agrarian economy. Such development was meant to be carried out through certain 'fundamental reforms' in the agricultural sector and included consolidation of holdings through cooperative farming, liquidation of the burden of agricultural indebtedness through cooperative societies, as also paying attention to and mitigating the problem of soil erosion through terracing arable lands, afforestation and other suitable methods in different areas.

The Plan also provided for transport and communication to assist in the movement of goods and services, resulting from the large volumes of industrial and agricultural production. It suggested a 50 per cent increase over the existing railway mileage and a 100 per cent increase over road mileage in British India. Shipping facilities were also sought to be improved upon by developing the small natural harbours along India's long coastline. The Plan excluded civil aviation.

In terms of providing a minimum standard of living to the citizens of India, the Plan went into details of minimum nourishment required and balanced diet, minimum clothing and housing needs, besides health and education for the Indian population. Within health, the architects of the Plan went into details of proper arrangements for sanitation and water supply, village dispensaries, general hospitals, maternity clinics in towns and even specialized institutions for the treatment of chronic diseases such as tuberculosis, cancer, leprosy and venereal diseases. Similarly, education was looked at from the aspects of primary, secondary, university and technical education, as also adult literacy.

Part II of the document touched upon other critical aspects such as minimizing temporary, as well as disguised unemployment in agriculture, evolving schemes of unemployment insurance for workers during prolonged periods of unemployment; minimum wages, which itself would be revised periodically; agricultural prices, keeping in mind the interests of both farmers and consumers; establishment of multi purpose cooperative societies; reforms in the system of land tenures and especially the abolition of the zamindari system, albeit gradually, ensuring uniform land revenue from across the different areas; taxation of agricultural incomes above a certain level; provision of free social services (primary and middle school education, adult education etc.); provision of essential utility services such as electricity and transport at low cost; introduction of social security through introducing sickness insurance, paid holidays in organized industries, maternity benefits in all industrial establishments; and regional development.

Thus, it was a Plan which covered a wide scope and was well ahead of its times.

Depth of Change: The Plan was rather shallow in its conception of the sources from which the capital expenditure required by the Plan could be raised. The capital expenditure involved in the Plan was estimated to be slightly above ₹10,000 crores (£7,500 million), comprising ₹9,170 crores (£6,877.5 mn) of non-recurring expenditure and ₹1,189 crores (£891.74 mn) of recurring expenditure.

Such expenditure could be financed from external and internal financing sources. External finance would involve hoarded wealth worth approximately ₹300 crores (£225 million), the return of which, from their places of concealment, the national government would facilitate. It would also comprise the short-term loans to the UK in the form of sterling securities held in the Reserve Bank of India (RBI). A favourable Balance of Trade as India reduced her dependence on imports through agricultural and industrial development and foreign borrowings, would bridge the gap through additional sources of external finance. External finance would contribute to about ₹2,600 crores, while the share of internal finance was estimated to be ₹7,400 crores.

Such internal financing would depend partially on domestic savings, estimated at 6 per cent of the national income, which would be available for investment during the plan period. The Plan was radical in that it proposed the monetization of deficit through 'created money'— money created by borrowing against *ad hoc* securities from the RBI, as a major source of internal finance. Such created money was estimated to provide ₹3,400 crores towards financing capital expenditure required of the Plan. It appears then that the need to restrict the dependence on external financing sources made the authors throw norms of 'responsible monetary policy' to the wind.[15]

Thus, the Bombay Plan envisaged more than 33 per cent of capital expenditure to be financed through deficit financing. It is pertinent to note here that even Keynes, during the Great Depression, referred to only the socialization of investment[16], which was not the same as the concept of deficit financing. It is also pertinent to note that this concept of created money was used by the Indian government right upto April 1997, which was the

---

[15]Tyabji, N. (n.d.): 'Imperialism, Big Business and Industrialization in India', http://www.revolutionarydemocracy.org/rdv21n1/tyabji.htm

[16]Brown-Collier, E.K and Collier, B.E. (1995), 'What Keynes really said about Deficit Spending', Journal of Post-Keynesian Economics, Vol. 17, No. 3, pp.341-355.

year when the automatic monetization through *ad hoc* bills was stopped. The Plan architects were aware of the inflationary consequences of this mode of raising finance, as also an increase in the inequalities between the societal classes. Their solution, surprisingly, is a recommendation of *'a rigorous control by the government of every aspect of economic life, [such that] individual liberty and freedom of enterprise will suffer a temporary eclipse.'*

The problem with this approach and the expected criticism to follow, do not seem to have escaped the architects of the Plan, for later they relegated the role of money or finance 'merely as a means of mobilizing the internal resources of the country in materials and man power', which is completely subservient to the requirements of the economy as a whole.

Pace of Change: The Plan envisaged a phenomenal transition of the economy in a mere fifteen years. It sought to execute this change through three plans, each covering a period of five years, christened the First, Second and Third Plans respectively. The total expenditure was to be allocated to each of the Plans in a geometric progression in the following manner—First Plan: ₹1,400 crores; Second Plan: ₹2,900 crores and Third Plan: ₹5,700 crores. The rationale for this was that the total amount would be increased gradually, as the availability of both material resources and the personnel required for such development would rise in increasing proportions, thereby facilitating accelerated progress.

CULTURAL EXPERIENCES IN CHANGE MANAGEMENT

Change Management has developed in the field of management largely after the Second World War. The fruits of theory and practice in behavioural sciences has permeated into corporate management and seeped a bit into public policy as well. The fact is that the *technical* attributes of change are by themselves complex—difficult to first, conceive and second, articulate into a cohesive wholeness. Having accomplished such a challenging task, transformers have realized that the *human* aspects of transformation are even more complex—wholly when articulated, and emotionally unpredictable during implementation. The cultural vector in executing change management is, in some respects, far more important to focus upon in transformation exercises at both corporate and national levels.

This has been made amply clear time and time again in the various initiatives that successive governments in India have tried to drive. One has to only look at the initial failed attempts to introduce Hindi as the national language in the South, the initial communications exhorting India to adopt family planning or even the recent Swacch Bharat campaign with its focus on building toilets, to understand how critical the *human vector* aspect of change management is, and the need for mindset change at the mass level.

Change management at the level of individual organizations is challenging enough. Executing a plan as wide in its conception as the Bombay Plan would be a herculean task by any standards. The architects of the Plan recognized the challenge in execution as that of 'getting the cooperation of the people'. However, this was then reduced to resolving such a challenge by getting people 'to read and write' so that they could be in a position to 'understand *for themselves* the broad implications of the developments embodied in the Plan'. The only other obstacle in the execution of the Plan, as per the architects, was the large-scale training of personnel for technical posts in agriculture, trade, industry and for general administration, resembling the Soviet system.

However, even seventy-one years after India has achieved Independence, whether adult mass literacy (of the sort achieved by India) has been a panacea to any of the ills plaguing it, remains a moot question. Nor has technical advancement resolved the development concerns of India. In this sense, again, the Plan was naïve in its conception and implementation.

With the benefit of hindsight and newly mined knowledge, we can today, in an act of constructive criticism, say that the Bombay Plan was woefully inadequate in the area of the human vector of change management. Indeed, it is a moot point whether, on an ongoing basis in national public policy, there is sufficient attention paid to, and learning derived from, cultural experiences in change management. Within companies, the awareness is high, and the attempt to incorporate behavioural techniques is expanding rapidly. It is, of course, far more difficult to do so in a country with as large and diverse a population as India. However, recognizing the cultural vector of change management is exceedingly important in planning and execution of change and must feature more prominently in national planning initiatives.

BOMBAY PLAN AND INDIA TODAY

The circumstances faced by India are vastly different in the new millennium. As such, the relevance of the Bombay Plan seventy-five years hence, appears to be merely academic. Nonetheless, it is an opportunity to revisit the statements in the Bombay Plan and the development of events over the last seventy-five years. Many important points emerge. However, what appears to be overwhelmingly clear is how despite years of planning and all the progress, India's development concerns have changed very little over time. The development narrative and its themes seem to remain the same; it only gets seen from different ideological lenses from time to time.

We refer to just three such concerns in the context of 'relevance' of the Bombay Plan in the interest of brevity.[17]

Education and Health: The hope and ambition of the planners in literacy, education and public health has been a repeated theme from the Bombay Plan right up to the contemporary plans. Statistics used to measure education and health, as reflected in Budget speeches or annual reports of the respective ministries, give the impression of great progress. However, the situation on the ground reveals that while the quantity parameters are reasonably impressive, the qualitative parameters are woefully inadequate. Any symptom that persists in the body requires urgent action. Similarly, inadequacy of quality education and healthcare require to be urgently addressed by planning.

Hoarded Wealth: It is fascinating to reflect on the important role that the Bombay Plan accorded to bringing back hoarded wealth. After seventy-five years, the present political and economic system is also battling with this problem. The practice of stashing money abroad is not

---

[17]We make these points with full awareness and respect for the enormous and impressive progress made in the country across several fronts in economic planning, strengthening democratic institutions and offering citizens an improving standard of living. One has to only compare India with her immediate neighbours to appreciate the point.

new, and so are the difficulties of bringing back this wealth to play a role in national economic planning. The idea of using this wealth is now old, but new executable planning models need to be considered.

Farming: The importance of farming (agriculture, horticulture, dairy and animal husbandry) has received emphasis all the way from the Bombay Plan to the latest Budget proposals. The authors have briefly scanned the speeches delivered by finance ministers since the first Budget to date—every finance minister, indeed every prime minister, has laid great emphasis on improving farming. Although India's aggregate production of agriculture and related sectoral goods has dramatically improved, especially with the successful green, blue and white revolutions, India's farm productivity is comparatively poor. Further, the marketing channels for India's produce are riddled with State regulations, ostensibly to protect the farmer, but providing rent to unworthy players in the agricultural chain. India needs to think of doing something new for farming—for example, adopting a novel 'holistic framework approach' to farm planning.[18]

---

[18] Gopalakrishnan, R.G. and Thorat, Y.S.P. (2015), 'What India can do Differently in Agriculture', *Sarthak Krishi Yojana*, http://www.rallis.co.in/imagesReusableFiles/Corporate_Sarthak-Krishi-Yojana.pdf

The Bombay Plan, from a business perspective, can be seen as largely preemptive, considering the socio-economic-political context against which it was framed. The Quit India Movement in 1942 launched by Mahatma Gandhi had made British rule in India largely untenable. There was the unprecedented famine in Bengal, and growing suspicion over the role of business. Then, there was the Nehruvian socialism on one hand and Gandhian socialism on the other. As for the economy, the positive Balance of Trade gave the architects of the Plan the confidence that such a plan could be financed and managed. These businessmen, thus, supported an increased State participation, reduction in income disparities, as also concentration of resources in the hands of a few rich, as a means of preventing the spread of foreign power and communism. This, in our studied view, bereft of any normative stance, was in their own business interests and aimed at the preservation of such interests.

The question of why the Bombay Plan was never mentioned after just one year of its presentation, and why it was never referred to in Indian planning, appears to be shrouded in mystery.[19] But adopting a business perspective, this does not seem so strange after all. Which company would use an eight-year-old plan document

---

[19] Sanyal, A. (2010), 'The Curious Case of the Bombay Plan,' Contemporary Issues and Ideas in Social Sciences, June.

for perspective planning in the current scenario? The Bombay Plan, published in 1944, had exactly a similar relationship to the first Five Year Plan implemented in 1951, eight years later. Little wonder then that the Bombay Plan was never used as an active plan document, although its principles were never ignored.

Finally, the Bombay Plan is testimony to the evolving public-private relationship over the years, and the continued debate on what ought to be the role of the State. From the private sector demanding the role of the State in transforming the economy in the Bombay Plan, to the State demanding the role of the private sector in 'nation-building', while understanding its own limitations thereof—whether it be in the conception of Public-Private-Partnership (PPP) models, or the mandatory Corporate Social Respnsibility (CSR) requirement under the Companies Act 2013—India seems to have come full circle.

◆

Tulsi Jayakumar is Professor of Economics and Chairperson, Family Managed Business at the S.P. Jain Institute of Management & Research (SPJIMR), Mumbai.

R. Gopalakrishnan is a former director of Tata Sons and is currently an Executive-in-Residence at SPJIMR, Mumbai.

WHATEVER HAPPENED TO THE INDIAN BOURGEOISIE?

Meghnad Desai

From a temporal distance of nearly seventy-five years, the Bombay Plan raises many intriguing questions. Why should a group of top industrialists and leading capitalists prepare and argue for a Plan where the State was to play a predominant role? Of course, there were other Plans—The People's Plan that M.N. Roy had put forward and a Gandhian Plan that Shriman Narayan had presented. Today, however, the other Plans are forgotten. The Bombay Plan commands attention.

The other important question is about the convergence of business leaders and the Planning Commission on the nature of the economic strategy. There are attractive policy proposals in the Bombay Plan which the Planning Commission did not take up—such as the need to aim for a minimum standard of living, production of consumer goods initially to forestall inflationary pressures, and emphasis on agriculture. But the fact remains that like the Planning Commission; the Bombay Plan downplayed the role of the private sector and overplayed the need for basic–capital goods–industries. Other Asian countries followed a bottom-up path of beginning with agro-industries and other consumer goods while importing capital goods. India reversed the time path to make machines first, consumer goods later and accorded low priority to agriculture (until the foodgrain shortage and US pressure on PL480 shipments drove India to the Green Revolution in the 1960's). The result was that while there were Asian Tigers and Asian Miracle economies which marched faster—South Korea, Taiwan, Singapore, not to mention Japan and China—India was left in the slow lane. While the business elite of Japan, the Keidanren, or the Chaebol in South Korea, harmonized with the State and thrived to their mutual benefit, the Indian capitalists stayed supine and neither wielded influence on the economic policy being followed, nor were they harnessed in a creative partnership by the State. The Rao-Singh turn in 1991 was a late correction, but forty years were already wasted. Business leaders may have been cronies but never were true partners of the political circles. Why did the industrialists not fight for their corner and go the route they knew best? Why don't Indian political parties, even today, praise the role that business plays in India's prosperity? Why was even Narendra Modi embarrassed to be called 'suit boot ki sarkar?'

A PLAN OR MANY PLANS?

Subhash Chandra Bose had established the National Planning Committee (NPC) during his Presidency of the Congress, putting Jawaharlal Nehru in charge. The NPC had been publishing its reports, which were more like stocktaking than blueprints. Not only was Soviet Planning well known but wartime in Great Britain had seen the Beveridge Plan. The US had gone through the Great Depression and the New Deal. The philosophy of State activism was the zeitgeist. The advocates of Free Market had been soundly defeated during the Great Depression as they had no cure for it except to urge everyone to wait till the Market had self-adjusted and equilibrium had been restored. The Free Market advocates had retired into obscurity then. The private corporate sector had understood the need for rational planning for its operations. Joseph Schumpeter, the celebrator of the 'entrepreneur as the dynamic agent of Capitalism' had pessimistically seen the triumph of corporate capitalism replacing the individualist ethos, and predicted that Capitalism and Socialism would converge in his *Capitalism, Socialism and Democracy*.[1]

One must also remember that to the extent that economics was taken on board in these deliberations, there was no Development Economics in the mid-1940's. Rosenstein-Rodan's pioneering article about development of South-Eastern Europe requiring the Big Push had just appeared in 1943.[2] Keynes's General Theory was adapted for a government Budget only in the UK Budget of 1944. The Harrod-Domar model had not yet been articulated, though Harrod's 1939 article had presentiments of a growth model which he later developed fully post-war in a series of lectures at the LSE.[3,4]

There was no data on India's national income. Dadabhai Naoroji had made some pioneering calculations in his critique of the British rule. But continuous estimates of national income were being developed in the 1930's for the US by Simon Kuznets and for the UK by Colin Clark, and we can see how preliminary they were from Keynes's citation of the data in his General Theory. V.K.R.V. Rao,

---

[1]Schumpeter, J.A. (1942) *Capitalism, Socialism and Democracy*. Harper, New York.
[2]Rosenstein-Rodan, Paul (1943) 'Problem of industrialization of Eastern and South Eastern Europe', *Economic Journal*, 53, 202-211
[3]Harrod, Roy (1939) 'An Essay in Dynamic Theory', *Economic Journal*, March, 14-33.
[4]Harrod, Roy (1949) *Towards a Dynamic Economics.* Macmillan, London.

who had done his PhD at Cambridge, produced national income estimates for India for 1931-32.

But there were no continuous income-series available. Input-Output analysis had been formulated by Wassily Leontief, but as yet it was not widely used. War time requirements had made governments aware of the contribution mathematical techniques could make to improve the efficiency and accuracy of logistical transfers. For instance, Linear Programming was being used to plan optimal routing for sea transportation (Tjalling Koopmans, the joint winner of the Nobel Prize in Economics, 1975, was the author), but this was only during the second half of the War.

However, the idea had taken root that the economic condition of a nation can be improved with the use of Planning. The Resolution for setting up the NPC had said, 'The problem of poverty and unemployment, of national defence and economic regeneration in general cannot be solved without industrialization. As a step towards such industrialization, a comprehensive scheme of national planning should be formulated. This scheme should provide for the development of heavy key industries, medium scale industries, and cottage industries.'[5]

Thus, industry was to be at the centre of new India.

---

[5]Nehru, J. (1946) *The Discovery of India*. Bidley Head, London pp.435-438

The perception of the Independence movement was that India had been de-industrialized by the British. Yet this was a misunderstanding of history. It was not because of foreign rulers that domestic handicraft industries had been destroyed. This was a result of the Industrial Revolution. This was not unique to India. Capitalism had destroyed the old handicrafts both at home and abroad just as Marx and Engels had written in their *Communist Manifesto*. (Marx's interest was drawn to the economic question because of the distress in the hand-weaving craft families of Upper Silesia. The spinning revolution had brought down the price of yarn and boosted the handloom weavers. But when weaving was industrialized fifty years after spinning, the weavers were wiped out just as cottage spinners had been when spinning was mechanized. Marx began to study Capitalism in an attempt to understand this development.) But within Asia, India had begun to acquire modern industry in the 1850's even before Japan. While Japan went ahead under the Meiji restoration, modern Indian industry grew at an astonishing rate of 8 per cent per annum between 1860 and 1900.[6] Of course, this was from a small base. But the two World Wars had forced the colonial power to help develop industries in India.

---

[6]Brahmananda, P.R. (2001), *Money, Income, Prices in Nineteenth Century India : A Historical, Quantitative and Theoretical Study.* Himalaya Publishing House Mumbai

By the 1940's, India had a large and world-class textile industry. It was the third or fourth largest in the world by the 1920's.[7] This was despite the insistence on handspun and woven khadi by Gandhi and the Congress. In Ahmedabad and Bombay, there were large mills which produced fine textiles. The jute industry in Calcutta, the largest in the world, was mainly foreign owned but the cotton textile industry was owned by Indians—largely family based ownership in Ahmedabad—and shareholders in Bombay. India also had the third largest rail network in the world by the 1920's. Iron and steel industry had been pioneered by Tata and by 1939; India was producing nearly a million tonnes. There were cement, paper and glass industries. Of course, industry was a small part of the economy in aggregate terms. One ranking showed that in 1947, India was the seventh largest by volume of industrial production. One of the reasons for this high rank was the wartime destruction in Japan and continental Europe. But India was not starting from scratch.

There was, however, the strong perception among Indian nationalists that India was de-industrialized by the imperial power. To recover, India had to build an

---

[7]Morris, M.D.(1984), *The Growth of Large Scale Industry to 1947*, in *The Cambridge Economic History of India Volume 2 1757-1970*, edited by Dharma Kumar. Cambridge University Press, Cambridge, UK

industrial structure from scratch. It could not, and should not rely on importing machinery from foreign countries. It should be self-sufficient even at the cost of paying a higher price. There was no need for such self-denial. The Soviet Union was forced to be self-sufficient because of the international blockade. India could have imported machinery but chose not to. Thus the advantages of international trade were to be shunned. But other Asian countries did not follow this logic except China, until it changed direction in 1978.

THE NATIONAL BOURGEOISIE

A remarkable fact about the industrialists who conceived of the Bombay Plan was that they were nationalists rather than 'comprador', as the Chinese capitalists were alleged to be. They had backed the Independence movement with financial support and were sympathetic with the programme that the Congress was about to put forward. Nationalism meant similar things to the Congress and the capitalists. India had to prosper and industrialization was the solution. But the industrialists had always cooperated with the existing State. They had thrived due to tariffs which required State support. India had been granted tariff autonomy since 1910. The Second World War had meant lucrative war contracts and tremendously rapid growth of output and profits. Some of them, especially the Ahmedabad textile magnates and the Marwaris, had openly supported Congress (less so the Bombay industrialists till the 1940's). But by and large, industrial development in India had never been along *laissez-faire lines*. Tariffs and rupee depreciation were constant issues on which the nationalist politicians and the industrialists had converged for the preceding sixty years.

Of course, in the then popular Leninist vocabulary, the bourgeoisie was a weak relative to the feudal elements in the ruling class. But these things are tricky to be precise about. The feudal classes had begun to invest in modern industry as they had done in Europe. The celebrated polymath and staunch communist D.D. Kosambi, in a trenchant review of Nehru's *The Discovery of India*, had remarked about the wartime boom and the character of Indian bourgeoisie:

> 'The best example of this perhaps is the Parsi community which, in its original situation in Gujarat, was one of the most oppressed of refugee minorities and is today one of the most advanced and powerful of communities in India because of their adoption of modern industrial and finance capitalism. On the other hand, the case is totally different with the Marwaris of Rajputana, who did control finance and moneylending in the old days but had no political rights whatsoever. If Nehru

would take the trouble to look up the records, he will see how often such moneylenders backed the British in the days of British expansion in India. Of course that may not lead him to realize a basic contemporary phenomenon: the change of pseudo-capital thus accumulated in modern productive money. The changeover is now actually so rapid that even the most backward and degenerate of Indians, the feudal princelings, are now becoming shareholders on a large scale.'[8]

Kosambi reflected the prevailing Left view that despite his good intentions, Nehru would not prevail over the powerful capitalists. Concluding his review, he says,

'History has thrust upon Nehru the mantle of leadership of a very powerful organisation which still commands greater mass support than any other in India, and which has shown by its unremitting and painful struggle that it is determined to capture political control of the entire subcontinent. But will Nehru's orientation towards Marxism change when the interests of the class which now backs Congress so heavily, diverge from the interests of the poorer classes, or will his lack of a class analysis

---

[8] The Bourgeoisie Comes of Age in India, *Science and Society*, Vol. X, 1946, New York; p.395

lead only to disillusionment? It would be silly to proclaim that Mahatma Gandhi, than whom no more sincere person exists, is a tool of the capitalists in India. But there is no other class in India today, except the new bourgeoisie, so strong, so powerfully organized, and so clever as to exploit for its own purposes whatever is profitable in the Mahatma's teachings and to reduce all dangerous enunciations to negative philosophical points. This bourgeoisie needs Nehru's leadership, just as India has needed the class itself. As I read the omens, the parting of the ways is clearly visible; what is not clear is the path Nehru himself will choose in the moment of agony."[9]

The contradictions of the orthodox Left analysis become clear. The bourgeoisie was a powerful class but not powerful enough. Nehru leads a popular movement which is determined to win political control but could be overwhelmed by the powerful capitalist class. There is also a lot of optimism that the condition of the poor will force Nehru into a revolutionary direction. As it happened, soon after Independence, the Communist Party of India (CPI) did launch a general strike with hopes of success, but it failed; its peasant revolt in Telangana was put down effectively. The Ranadive line was abandoned

---

[9]ibid.

and he was replaced by Ajoy Ghosh as Secretary of the CPI which agreed to tread the Parliamentary path. Nehru carried Congress to a large majority in the Lok Sabha in 1952 and ruled for the next twelve years. He shaped India's economic path as he wanted.

Nehru was able to co-opt Mathai, who was the brain behind the Bombay Plan. The first Five Year Plan was a makeshift exercise with some schemes launched even before Independence. The theoretical structure was conventional. K.N. Raj, who had joined the Planning Commission having completed his Masters at LSE, warned that high and ambitious growth targets envisaged in the NPC's early drafts would not be achievable. Nehru thought he was influenced by Western pessimism. But Raj was proved correct. The growth rate of income over the first Five Year Plan was 18 per cent. This was several times what the economy had got over the first half of the century but much less than the ambitions of the NPC.[10]

A radical break came during the preparation for the second Five Year Plan. The 1954 harvest was extremely good. After years of rationing and problems of rehabilitating Partition refugees, India felt at ease. India could now plan ambitiously. There is another change which seems to have taken place around this time which

---

[10]Desai Meghnad (2017) *Raisina Model : Indian Democracy at 70*. Penguin, Delhi; chapter 3

has not been fully discussed till now. Nehru had hoped that India would convey to the world the Gandhian message of peace and nonviolence. But he seems to have felt the need for strengthening India's fighting capability. The only evidence I have seen is what he is reported to have said to Marie Seton, the film critic and his friend. She says, he told her that he was embarking on a capital-intensive growth strategy because he wanted India to be self-sufficient in its arms supplies.[11] It could be that he had heard the rumblings of China's interest in the border or realized that Pakistan was going to be a permanent enemy. Either way, the second Five Year Plan adopted the Mahalanobis strategy of 'machines to make machines' approach to investment. Agriculture was given a lower allocation. A new Industrial Policy Resolution was announced in 1956. The State was to have a monopoly in a number of new sectors to start industries. Nehru had persuaded Congress to adopt 'A Socialist Pattern of Society' as its goal at the Avadi session in January 1955. Whatever Kosambi's fears, the political leadership was in vanguard and the bourgeoisie was meekly following. Rama Krishna Dalmia, head of a rich Marwari family and owner of the old publishing firm Bennett Coleman which published *The Times of India*, was sent to prison for violating tax laws.

---

[11]ibid.

It was a very ambitious plan in terms of the investment required. The gap between investment planned and the savings likely to be available was unbridgeable. By now, the large sterling balances accumulated during the Second World War had been spent, mainly on facilitating the buying out of British-owned capital by Indian capitalists. C.D. Deshmukh, who was finance minister during the first Plan period, was to say later that the money was 'spent like there was no tomorrow'.[12] The worry the Bombay Plan architects had was now real. Deficit financing was followed systematically. There would also be a need for foreign aid. India was going to be ecumenical in seeking aid from the US, USSR, UK and even West Germany.

Even so, the bourgeoisie were not stupid. Foreseeing a foreign exchange shortage, imports had been brought forward and India was running out of reserves. T.T. Krishnamachari, who was commerce minister, was blamed at that time but he survived. The Plan had to be 'pruned'. Strict import controls had to be imposed. But the basic capital intensive path was not abandoned. Yet the neglect of agriculture was telling. Harvests were lower in 1957 than in 1956 and inflation was becoming a problem. The issue of marketable surplus of foodgrains became a big issue.

At the same time, Nehru's favourite scheme

---

[12]ibid.

for agricultural growth—cooperative farming—was introduced at the Nagpur Congress but despite Nehru's enthusiasm, nothing seems to have been done to implement it.

The bourgeoisie now began to get restless. The cooperative farming decision incensed some politicians. The few senior politicians who could openly disagree with Nehru got together. The Swatantra Party was established by C. Rajagopalachari and Minoo Masani. Jayaprakash Narayan was present at the launch of the Swatantra Party in Bombay. Nehru was annoyed and perhaps amused but not intimidated by the birth of this party.

India had a plan to increase its steel production from under 2 tonnes to 6 tonnes. Steel plants were sponsored as foreign aid by the UK (Durgapur), USSR (Bhilai) and West Germany (Rourkela). There was a request to the US to add to that list. But G.D. Birla, in a testimony to the Joint Economic Committee of the US Congress, advised against it. This was an unusual show of hostility to Nehru's policy. The US decided not to build a steel plant in India. The USSR stepped in and built a second steel plant for India. (I report this from memory of what I read at that time sixty years ago.)

The second Five Year Plan was successful in as much as income went up 23 per cent in five years. Thus India experienced a growth of income of 45 per cent over the ten years of the two Plans, the highest India had experienced as far as available data goes. What is more, while new industrial sectors had been reserved for the public sector, and output expansion in private sector industries was restrained, Nehru did not nationalize more than two enterprises—the Imperial Bank was made into a State Bank and Life Insurance Corporation. The bourgeoisie could therefore rest easy.

The third Five Year Plan (1961-66) was inaugurated during Nehru's final years. But it failed to deliver. Growth fell short of targets in the first two years. So the targets of the last three years were jacked up. But much of the 1960s was a disaster for India. Unlike the careful dovetailing of the Bombay Plan, the third Five Year Plan began as more of the same. But then the food situation became acute. There were two famines in 1965-66 and 1966-67. Lal Bahadur Shastri suspended the implementation of the fourth Plan and introduced annual plans. He clearly saw that Planning hadn't benefited the common man. He even used the expression 'Aam Admi'. He would have altered the direction of economic policy. He was also much friendlier towards the US than Nehru had been. But he died in January 1966. Soon the equation between the bourgeoisie and the politicians began to change.

Not immediately, of course. Indira Gandhi, who succeeded Nehru, took time to assert herself. She barely won the 1967 elections. In many states, coalitions of Opposition parties formed the government—an unforeseen erosion of Congress power. The more Right Wing forces within the Congress were asserting themselves. Finance minister Morarji Desai was known to be business-friendly, if not market-friendly. The syndicate—S.K. Patil, Atulya Ghosh and Kamaraj Nadar—were powerful regional leaders and determined who got what. Indira Gandhi had been prevailed upon to devalue the Rupee under pressure from the World Bank. But the promised loan did not arrive because Lyndon Johnson was not happy with India's stance on Vietnam. Indira Gandhi felt threatened by the Right both at home and abroad.

She broke the syndicate's power in 1969 by splitting the Congress. From then on, the Congress (I) took a much more determined Leftist stance than it had done under Nehru. This was the time when forgetfulness about things such as the Bombay Plan became general. Manichean distinction was made between the Left-oriented economics and politics, and the rest who were castigated as reactionaries and friends of sinister foreign (read American) forces. Drastic restrictions were put on the private sector. Several companies were nationalized, beginning with large commercial banks. The bourgeoisie was warned to truckle down or face nationalization.

The Green Revolution was accomplished during the sixties. Now there was a new class to flex its muscles—the large farmers who benefited from the Green Revolution.

They wanted input price subsidies, output price guarantee and generous bank loans from the newly nationalized banks. These farmers were closer to the regional leadership than the bourgeoisie were to the Central leadership. Income growth during the 1960's was 3.8 per cent per annum. This was a wasted decade. Then a more radical turn was taken on the expectations that growth would be speeded up. That, after all, was the Left orthodoxy—more centralization, more nationalization, higher investments in manufacturing.

The creation of linguistic states had allowed the emergence and growth of the local, same-language-speaking bourgeoisie. These were capitalists who relied on political favours and of course, paid back. Many who began as local manufacturers such as Kirloskar, grew to become national and even international over time.

The decade of the seventies was worse than the sixties. Income growth fell to 3.2 per cent per annum. Inflation surged due to devaluation and higher oil prices. Indira Gandhi responded the only way she knew. She moved further to the Left. She was rewarded with electoral success in 1971 and later consolidated her position, thanks to her intervention in Bangladesh. She proceeded to tame the industrialists and the traders. To prevent Swatantra Party from receiving donations from business, a law was made forbidding corporate donations to political parties. The perennial shortage of foreign exchange made the passing of drastic legislation on foreign exchange—The Foreign Exchange Regulation Act (FERA)—inevitable, giving the government one more weapon to blackmail the business community. At one stage in 1971, wholesale trade in foodgrains, the mandis, were nationalized but wisdom prevailed and that was reversed.

Inflation persisted and people took to the streets. In Gujarat, a student movement, Navanirman, became popular. In Bihar, Jayaprakash Narayan gave leadership to the masses. To Indira Gandhi, this was the Right's reaction challenging her socialist policies. Emergency followed, and after twenty one months, ended in her defeat. But in her ten years in power, Indira Gandhi met the challenge Kosambi had put before Nehru. She asserted the power of political leadership over the bourgeoisie. The entire class was transformed from a nationalist and strong class to a whimpering subordinate of the political classes, harassed by income tax officers, threatened with nationalization if it did not do the bidding of the ruling party (most often demands for cash donations, no receipts given), and kept under the thumb by inspections of factories and shops. The more successful were those who could become poodles of the prime minister—crony would be too grand a word—while she was in power. There was no revolt, no murmur, and no attempt to revive the spirit of the Swatantra Party. The middling sort of businessmen learnt jugaad. They knew how to evade regulations, bribe their way across the bureaucracy and deal in black money. They could stay below the radar unlike their bigger brothers. An active circuit of black money developed.

THE REPRIEVE

There is no doubt that the high tide of (Indira) Gandhian socialism passed after her defeat in 1977 and return in 1980. A more balanced Indira Gandhi began to move slightly more to the Centre and became less high handed. There was an application to the IMF for loan. Old capitalist families such as Tatas and Birlas were now in the next generation. Rusi Mody succeeded in the Chair at Tata. Birla had passed on the torch to his children and grandchildren. Capitalists less respectful of government regulations and more adept at finding their way around obstacles began to arrive on the scene. The best example was Dhirubhai Ambani who laid the foundation of the largest fortune made by an Indian family. Petrochemicals emerged as a new growth area, a development not expected in the days of the Bombay Plan.

Rajiv Gandhi was a liberalizer at least in terms of relaxing import controls. He was young, had worked in the airline industry as a pilot and had friends who were known as 'MBA types.' Rajiv was happy with private sector growth though he did not denationalize. The GDP growth rate perked up to 5 per cent and India began to relax a bit.

WHATEVER HAPPENED TO THE INDIAN BOURGEOISIE?

Rajiv Gandhi was quite relaxed about the rich displaying their wealth. The slogan was that there were enough rich middle-class in India to match the population of Belgium or Bel-India as it was called. Money was borrowed from NRIs thus opening a breach in the old doctrine of national self-sufficiency. But secularism and socialism remained the catchwords.

The Rao-Singh liberalization continued the progress in relaxation of constraints amid much controversy. Rajiv had an easier time as he was a Nehru-Gandhi after all; Rao was an interloper at the helm only because of the sudden and tragic demise of Rajiv Gandhi. Rao and Singh were forced to liberalize as the old economy finally imploded. India ran out of foreign exchange reserves and had to borrow from the IMF. This meant a lot of opposition from Congress veterans as well as professional economists. There was a double devaluation and greater opportunity for exports and imports. After a year of difficulty, the economic growth rate picked up.

Liberalization increased the value of output and trade. Government corruption became endemic. Stock market scam cases became public during the Rao government. Now the government could offer lucrative contracts by selling some of its assets. The bourgeoisie slowly rose from its poodle position to a crony one. Many acquired an international profile by living as NRIs. The international nexus had already been exposed in the Bofors scandal. The bourgeoisie was now spreading its wings. The class was still dependent on favours bestowed by the government, ministers as well as babus. Nationalized banks were harnessed to give large loans which might not be repaid if the crony had reached near the influential top.

It was in the 1990s that globalization began to benefit India. After forty years devoted to building up the hardware base for a self-sufficient manufacturing industry, India discovered its genius was in software. The multinational reach of the IT sector doing the back office work for Western multinationals became a booming business. Infosys became the first well-known Indian multinational. Bollywood acquired a global market thanks to the diaspora as well as its ability to tell stories that transcended language. Later, during the National Democratic Alliance (NDA) period, the film industry was granted industry status and could get bank credit as well as be on the stock market. Foreign capital began to feel welcome first as portfolio investment and later, though in the face of much political reluctance, as Foreign Direct Investment (FDI). At first, the local bourgeoisie resisted opening up of the economy. The Bombay Club was the name of an informal group of capitalists, whose ancestors had drafted the Bombay Plan, who resisted the opening up. But luckily the received opinion now among many US-trained Indian economists is that there was much synergy between domestic and foreign capital. Pharmaceuticals also became competitive after decades of reverse engineering.

Over the twenty-four years between 1991 and 2014, India got more comfortable with foreign capital and even domestic capital. But there is still a pervasive distrust of business and in the World Bank 'Ease of Doing Business' scale, India scores very low.

Nothing much has changed since the advent of the Bharatiya Janata Party (BJP)/NDA, except the stemming of very large scale corruption with the involvement of Cabinet ministers—'scams' as were seen during UPA 2. The issue of Non-Performing Assets (NPAs) of public sector banks has become public and very serious. The BJP/NDA government has passed the insolvency legislation which should make it possible, though neither quick nor easy, for creditors to seize assets of defaulting borrowers. But otherwise, the idea that a bourgeoisie can be independent of, if not antagonistic to, the State is alien to the Indian political economy.

Twenty-five years later, India has moved on to growth rates in high single digits and now 7 per cent is thought to be the norm with drastic forebodings when growth slips to 6.5 per cent! The Indian economy is much more versatile and the bourgeoisie have spread their wings abroad. The Indian economy is the third largest in the world by PPP standards. Yet nothing much has changed in the relative positions of the bourgeoisie vis-a-vis the political class.

Seventy-five years since the publication of the Bombay Plan, one can confidently say that there is neither the desire nor the courage among the bourgeoisie and their organized bodies FICCI, CII, Assocham etc, to repeat such an exercise. More is the pity.

THE SURPRISING GENESIS OF OUR STATE ALBATROSS

Ajay Chhibber

'I do not want India to be an economic superpower. I want it to be a happy country.'

—J.R.D. TATA

For a document put together by India's leading businessmen, the Bombay Plan gave amazing importance to the role of the State and central planning. There is no doubt that the Second World War had expanded the role of the State hugely. But a return to peacetime would have justified a reversal to a reduced role for the State, and not the expanded one that was postulated in the Bombay Plan.

How did this happen? What were the fears, motivations and conditions that led a group of businessmen to propose such a dominant role for the State in independent India's economic and social development?

One obvious motivation could have been the amazing ability of the Soviet Union to industrialize rapidly from a backward economy to an egalitarian industrial society. This, no doubt, loomed large in the thinking on development at that time. The Soviet Union had suffered huge losses in the War but had nevertheless emerged as a victorious nation, dictating peace.

A second factor driving the thinking behind the Bombay Plan was the perilous state of the Indian economy—despite its sound finances. As has been convincingly shown by the works of Dadabhai Naoroji (1902), R.C. Dutt (1902), Kumar and Desai (1983), and most recently by Tharoor (2016), India had been left by the British after almost two hundred years of rule in a state of deep underdevelopment.

The bulk of the population was at, or below, the poverty line and India had been consciously de-industrialized by trade and industrial policies that favoured British industry over Indian. The agriculture sector was also in a state of extreme penury and underdevelopment, with pockets of development favouring British-owned estate farming. A Rosentein-Rodan (1943) style big push was needed to reach the take-off velocity for growth to occur.[1]

---

[1] Paul Rosentstein-Rodan argued that the economy would need a big push initially, similar to an airplane needing a boost at take-off to achieve sufficient height and a cruising speed. He favoured heavy investment to achieve momentum for an economy to get

A third factor, perhaps, was that during the World War, governments all over the world—even in the US—had taken a larger role in running the economy. The war effort required a command and control economy to make more guns versus butter. Shortages called for price control to manage inflation. For example, in the US, the war time effort raised confidence in the government's ability to manage the economy, which had declined sharply during the Great Depression. This more active government role then translated into the Marshall Plan, designed to help the losers of the Second World War recover. It was felt that a similar approach could then be used to deal with the problems of underdevelopment.

One would have expected a Bombay Plan written by a business group composed of India's leading industrialists to look towards the other major victor of the War—and easily the richest country on the planet—the US as a role model and push for an American-style capitalism—with free enterprise driving economic growth, not Soviet-style centralized planning. But there was, surprisingly, no trace of this approach in the Bombay Plan. In Korea, the Chaebols—family conglomerates quite similar to India's business houses—prospered under a system of 'guided capitalism' and helped propel Korea from a poor, underdeveloped

---

on a path of rapid growth to catch-up. His ideas were initially developed for South and Southeast Europe.

country devastated by war into an industrial country.[2] But such an approach—later formulated by Alexander Gerschenkron as a Theory of Backwardness—was not even properly considered in the Bombay Plan.[3]

Perhaps the biggest fear among the business community was the spectre of communism, and that

---

[2] There are many different interpretations and factors underlying the rise of Chaebols in Korea but no one disputes the basic model of the State working with Chaebols to drive Korea's industrialization. A similar story occurred in Japan between the two World Wars when the Zaibatsu firms propelled Japan's industrialization. A less family-oriented and more managerial elite worked after the Second World War to rapid recovery through large complex firms called the Keiretsu coming together under large business groups called the Keindranen. It is interesting that India's big business houses have never set up a separate business grouping.

[3] The Backwardness Model is a theory of economic growth created by Alexander Gerschenkron. The model postulates that the more backward an economy is at the outset of economic development, the more likely certain conditions are to occur, namely: Special institutions, including banks or the State, will be necessary to properly channel physical capital and human capital to industries. There will be an emphasis on the production of producer goods rather than consumer goods. There will be an emphasis on capital-intensive production rather than labour-intensive production. There will be a great scale of production and enterprise. There will be a reliance on borrowed rather than local technologies. The role of the agricultural sector, as a market for new industries, will be small. There will be a reliance on productivity growth.

India after Independence would be swept by a wave of insurrections and all private property would be expropriated. Or perhaps the authors were swayed by the argument that the State alone had the capacity and broader organizational ability to move India forward. Whatever the motivation, the ideas, even if they were subsequently more or less forgotten, may have helped push India in the direction of State ownership and control under planning for at least another seven decades.[4]

THE PUSH FOR INDUSTRIALIZATION

Industrialization was to be the key driver of India's development under the Bombay Plan. Indian industry had been held back by colonial policies designed to extract agricultural products and minerals from India and in turn, try to sell British industrial products to India.

---

[4] It is not fair, of course, to blame all the excesses of the State control that followed only on the Bombay Plan. Nehruvian planning had many proponents. And these were expanded under the 'Garibi Hatao' programme of Mrs Indira Gandhi when all the banks were nationalized and price controls imposed on a range of commodities leading to shortages and a sharp increase in corruption (WDR 1997). Where the Bombay Plan can be faulted is that it did not offer a credible alternative to and in fact, supported the basic ideas that were adopted from 1947 to 1964. Mrs Gandhi did reverse the terms of trade against agriculture after the 1965 Bihar famine and ushered in the Green Revolution.

The Bombay Plan proposed to rectify this deliberate de-industrialization with a big push for it. The role of agriculture and services was seen as a support for industrialization.

Over a fifteen year period, from 1947 to 1962, the proportion of industry to agriculture and services was to go from 17:53:22 to 35:40:20. Industry share would double and that of services would decline. This was not surprising, especially as the IT revolution, which brought services into a central role in development, was nowhere on the horizon. In reality, the opposite happened as the share of services in India's economic development increased hugely. India industrialized for a while, but eventually services, not industry, became the main engine of growth.

It emphasized not just basic industry but also consumer goods. There was a strong sense that while the Soviet Union had made huge progress in industrializing rapidly, it had come at a very high cost to the population, who had to suffer many years of deprivation.[5] The authors

---

[5] The Soviet growth model was best exemplified by Grigory Feldman in a report *On the Theory of the Rates of Growth of the National Income* to the Gosplan committee for long-term planning in 1928. The Feldman model suggests in order to reach a high standard in consumption, investment in building a capacity in the production of capital goods is firstly needed. A high enough capacity in the capital goods sector in the long run expands the

of the Bombay Plan felt that such deprivation may lead to a revolt among the populace and could not, in any case, be pursued in a democratic setup. Therefore, the plan emphasized the production of consumer goods even as it admitted such an approach may slow down the rate of economic growth.

These goods were to be produced as much as possible by small industry and cooperatives, as this would maximize employment and reduce the need for scarce capital. This was needed for the development of basic industries such as power (electricity), mining and metallurgy, engineering goods, transport equipment, and cement, as these would need a higher capital–labour ratio.

The Plan did not give too much importance to agriculture. This sector was to grow by 130 per cent over fifteen years: just enough to feed the people and provide raw materials for agro-based industry. One of the ways this was to be achieved was to shift the cropping pattern from cash crops to food crops. It also emphasized the importance of cooperative farming as it argued that the average farm size was too small for productive farming. There was a recognized need to increase irrigation and efforts to fight soil erosion. The role of agriculture was to grow fast enough to feed the population and provide raw materials for industry.

---

capacity in the production of consumer goods.

IMPORT SUBSTITUTION VS EXPORT-LED GROWTH

The Plan's focus was import substitution, not export-led growth. The emphasis was on domestically producing basic goods: machinery, transport equipment, power equipment and consumer goods that were being imported. This was not surprising, as much of the developing world coming out of colonialism turned its back on the global economy. The depression had also turned many economists away from free trade—the most prominent of these were Raúl Prebisch and Hans Singer, who developed the Prebisch-Singer dependency theory, which postulated that the terms of trade would move against primary commodities and so commodity producers would remain dependent on industrialized countries.[6] Therefore, the less developed countries must intervene through import substitution policies to encourage faster industrialization in the developing world.

In addition, global trade conducted under colonial rules had kept the developing world agrarian and prevented its industrialization. Whatever industrialization had occurred had happened during the war, when shipping was blocked and the war effort needed to be

---

[6]Prebisch later became head of the UN Commission for Latin America (CEPAL) and eventually the Head of the United Nations Conference on Trade and Development (UNCTAD), where he pushed these ideas forcefully across the world.

supplied from the nearest source.

Most development experts at that time were also in favour of import substitution. One of the exceptions was Burmese economist Hla Myint who argued in favour of export-led growth. To be fair to the authors of the Bombay Plan, Myint's writings came a decade after the Plan was written. Myint's ideas were rejected even in his own country, but many so called 'Asian tigers' subsequently adopted his ideas—although without giving him any credit.[7]

India, on the other hand, unfortunately persisted with import substitution until the 1991 reforms. But even after that, it simply liberalized its economy by reducing import barriers and delicensing the economy. It did not aggressively pursue an export-led growth strategy through exchange rate, credit and industrial policies, which was the central plank of the development strategy of the Asian tiger economies, and subsequently China.

Indian business was never in favour of an export-led growth strategy and even today would prefer to grow behind import tariffs and preserve the domestic market for themselves. This lack of focus on exports has

---

[7] UNDP organized a seminar in Nya Pi Daw in 2012 in which Hla Myint was invited along with Prof Ron Findlay and Joe Stiglitz to present ideas on economic reform to a new government. It's a pity Prof Myint's views were not taken up 60 years earlier. The trajectory of Myanmar (Burma) might have been very different.

forced the Indian consumer to buy shoddy and expensive consumer goods for a long time. It also ensured that when India liberalized, its markets were inundated with cheaper products from China and East Asia.

In the transport sector, the Plan focused on roads and small ports at the expense of railways. Since railways were seen as a colonial project largely designed and laid out to produce extractive crops, they were not seen as contributing to India's development. The railways had also been built at an enormous cost to benefit British companies at the expense of the Indian taxpayer. The emphasis was on roads, with an effort to build greater connectivity, especially to rural areas. But India did not give the road programme as much emphasis as was needed until this century, when it intensified under the first NDA government. Small ports were also to be given emphasis as the shipping was concentrated on large ports such as Bombay, Karachi, Madras and Calcutta.

A MULTI-DIMENSIONAL HUMAN DEVELOPMENT APPROACH

The Bombay Plan was ahead of its time in some aspects of development thinking. Its focus went beyond income to a multi-dimensional approach to development, well before the concept of human development or happiness came into discussion. It laid out in detail the need to provide education, health, clothing, housing and shelter, and food and basic consumer goods. This focus beyond just increasing the growth of the economy later became the human development approach pioneered by Nobel laureate Amartya Sen and Mahbub-ul-Haq. Their work led to the Human Development Index (HDI) at UNDP (1990), an index that is still used as a yardstick to measure progress in human development. That the Bombay Plan consciously emphasized these aspects of human development deserves positive mention.[8]

It paid attention to water and sanitation, something the development and aid community neglected until recently. The community has belatedly realized the cost of neglecting water and sanitation, and focusing excessively on population control. This has also meant that the benefits of health programmes have not been fully realized. A gnawing paradox of India's development has been the fact that the decline in malnutrition has not kept pace with the decline in income poverty. The neglect of water and sanitation is the missing factor here. The link between malnutrition and sanitation has been explored from many angles, but the latest survey data from 112 districts analysed by Spears, Ghosh and Cummings (2018)

---

[8]And reflected perhaps the thinking of J.R.D Tata, who felt India should not aspire to be merely an economic superpower but a happy country.

provides convincing evidence of this linkage.[9]

India has spent huge sums of money on fighting poverty and malnutrition, but by neglecting water and sanitation until recently, the returns on that spend have been low. The current government is now focusing on this issue—building toilets at a rapid pace. Whether this alone will solve the problem of open defecation remains to be seen, especially in water scarce parts of the country.

The Bombay Plan placed emphasis on education, but given the abysmal levels of literacy and basic education, it focused mainly on universal primary and middle school education as well as adult literacy. There were to be efforts at tertiary education as well, but it was not given the kind of importance it acquired in the Five Year Plans that were eventually enacted. East Asian countries placed heavy emphasis on basic education, which helped in their success in the initial stages of industrialization.

Unfortunately, India is yet to achieve universal literacy and quality basic education. India's heavy focus on higher education helped develop the IT and pharma industries and helped it become a nuclear power and achieve success in outer space, but it came at the cost of faster progress in quality basic education. This has had many implications for India's economic development. Had the

---

[9] There is also the view that India's high rate of open defecation and lack of toilets is due to the caste system.

priorities laid out in the Bombay Plan on health and education been pursued, India's development may have taken a very different path.

INEQUALITY AND UNEMPLOYMENT

The Bombay Plan focused quite a bit on the issue of inequality. The role model of economic development at that time was the Soviet Union, which had managed to achieve very rapid growth without rising inequality. In the minds of the authors of the Bombay Plan, there were concerns that if inequality was allowed to get too high, it could generate social tensions and even revolution. It laid out ideas to control rising inequalities through death taxes, some land reform, widespread distribution of shares in joint stock companies, regional distribution of industry, and cooperative and State-owned enterprises. These were not radical ideas but were seen as the relevant toolkit of a democratic setup. Even the type of land reform that several East Asian countries later carried out was not envisaged.[10]

The Bombay Plan was concerned with the issue of unemployment and underemployment. In the initial phases, it opted to rely on imported skilled labour. This

---

[10] Korea and Taiwan carried out substantive land reform after the war and their subsequent rapid agricultural growth has been attributed to these reforms.

was seen as necessary because the push for basic industry would be needed at a time when India did not have the requisite skilled labour. While it was recognized that the capital–labour ratio would be high in the basic goods sectors, the overall capital–labour ratio was to be kept low through reliance on small-scale industry to produce consumer goods.[11]

The Bombay Plan did envisage a major shift in employment from agriculture to industry, and to some extent, to services as well. The share of sectoral employment between agriculture, industry and services was to go from 72:15:13 in 1931 to 58:26:16 by 1962. The Plan also surprisingly proposed setting up industry specific minimum wages in select industries such as mining, cement, sugar, textiles, engineering and jute. It also suggested setting up agricultural commodity reserves and fair producer prices to ensure that farmers were not subject to large fluctuations in farm income. India eventually adopted an elaborate system of fair price shops, producer support prices and a massive food reserve system under the Food Corporation of India (FCI) after the Bihar famine of the mid-1960's, and then embarked on huge investments in agriculture under the Green Revolution.

---

[11] Subsequently, India set up IITs and IIMs to handle the shortage of skilled manpower and managerial shortages, but neglected to have universal adult literacy and basic education.

The Plan correctly recognized that in the agriculture sector, the problem was not unemployment but underemployment. Much of the farming was rain-fed and single-crop. To address this, emphasis was given to mixed farming and double cropping, with expansion of irrigation. At the same time, agro-based industries were to be encouraged and developed so that employment opportunities could be increased in rural areas. The Plan did call for Keynesian-style temporary work programmes to provide seasonal employment. As we see, these ideas were eventually incorporated into the Maharashtra employment guarantee scheme and then to the much bigger Mahatma Gandhi National Rural Employment Guarantee Scheme (MGNREGS).

No major scheme for land redistribution was proposed in the Plan. But the Plan did suggest shifting away from the zamindari system and more towards ryotwari systems of farm tenure. This was because the zamindari system provided very little incentive either to the landowner or to the tenant to invest in the land. The ryotwari system was seen to generate greater interest from the cultivator in land improvement. It did propose changes in land revenue taxation, but also suggested that agricultural income above a threshold should be taxed like any other income. India is still awaiting such a threshold as all agricultural income remains untaxed today.

The Plan also recognized the need for regionally

balanced development. The regions under direct British Rule had progressed better on the whole than those under the Princely States. The Plan envisaged greater efforts for more balanced development between these two parts. It emphasized the need for a strong national government that would be able to manage this process.

STATE PLANNING AND STATE CONTROL OF THE ECONOMY

The Bombay Plan placed very heavy emphasis on State intervention and control. There was a long discussion on State control versus ownership versus management. It was recognized that the State could control without necessarily owning or managing, and that not all State-owned enterprises needed to be managed by the State. As events unfolded, the industrial policy resolution of 1956 shifted huge control into State hands, with nationalization of large swathes of the basic goods industry and even slices of the consumer goods sector.

What was surprising was that the Bombay Plan did not delineate boundaries for State ownership. It suggested a case by case flexible approach. In hindsight, had it suggested that the consumer goods sector should remain in private hands while the basic goods sector would need more State ownership, perhaps India's development story may have been different. In many East Asian countries, the State played a controlling role, but left ownership and management to the private sector.

To finance development, the Bombay Plan also gave huge importance to the State, relying on gold, credit creation (inflationary financing), reserves, and foreign borrowing. Heavy reliance on Foreign Direct Investment (FDI), which later led to East Asian style industrialization, was not part of the Plan. Instead, the emphasis was on using the sterling reserves held at the British India account, trying to get people to shift from gold to gold backed securities, as well as on money creation and foreign borrowing.

The huge inflow of FDI from the US to East Asia for export-led industrialization was not envisaged in the Bombay Plan. This was because British investments in India had largely been seen as exploitative and therefore FDI was seen as competing for the local market with domestic business. India is now trying to attract FDI and has opened up many areas to full 100 per cent foreign ownership—but some say that it is perhaps too late, as India missed the opportunity for the export-led, employment generating growth which East Asia enjoyed.

One of the challenges faced by the drafters of the Bombay Plan was the need to marry State planning with democracy. State planning and control had been successfully applied in a totalitarian setup like the Soviet

Union. But never before, except during emergency wartime conditions when normal democratic systems were often suspended, had State control and planning to the extent envisaged under the Bombay Plan been applied during peacetime. One way suggested in the Plan was not to do things too abruptly, but in a gradualist manner.

It suggested a transition phase so that the conditions for State planning could be prepared in steps. It also wanted to manage the sacrifice such an approach would inflict on the common man—so as to ensure the success of this approach.

The role model for the Bombay Plan was a Pigouvian State (Pigou 1949) where the lines between socialism and capitalism were somewhat blurred and a more pragmatic practical approach towards each was to be followed. The Plan recognized the need, especially in the initial phases, for development of enormous State control—including even rationing and targets for private industry—later to be implemented on a wide scale and called the 'Licence Raj'.

State control was to be applied to production, distribution, consumption, investment, foreign trade and exchange and wages and working conditions. So the scope of State control envisaged was very wide.

The Plan called for decentralization, with the national government responsible for broader policymaking and coordination, but its implementation to be delegated to state governments and local bodies. It also called for the establishment of an economic civil service to manage the planning process and its implementation.

The Plan did suggest that State control did not necessarily imply State ownership, which was to be reserved for industries that required State financing, particularly new industries, and those where State control could only be exercised by State ownership. It did say that while State ownership would be needed in new industries where private finance was not forthcoming, once private finance became available these could then be passed onto the private sector. India built up a large public sector through new State investment and nationalization of private firms in basic goods sectors, but failed to privatize them even when private finance could be raised. The country is still struggling with this socialistic legacy.

The Bombay Plan itself proposed considerable flexibility in the management of State enterprises. It discussed their management by the State, by the private sector and by public corporations, depending on the degree of control needed and the nature of the industry. It also saw the possibility of private and State-owned enterprises functioning in the same industry and learning from each other's performance. Such a mixed up approach has not been very successful. In reality, with the benefit of hindsight, it would have been better to have a clearer delineation of industry.

THE DISASTER THAT FOLLOWED

But what followed was in hindsight a huge disaster for the Indian economy. India introduced the Five Year Plans, with the First Plan basically helping it recover from the War. But the main direction was laid in the Second Five Year Plan, which followed the Mahalanobis–Feldman model,[12] with heavy emphasis on capital goods industry at the cost of a consumer goods industry (which was to be kept for the small-scale sector). During the period 1950–1980, public sector investment reached over 50 per cent of total investment. Many new public sector companies were established and a large number of companies in sectors such as coal, airlines, banking and insurance were nationalized. Industrial licensing was introduced mimicking the Soviet Union—prescribing what the private sector could produce. India was not the only country in the developing world that went down this path after WWII. Most postcolonial countries across Africa and Asia followed this approach, but so did countries like China and others in Latin America.

In India, this involved not only setting up State-owned enterprises, but also efforts to control and plan

---

[12] Grigory Feldman developed the basic Soviet growth model in 1928 whereas Mahalanobis developed a similar model for India in 1950. There is no clear evidence that Mahalanobis was aware of the Feldman model.

private sector development. An entire apparatus was established to make decisions on the number and types of licences, all run by arcane bureaucratic procedures. The Licence Raj, combined with inefficient public enterprises, nurtured inefficiency and corruption, producing a bevy of intermediaries whose main function was to grab these licenses and sell them off to the highest bidder. Raj Krishna called the Licence Raj, 'socialist allocation in the first round followed by market allocation in the second round.' In some cases, large private business houses would grab the licence to expand production but delay its execution in order to benefit from the shortages, or just keep the licence unutilized to stave off a competitor from entry into the industry.[13]

One of the original objectives of the policy to establish State-owned enterprises was to help industrialize the economy and build infrastructure, especially as it was then believed that the private sector was unwilling to enter. Soon after Independence, the consensus was that the private sector was too weak to be able to handle risks, especially in capital intensive sectors. But unlike Japan, Korea and Taiwan,[14] which relied on a strategy of

---

[13] Mohan and Agarwal (1990) argue that the kind of planning introduced was more suited to a Soviet economy which had no private sector—just State-owned enterprises or cooperatives.

[14] The interesting question is why the close nexus between big business and the State, which often ends up in cronycapitalism

(cont)

helping the private sector grow and reduce their risks, India followed the approach adopted by many developing countries of setting up public sector companies. India even nationalized many private industries under the guise of putting so-called 'strategic' industries under State control. Many areas of the mining industry, such as coal, were brought under State control.

But this approach proved disastrous and India's GDP growth remained low, averaging only 3.5 per cent between 1950 and 1980, in the first three decades after Independence—with per capita GDP growing at only 1.3 per cent on average. It was famously called the 'Hindu growth rate' by Raj Krishna, suggesting that Hindu fatalism was responsible for this slow growth. But as we saw later, when with better policies India grew faster, Hinduism had nothing to do with it. India's poverty rose during this period and India fell behind many countries on social and economic indicators. Some internal liberalization was pursued in the 1980's, but it was insufficient to address the growing problems in the economy. It eventually took a balance of payments crisis in 1991 to force the political establishment to accept the need for reform.

---

with large private monopolies or duopolies getting huge benefits under protected markets, did not happen in these countries. One reason would be that the State promised to help industry compete under export-led growth in global markets. This export-orientation ensured high productivity growth and competitiveness.

After pursuing State-led capitalism for four decades after Independence, triggered by a major economic and financial crisis, India introduced a new industrial policy in the 1990s. Given the perception that State-led capitalism had failed, there was a significant change in thinking after liberalization in 1991. The private sector was allowed to enter many restricted areas, especially mining, telecommunications and airlines. The State expanded its role in certain priority areas like electricity. But subsequently, State control on the economy was reduced. The Electricity Act 2003 delicensed power generation and permitted captive power plants. It also facilitated private sector participation in transmission and provided open access to the grid sector. Various policy measures facilitated increased private sector participation in key infrastructure sectors such as telecommunication, roads, and ports. Foreign equity participation up to 100 per cent was allowed in construction and maintenance of roads and bridges. Monopolies and Restrictive Trade Practices (MRTP) provisions were relaxed to encourage private sector financing by large firms in the highway sector.

IT COULD HAVE BEEN DIFFERENT

Much of our thinking about the role of planning and the shift to State-led and controlled economy—so-called 'Nehruvian Socialism'—has focused on the idea that all this was the brainchild of India's first prime minister Jawaharlal Nehru and his advisors[15]. But the Bombay Plan shows that the parenthood of India's shift to State planning is hard to pin on Prime Minister Nehru alone. Even the top industrialists of that time, J.R.D. Tata and G.D. Birla, were pushing for State control and planning as co-authors of the Bombay plan.

Many of the elements of what later became the infamous 1956 Industrial Policy resolution which introduced State control, licensing, and State-owned enterprises in the commanding heights of the economy can be found in the Bombay Plan. While the Plan was forgotten, its ideas lived on and were further embellished into an elaborate system of State control and planning from which we are yet to recover.

There were other ideas in the Bombay Plan—such as the focus on universal adult literacy, primary education, basic healthcare and water and sanitation—which were subsequently ignored. India spent far too much on higher education and neglected the importance of access to water and sanitation.[16] But the broad thrust

---

[15] Nehru had, of course, laid out his ideas for a more socialistic economy as early as in 1929 at his address as the Congress President.

[16] Had India paid as much attention to health and education as Mao's China did, its GDP growth may not have increased immediately, but its HDI would have grown much faster and

of the Bombay plan—State planning and State control and import substitution—was what came subsequently.

In hindsight, the Bombay Plan could be blamed for having supported the intellectual groundwork for the State albatross that still holds back this great country. It could have been different had we followed a different economic path and would by now possibly be both an economic superpower and a happier country.

◆

Ajay Chhibber is Distinguished Visiting Professor at The National Institute of Public Finance and Policy (NIPFP) and Chief Economic Advisor, FICCI.

REFERENCES:

Sabina Alkire, James Foster et al (2003). *Multidimensional Poverty Measurement and Analysis.* 1st Edition, Oxford University Press.

Baru, Sanjaya (1998-01-01). 'Mahbub ul Haq and Human Development: A Tribute'. *Economic and Political Weekly.* 33 (35): 2275–2279.

Chandrashekhar, C.P. (2017). *The Rise and Fall of South Korea's Chaebols.* http://www.networkideas.org/news-analysis/2017/03/the-rise-and-fall-of-south-koreas-chaebols/. Retrieved 15 March, 2017.

---

would have helped lay the basis for much faster growth later (Meghnad Desai, 2003).

Desai, Meghnad (2003). *'India and China: An essay in comparative political economy'.* Delivered at the IMF Conference.

Dutt, R.C. *The Economic History of India Under Early British Rule. From the Rise of the British Power in 1757 to the Accession of Queen Victoria in 1837.* Vol. I. London, Kegan Paul, Trench Trübner (1902). 2001 edition by Routledge.

The Economic History of India in the Victorian Age: From the Accession of Queen Victoria in 1837 to the Commencement of the Twentieth Century. Vol. II. London, Kegan Paul, Trench Trübner (1904).

Feldman, Grigory (1928). *On the Theory of the Rates of Growth of the National Income.* Report to the Gosplan committee for long-term planning, Moscow.

Gerschenkron, A. (1962). *Economic Backwardness in Historical Perspective: A Book of Essays.* Cambridge, MA: Belknap Press of Harvard University Press, 1962.

Kumar, D. and Meghnad Desai (1983). *The Cambridge Economic History of India, Volume 2, 1751-1970.* Cambridge University Press.

Mahalanobis, P. (1953). *Some Observations on the Process of Growth of National Income.* Sankhya. pp.307–312.

Mahbub-ul-Haq. *Reflections on Human Development* (1996). 1st Edition, Oxford University Press (1996).

Mohan, R. and V. Aggarwal (1990). 'Commands And Controls: Planning for Indian Industrial Development, 1951-1990'. *Journal of Comparative Economics* 14, 68 1-7 12 (1990).

Myint, H. (1958) 'The "Classical Theory" of International Trade and the Underdeveloped Countries.' *Economic Journal* 68. 270: 317-37.

Economic Theory and the Underdeveloped Countries (1971). Oxford University Press.

Southeast Asia's Economy: Development Policies in the 1970s (Penguin Modern Economics Texts). Penguin Books, 1972.

Naoroji, Dadabhai (1902). *Poverty and Un-British Rule in India.* Publications Division, Ministry of Information and Broadcasting, Government of India; Commonwealth Publishers, 1988.

Pigou, A.C. (1949). *Socialism versus Capitalism.* Macmillan.

Prebisch, Raul (1950). *The Economic Development of Latin America and its Principal Problems.* CEPAL (New York: United Nations, 1950)

Raúl Prebisch (1970). *Change and Development: Latin America's Great Task.* Inter-American Development Bank.

Rosenstein-Rodan, Paul N. (1943). 'Problems of Industrialization of Eastern and South- Eastern Europe'. *Economic Journal* v 53, No. 210/211, (1943), pp.202–11.

Sen, Amartya (1982). *Poverty and Famines: An Essay on Entitlement and Deprivation.* Oxford New York: Clarendon Press Oxford University Press.

Development as Freedom. New York: Oxford University Press.

Spears, Dan, A. Ghosh and O. Cummings (2018). *Open Defecation and Childhood Stunting in India: An Ecological Analysis of New Data from 112 Districts.*

Tharoor, Shashi (2016). *An Era of Darkness: The British Empire in India.* Aleph Book Company.

UNDP (1990). *Human Development Report 1990: Concept and Measurement of Human Development.* Oxford University Press.

WDR (1997). *The State in a Changing World.* World Development Report, World Bank. Oxford University Press.

APPENDICES

APPENDIX I: THE VICEROY'S EXECUTIVE COUNCIL

Portfolio	Name	Tenure
Viceroy and Governor-General of India	The Marquess of Linlithgow	8 August, 1940–1 October, 1943
	The Viscount Wavell	1 October, 1943–21 February, 1947
Commander-in-Chief, India	General Sir Robert Cassels	8 August, 1940–27 January, 1941
	General Sir Claude Auchinleck	27 January, 1941–5 July, 1941
	General Sir Archibald Wavell	5 July, 1941–5 January, 1942
	General Sir Alan Hartley	5January, 1942–7 March, 1942
	Field Marshal Sir Archibald Wavell	7 March, 1942–20 June, 1943
	General Sir Claude Auchinleck	20 June, 1943–21 February, 1947
Home	Sir Reginald Maxwell	1941–1944
	Sir Robert Francis Mudie	1944–1946
Finance	Sir Jeremy Raisman	1941–1946

BOMBAY PLAN

Defence	Sir Malik Feroz Khan Noon	1942–1944
Civil Defence	Dr. Edpuganti Raghavendra Rao	1941–1942
	Sir Jwala Prasad Srivastava	1942–1943
Law	Sir Syed Sultan Ahmed	1941–1943
	Asok Kumar Roy	1943–1946
Information and Broadcasting	Sir Akbar Hydari	1941–1942
	Sir Syed Sultan Ahmed	1941–1943
Communications	Sir Andrew Clow	1941
Supply	Sir Homi Mody	1941–February 1943#
	Sir Ramaswami Arcot Mudaliar	1943
Commerce	Sir Ramaswami Arcot Mudaliar	1941
	Sir Nalini Ranjan Sarkar	1942–February 1943#
Health, Education and Lands	Sir Nalini Ranjan Sarkar	1941
	Sir Jogendra Singh	1942–1946
Labour	Sir Feroz Khan Noon	1941
	Bhimrao Ramji Ambedkar	1942–1946
Indians Overseas and Commonwealth Relations	Madhav Shrihari Aney	1941–February 1943#
	Narayan Bhaskar Khare	1943–1946

APPENDICES

India's Representative at British War Cabinet and on Pacific War Council	Sir Ramaswami Arcot Mudaliar	1942–1944
	Sir Feroz Khan Noon	1944–1945
War Transport	Sir Edward Charles Benthall	1942–1946
Posts and Air	Sir Mohammad Usman	1942–1946
	Sir Gurunath Venkatesh Bewoor	1946
Food	Sir Jwala Prasad Srivastava	1943–1946
Commerce, industries, civil supplies	Sir Mohammad Azizul Haque	1943–1945
Post-war Reconstruction	**Sir Ardeshir Dalal**	**August 1944–January 1946**

#resigned in support of Mahatma Gandhi's fast (10 February–3 March, 1943).

APPENDIX II: COUNCIL OF SCIENTIFIC AND INDUSTRIAL RESEARCH (CSIR) CONSTITUTED: SEPTEMBER 26, 1942

List of Members of the First Governing Body

PRESIDENT

Sir Nalini Ranjan Sarkar, Member, Council of the Governor-General

MEMBERS

1. Shanti Swaroop Bhatnagar, Director, Scientific and Industrial Research, Delhi.
2. Ghulam Mohammad, Finance Minister, Government of Nizam, Hyderabad.
3. Sir Bortio Staig, Additional Secretary to Government of India, Finance Department, New Delhi.
4. T.S. Pillay, Joint Secretary to Government of India, Department of Commerce, New Delhi.
5. Jehangir Ratan Dorab Tata, Industrialist, Bombay.
6. Sir Ardeshir Dalal, Director, Tata Iron and Steel Company, Bombay.
7. Sir Shri Ram, Agent, Delhi Cloth & General Mills Ltd, Delhi.
8. Sir Abdul Halim Ghuznavi, Member, Central Legislative Assembly, Calcutta.
9. Sir Henry Richardson, Managing Directors, M/s Andrew Yule & Company, Calcutta.
10. Kasturbhai Lalbhai, Managing Agent, Arvind Mills Ltd, Ashoka Mills Ltd, Ahmedabad.
11. Dr J.C. Ghose, Director, Indian Institute of Science, Bangalore.
12. Dr Nazir Ahmad, Director, Technological Laboratory, Indian Central Cotton Committee, Bombay.
13. Dr M.N. Saha, Palit Professor of Physics, University College of Science, Calcutta.

APPENDICES

14. Diwan Bahadur A.N. Mudaliar, Vice-Chancellor, University of Madras, Madras.

APPENDIX III: INDIAN CIVIL SERVICE APPLICATION AND RESULTS, 1870-1914

Year	Vacancies	Candidates	Indian Candidates	Successful Indians
1870	40	332	7	1
1880	27	182	2	0
1890	47	205	10	5
1900	52	213	17	2
1910	60	184	20	1
1914	53	183	26	7

Source: Russi M Lala. 'For the Love of India'. Penguin: Delhi, 17 May, 2006. p.86

APPENDIX IV: ARDESHIR DALAL LIFELINE

April 24, 1884	Born
	Elphinstone School
1905	Sir Dorab Tata grants Dalal a JN Tata Endowment scholarship to attempt entry in the ICS
	Graduates with a Tripos in Natural Science, St John's College, Cambridge
1907	Passes the ICS examination
1908	Returns to India, enters ICS
1912	Marries Mane bai Wadia
	Assistant Collector, Bombay Presidency

	Collector, Bombay Presidency
	Deputy Secretary, Government of Bombay in the finance department
28 Jul, 1914 – 11 Nov, 1918	World War 1
1923	Member, Bombay Legislative Council
	Acting Secretary, Government of Bombay
1927	Acting Secretary, Government of India, Education, Health and Lands Departments
1927	Member, Indian Legislative Assembly
1928–31	Municipal Commissioner, Bombay (1st Indian to hold this position)
1931	Joins the Tata Group as Tisco's Resident Director
1931	Opens the Agents' office in Calcutta
*	Appointed Tisco's Director-in-Charge
*	Appointed Director and Partner in Tata Sons
26 July, 1938	Tata Sons board meeting. Dalal seconds the proposal that JRD Tata be appointed chairman of the board of directors of Tata Sons
* – 1944	Director, Andhra Valley Power Supply
* – 1944	Director, Associated Cement Companies
* – 1944	Director, Tata Oil Mills
* – 1944	Director, Taj Mahal Hotel
* – 1944	Director, Tata Chemicals
1 Sep, 1939 – 2 Sep, 1945	World War II
1937–38	President, Rotary Club, Calcutta
1938–39	Member, Indian Chamber of Commerce, Calcutta

APPENDICES

1939	Strike in Jamshedpur Profit-sharing scheme and retiring gratuity scheme for labour An Indianization programme was gradually introduced
1939	First knighthood
1941	Tisco's liaison officer for the Ministry of Supplies
1941	Member, Indian Science Congress Association
20 Aug–3 Sep, 1942	Dalal and the Jamshedpur strike after Gandhi's announcement of the Quit India movement
Sep 6, 1942	Council of Scientific and Industrial Research (CSIR) launch
Dec 11, 1942	Bombay Plan meeting, Bombay House
Nov 1942 - Mar 1943	Vivian Archibald Hill visit to India
Jun 1944	Resigns from Tatas
Aug 1944 - Jan 1946	Member, Viceroy's Executive Council
Aug 1944 - Jan 1946	Planning and Development Department created. Dalal appointed head. Department wound up in 1946.
Sep 1944	Dalal visit to the Massachusetts Institute of Technology (MIT) along with a member of the Department of Planning and Development
Oct 1944	Dalal joins in his role as Member for Planning and Development in the Viceroy's Executive Council
Nov(?) 1944	Dalal press conference calls for Indian version of MIT
11 Apr, 1945	Sarkar Committee recommends MIT structure
23 Apr, 1945	Dalal-headed Planning and Development Department issues a statement of India's future industrial policy.
1 Sep, 1945	Telco's incorporation
Jan 1946	Dalal resigns from Viceroy's Executive Council and rejoins Tatas Sir Ramaswami Arcot Mudaliar takes over the portfolio

Jan 1946	J.R.D. Tata appoints Dalal as Tisco's vice-chairman
Mar 1946	Dalal and Sir Jogendra Singh urge the Viceroy's Executive Council to set up a committee to define the direction of technical education for post war India
*	Dalal brought into Telco
Oct 1946	*Interim Government sets up a planning advisory board*
1946	Higher order of knighthood, the KCIE
15 Aug, 1947	*Independence*
8 Oct, 1949	Died
May 1950	*1st IIT opens temporarily in Calcutta*
September 1950	*1st IIT established at Hijli Detention Centre, Kharagpur*

APPENDICES

APPENDIX V: THE BOMBAY PLAN DOCUMENT

MEMORANDUM OUTLINING

A PLAN OF ECONOMIC DEVELOPMENT FOR INDIA

PARTS ONE AND TWO

by
SIR PURSHOTAMDAS THAKURDAS
J.R.D. TATA
G.D. BIRLA
SIR ARDESHIR DALAL
SIR SHRI RAM
KASTURBHAI LALBHAI
A.D. SHROFF
AND JOHN MATHAI

CONTENTS OF PART ONE

		Page
I.	INTRODUCTORY	7
II.	REQUIREMENTS OF A MINIMUM STANDARD	12
III.	ECONOMIC PLAN EXPLAINED	27
IV.	SOURCES OF FINANCE	51
V.	STAGES OF DEVELOPMENT	56
	INDEX	103

APPENDICES

PART ONE

1
INTRODUCTORY

1. *Aim of Memorandum*

This memorandum presents in brief outline a plan of economic development for India. The plan set out in it is not in any sense a complete scheme nor is its scope so comprehensive as that of the National Planning Committee to whose labours the conception of a planned economy for India is very largely due. Our object is merely to put forward, as a basis of discussion, a statement, in as concrete a form as possible, of the objectives to be kept in mind in economic planning in India, the general lines on which development should proceed and the demands which planning is likely to make on the country's resources. It contains no reference to such essential matters as the organization, methods and technique required for carrying out a plan. For instance, neither the problem of distribution, which is vital to any scheme for raising the standard of living, nor the allied question of the control to be exercised by the state over economic activities are discussed in it. These matters, the importance of which is fully present to our minds, are at present under examination by us. The results of this examination will form the subject of a separate report which we hope to issue at an early date. Meanwhile, in view of the prevailing interest in problems relating to post-war economic development in India, we have thought it desirable to publish in advance our views regarding some of the more fundamental aspects of planning so as to stimulate discussion and criticism of our proposals before our investigations of other aspects of planning are completed.

SECTIONS 2, 3

2. *Political Assumptions*

Underlying our whole scheme is the assumption that on the termination of the war or shortly thereafter, a national government will come into existence at the centre which will be vested with full freedom in economic matters. The maintenance of the economic unity of India being, in our view, an essential condition of any effective planning, we have assumed for the purpose of our plan that the future government of India will be constituted on a federal basis and that the jurisdiction of the central government in economic matters will extend over the whole of India. We should, however, explain that this does not preclude the possibility of a regional grouping of provinces and States as an intermediate link in a federal organization. Such regional grouping will not disturb the economic unity of India, provided that, in important matters affecting economic development, the authority of the central government is not impaired. We draw attention to this aspect of the problem because we think that no development of the kind we have proposed will be feasible except on the basis of a central directing authority which enjoys sufficient popular support and possesses the requisite powers and jurisdiction.

3. *Planning Organization*

We contemplate that under the central government there will be a national planning committee in which the various interests concerned will be represented and to which the responsibility for drawing up plans will be delegated. The actual execution of the plans will be the function of a supreme economic council working alongside the national planning committee under the authority of the central government. The co-ordination of the duties assigned to these two committees and their relation to the various provincial and regional governments will be among the most important problems that will arise in connection with the constitutional aspect of our proposals.

4. *Objective of Plan*

The principal objective of our plan is to bring about a doubling of the present *per capita* income within a period of fifteen years from the time that the plan comes into operation. Allowing for an increase in population of 5 million per annum, which is the rate disclosed by the last decennial census, we estimate that a doubling of the *per capita* income within a period of fifteen years will necessitate a trebling of the present aggregate national income. To achieve this increase, we propose that the plan should be so organized as to raise the net output of agriculture to a little over twice the present figure, and that of industry, including both large and small industries, to approximately five times the present output. This would still leave our economy mainly agricultural in the sense that the greater part of the population would continue to be engaged in agriculture and allied occupations although the present preponderance of agriculture would be considerably reduced.

5. *Industrial Development*

It is an important part of our proposals regarding industrial development that in the initial stages attention should be directed primarily to the creation of industries for the production of power and capital goods. Nothing has more seriously hindered the development of India's industrial resources during the war than the absence of these basic industries, and we consider it essential that this lack should be remedied in as short a time as possible. Apart from its importance as a means of quickening the pace of industrial development in India, it will have the effect of ultimately reducing our dependence on foreign countries for the plant and

SECTION 6

machinery required by us and, consequently, of reducing our requirements of external finance. The proposal, however, is subject to this important qualification that provision should be made at the same time for the manufacture within the country of the most essential classes of consumption goods, as otherwise a great deal of unnecessary hardship may be caused during the planning period. We suggest that, in the production of these essential consumption goods, the fullest possible use should be made of small-scale and cottage industries. This will, besides providing employment, reduce the need for purchasing expensive plant and machinery.

6. *Difficulties Anticipated*

We are well aware of the difficulties which may stand in the way of our objective being attained within so short a period. The execution of the plan will run counter to many deep-seated prejudices and traditions. In the initial stages it will call for a very large measure of personal discomfort and sacrifice. Political differences may make it difficult to set up the necessary constitutional machinery. The international situation after the war may be such as not to permit of the orderly continuance of constructive activities on this scale. If difficulties of this character supervene, the progress of the plan will be materially hampered. Nevertheless, we think that it is worth while placing before the country a plan which, given favourable conditions, can be realised. The difficulties we have indicated may delay the scheme but will not necessarily make it impossible of achievement. We have some hope that if the programme we have put forward makes an appeal to the country, that by itself will help in some measure towards securing the conditions necessary for its fulfilment. It may be pointed out that the fifteen-year period we have suggested is intended to cover only the execution of the plan and does not include the time required for the necessary preparatory work, which may take about three to five years. Once the machinery required for executing the plan is properly organized, and given sufficient courage and energy in those responsible for carrying it out, we do not think that the attainment of our objective within the period indicated is an extravagant hope.

7. *Problem of Finance*

The estimates of capital expenditure contained in the memorandum are of such colossal dimensions that the whole scheme may appear impracticable to people whose minds are still dominated by orthodox financial concepts. In matters of this kind, the war has been a great educator. Lord Wavell, in a recent speech in London, remarked: "It has always seemed to me a curious fact that money is forthcoming in any quantity for a war, but that no nation has ever yet produced the money on the same scale to fight the evils of peace—poverty, lack of education, unemployment, ill-health." The answer to this question, which has puzzled many an inquiring mind since the commencement of the war, is that money or finance is not the master of a country's economy, but its servant and instrument. The real capital of a country consists of its resources in materials and man-power, and money is simply a means of mobilizing these resources and canalizing them into specific forms of activity. Looking at the problem from this angle, we are convinced that the capital expenditure proposed under our scheme is well within the limits of our resources and that, from a business point of view, such expenditure will constitute a sound and profitable investment for the country.

8. *Explanatory Remarks*

With regard to the several estimates of expenditure, production and income contained in the memorandum,

SECTION 9

it is necessary to explain that, in view of the inadequate data on which many of them are based, they are to be regarded merely as rough approximations and their value as more illustrative than absolute. Further, although most of the estimates are stated in terms of money, it is the quantum of commodities and services they represent that we have primarily in view. Money is used throughout as a measuring rod only; and in order to keep the measure uniform, we have based all money figures on the rupee at approximately the average price level which prevailed during the period 1931-39.

II

REQUIREMENTS OF A MINIMUM STANDARD

9. *Minimum Standard Defined*

The ultimate objective of any planning should be to increase the volume of India's economic production to the fullest extent which its natural resources would allow. The plan we propose, however, is limited to a period of 15 years and has the modest aim of securing a general standard of living which would leave a reasonable margin over the minimum requirements of human life. In order to give some idea of the standard of living at which we aim, we propose in this section to define in concrete terms what, in our opinion, are the minimum requirements of human life under existing conditions in India. These include, besides the physiological necessities of life like food, clothing and shelter, also some provision for medical relief and education. In a later section we shall discuss what further provision is required for a reasonable standard of living such as we aim at and on what lines a plan for securing this should be framed.

SECTIONS 10, 11, 12

10. Balanced Diet

Although India is an agricultural country, a large proportion of its population does not get enough food to eat. A still larger proportion fails to obtain the right kind of food. Studies made by nutrition experts suggest that a well-balanced nutritive diet for an adult person in India should be as follows:

OUNCES PER DAY PER ADULT

Cereals 16	Fruits	2
Pulses 3	Fats and oils ..	1.5
Sugar 2	Whole milk ..	8
Vegetables .. 6	or Meat, fish and eggs	2.3

11. Cost of Nourishment

The energy value of this diet is 2,600 calories. Making allowance for some wastage in the kitchen and at the table, the *per capita* requirements of a balanced diet in India would amount to about 2,800 calories per day. The available supplies of food, even if they are equitably distributed, would, however, fall short of this by a large margin. To secure a balanced diet for our population, a considerable increase in our food production would therefore be necessary. It is estimated that at pre-war prices the cost of a balanced nutritive diet of the type mentioned above would be approximately Rs.65 (£4 17s. 6d.) per annum for a growing adult and very little less for a growing child. At this rate an annual expenditure of Rs.2,100 crores (£1,575 millions) would be required to keep our existing population, 389 millions, well nourished.

12. Clothing Needs

Next to food comes clothing, considered in its utilitarian rather than its social aspect. The quality of cloth required differs according to the climatic conditions

SECTION 13

of the country, the habits and manners of living of the population and its income. Conditions in these respects differ widely in the different parts of India and it is therefore difficult to fix any particular standard for the country as a whole. On the basis of consumption in other countries it is, however, possible to arrive at a rough standard. At the peak level of textile output, which was reached in 1928-29, the average *per capita* consumption of textiles, consumed largely in personal and household uses, amounted to 42 yards for the world as a whole. For some of the individual countries for which comparable data are available, the consumption of cotton textiles alone was as follows:

CONSUMPTION OF COTTON PIECE GOODS PER CAPITA IN 1929[1] (IN YARDS)

U.S.A.	..	64.0[2]	Japan	..	21.4
Canada	..	37.7	Egypt	..	19.1
Sweden	..	36.0	Brazil	..	18.9
Germany	..	34.0	Iraq	..	16.9
Malaya	..	30.6	India	..	16.1
Denmark	..	30.0	Greece	..	15.0

13. *Cost of Clothing*

In the light of these figures, the estimate made by the National Planning Committee of the minimum requirements of clothing in India, *viz.* 30 yards per person, may be regarded as reasonable. To reach this norm, India would require on the basis of the 1941 population figure 11,670 million yards of cloth and its cost at the rate of 3½ annas (3¾d. approximately) a yard would amount to Rs.255 crores (£191¼ millions).

[1] *The World Textile Industry—Economic and Social Problems.* Vol. I, page 168.
[2] Sq. yds.

14. Housing Needs

Adequate shelter against sun and rain and against the inclemencies of weather is yet another of the essential primary needs of human life. On the basis that a person should have about 3,000 cubic feet of fresh air per hour, the accommodation required would be about 100 square feet of house room per person.[1] The quality of houses required, however, depends to a large extent on social traditions far more than on physical needs. "The house is not only a shelter from the weather and a place for preparing food and sleeping: it is also a centre of a complicated social ritual." The figure we have taken is the minimum determined by physical needs alone. The number of houses in India according to the 1941 census is 76 million: 10 million in towns and 66 million in villages. The number of persons per house, which was 5 in 1931, increased to 5.1 in 1941. It is not possible to indicate the average housing space available per person, although the information regarding industrial cities shows the existence of overcrowding of an extreme type. In the Bombay province, for example, the average floor space per person in industrial areas was 27.58 square feet in Bombay, 43.04 square feet in Ahmedabad and 24.03 square feet in Sholapur in 1938.

15. Cost of Housing

If we are to provide 100 square feet of house room per person, which has been mentioned above as the minimum needed, the average house should have an area of at least 500 square feet so that it can accommodate 5 persons. In rural areas the cost of building such a house is assumed to be in the neighbourhood of Rs.400 (£30) and in urban areas twice as much. In order that housing may come up to the standard we

---

[1] *Report of the Rent Enquiry Committee, Bombay*, Vol. III Part VI, page 21.

SECTIONS 16, 17

have laid down, a fairly large proportion of the existing houses both in rural and urban areas should be rebuilt and substantial provision should also be made for new houses. On a rough estimate, the total expenditure required for this would be about Rs.1,400 crores (£1,050 millions). At $7\frac{1}{2}$ per cent. of the total capital expenditure, including the value of existing housing, the yearly cost of maintenance would be Rs.258 crores (£193$\frac{1}{2}$ millions).

16. *Standard of Housing*

If the house is to serve its purpose also as a social centre, in addition to providing accommodation, it must conform to certain standards regarding site, type, ventilation, lighting, heating, waste disposal, water supply, etc. But these standards will vary according to a number of factors, such as climatic conditions, availability of land, traditions, etc., and will have to be fixed to suit local conditions.

17. *Present State of Health*

Apart from meeting the physiological needs of life mentioned above, an important aspect of the minimum standard of living which we wish to lay down for India is that every individual should be able to maintain a reasonable standard of health. At present the general standard of health in India is admittedly poor. The following figures would give some idea:

	Birth and death rate per 1000		Infant mortality: deaths under one year per 1000 live births.	Expectation of life. (years)	
	Birth	Death		Male	Female
Canada	20.3	9.6	61	58.96	60.73
U.S.A.	17.3	10.6	48	60.60	64.50
Germany	20.3	12.3	60	59.86	62.81
U.K.	15.3	12.2	53	60.18	64.40
Australia	17.7	9.9	38	63.48	67.14
Japan	27.0	17.6	114	46.92	49.63
India	33.0	21.8	167	26.91	26.56

18. Needs of Public Health

Satisfaction of the primary needs of life would go a long way towards attaining a reasonable standard of health for our population, but measures specially directed towards this purpose would be essential. These broadly fall into two categories: (*i*) preventive measures like sanitation, water supply, vaccination and anti-epidemic precautions, maternity and child welfare, etc., and (*ii*) curative measures like the provision of adequate medical facilities.

19. Inadequate Preventive Measures

Such preventive measures as have been adopted so far have touched but the fringe of the problem. Only in respect of vaccination against smallpox has some progress been made, but the number of deaths due to this disease still continues to be large. The average figure for the quinquennium 1935-39 was 67,130 in British India alone. "The fact that vaccination and re-vaccination should eliminate the disease altogether emphasizes the importance of making further efforts for the effective immunization of the people."[1] In respect of water supply it is known that out of the 1,471 towns in British India in 1939, only 253 towns with a population of 13 million had protected water supplies, and the position of conservancy and sanitation was no better. In rural areas the position is still worse. Provision for maternity and child welfare work both in urban and rural areas is extremely inadequate. The fact that more than 50 per cent. of the deaths that occurred in 1939 were among those who come within the scope of maternity and child welfare services fully bears this out.

[1] *Annual Report of the Public Health Commissioner with the Government of India for* 1939, page 20.

SECTIONS 20, 21, 22

20. Lack of Medical Facilities

So far as medical facilities are concerned, in 1939 there were about 7,300 hospitals and dispensaries in British India with provision for about 74,000 beds. The average population served by each hospital and dispensary works out to about 41,000 and the proportion of population per bed is 4,000. The number of doctors and nurses in India is 42,000 and 4,500 respectively,[1] which means one doctor per 9,000 persons and one nurse per 86,000 persons. The comparative figures for the U.K. are one doctor per 776 persons and one nurse per 435 persons.

21. Minimum Health Standard

For a minimum standard of living the criteria which we should like to lay down in respect of preventive and curative measures include the following: (*i*) proper arrangements in respect of sanitation and water supply in rural and urban areas; (*ii*) a dispensary for every village; (*iii*) general hospitals and maternity clinics in towns; and (*iv*) specialized institutions for the treatment of tuberculosis, cancer, leprosy, venereal diseases, etc.

22. Sanitation and Water Supply

Sanitation and conservancy in rural areas depend largely on proper instruction and education and could be substantially improved by means of well-organized effective propaganda. In urban centres, however, special measures would be necessary. Arrangements for adequate water supply will be required not only in urban areas but also in villages, many of which suffer from scarcity of water. It is difficult to estimate the amount of capital expenditure that sanitation and water supply on this scale will involve, but a figure of 100 crores of rupees (£75 millions) will not be wide of the mark. At

---

[1] J. B. Grant: *The Health of India* (Oxford Pamphlets on Indian Affairs), page 24.

SECTIONS 23, 24

7½ per cent. the cost of maintenance would be Rs.7½ crores (£5⅝ millions) per annum.

23. Village Dispensaries

The village dispensary should be in charge of a qualified doctor assisted by two qualified nurses, one of whom at least should be a trained midwife. This staff would be able to carry out most of the preventive and curative services necessary for improving the health of the village. As the average population of a village according to the 1941 census is only 517, normally they would be able to attend to vaccination against smallpox and inoculation against other infectious diseases whenever they show signs of breaking out in an epidemic form. They would render adequate medical aid to the sick and also attend to maternity cases. They might also be entrusted with the work of medical inspection of the village school.

24. Cost of Dispensaries

The cost of building a dispensary with an area of about 1,200 square feet would roughly amount to Rs.1,000 (£75) and the initial equipment would cost an equal amount. The running expenses of the dispensary which would include the salary of the staff and the cost of medicines are likely to be in the neighbourhood of Rs.2,000 (£150), assuming that a certain amount of voluntary and part-time help of practising doctors would be available. The total cost of maintaining rural health on the basis would amount to:

Buildings and initial equipment ..	Rs.132 crores (£99 millions)
Running expenses per year ..	Rs.132 crores (£99 millions)
Maintenance of buildings and equipment at 7½ per cent. per year of capital expenditure	Rs.9.9 crores (£7.425 millions)

SECTIONS 25, 26

25. General Hospitals

For urban areas we would suggest on an average a hospital with 40 beds for every 10,000 persons. As the average population of a town in India is 18,365, this would mean generally two hospitals per town of 40 beds each or one hospital of 80 beds. In addition to meeting the needs of the local population, the general hospitals in towns should serve as centres for expert advice and specialized treatment to sick persons in neighbouring rural areas. The capital cost of a hospital of this nature with 40 beds would be in the neighbourhood of Rs.40,000 (£3,000), and the running expenses, which would include the salaries of doctors and nurses, expenses of indoor patients, etc., would amount roughly to Rs.28,000 (£2,100) per annum. Here again it is assumed that to some extent voluntary and part-time services would be forthcoming. The total cost of general hospitals in towns would thus amount to:

Buildings and initial equipment	Rs.22 crores (£16½ millions)
Running expenses per year	Rs.15 crores (£11¼ millions)
Maintenance of buildings and equipment at 7½ per cent. per year of capital expenditure	Rs.1.5 crores (£1⅛ millions)

26. Maternity Hospitals

Besides general hospitals, every town in India should have adequate provision for maternity services. In the year 1939 the number of maternal deaths arising out of childbirth amounted to 200,000, and it is considered that 80 per cent. of these deaths could have been prevented if adequate maternity services had been available. As the *Indian Medical Review* puts it, "it is the

APPENDICES

SECTION 27

right of every woman to have skilled attendance during pregnancy, labour and the puerperium."[1] In rural areas the midwives attached to the dispensary should be able to render all necessary help in this respect to expectant mothers in their homes. But in towns it is necessary to have special institutions for this purpose. A maternity hospital with 30 beds should meet the requirements of the average population of a town in India in this matter. The cost of building such a hospital and providing it with initial equipment would be in the vicinity of Rs.30,000 (£2,250) and a sum of Rs.24,000 (£1,800) would cover its running expenses. The total cost of maternity clinics for all the towns in India on this basis would be:

Buildings and initial equipment ..	Rs.8 crores (£6 millions)
Running expenses per year ..	Rs.6 crores (£4½ millions)
Maintenance of buildings and equipment at 7½ per cent. per year of capital expenditure	Rs.60 lakhs (£450,000)

27. *Specialized Treatment*

Special institutions for the treatment of tuberculosis, cancer, venereal diseases, mental disorders, etc., would have to be provided at suitable places and would probably require accommodation for about 150,000 beds. The capital cost of housing these institutions and supplying them with equipment would on a very rough estimate amount to about Rs.19 crores (£14¼ millions) and would require a recurring expenditure of about Rs.11 crores (£8¼ millions). The cost of maintaining buildings and equipment would be Rs.1.5 crores (£1⅛ millions).

[1] *Indian Medical Review*, 1938, page 185.

SECTIONS 28, 29, 30

28. Cost of Public Health

The total cost of the various health and medical services mentioned above would be:

	Non-recurring cost (Rs. crores)		Recurring cost (Rs. crores)	
Sanitation, water supply, etc.	100	(£75,000,000)	7.5	(£5,625,000)
Rural dispensaries	132	(£99,000,000)	141.9	(£106,425,000)
General hospitals	22	(£16,500,000)	16.5	(£12,375,000)
Maternity clinics	8	(£6,000,000)	6.6	(£4,950,000)
Specialised institutions	19	(£14,250,000)	12.5	(£9,375,000)
Total	281	(£210,750,000)	185.0	(£138,750,000)

29. Minimum Educational Needs

That every person above the age of 10 should be able to read and write and to take an intelligent interest in private and social life is yet another of the constituents of a minimum standard of living which we should like to bring within the reach of every individual in the country. The percentage of literacy above the age of 5 in India to-day is 14.6. In the advanced countries of the world it is more than 80. "Extreme forms of poverty", it is maintained, "will prevail amongst the masses in India as long as the overwhelming majority of the Indian people are able neither to read nor write."[1]

30. Primary Education: Capital Cost

To provide adequate facilities for primary education, it is necessary to have a school for every village at least up to five forms. Construction of suitable buildings

[1] W. M. Kotschnig: *Unemployment in the Learned Professions*, page 316.

with equipment for this purpose, consisting of two rooms, 20 ft. × 30 ft. each, in rural areas would cost nearly Rs.66 crores (49½ millions). In urban areas, assuming that a room of 20 ft. × 30 ft. is necessary for about 30 students and that the cost of buildings would be twice as high as that in rural areas, the cost of establishing primary schools would amount to Rs.20 crores (£15 millions).

31. *Primary Education: Recurring Cost*

The recurring expenditure on primary schools consists largely of the salaries of teachers, which are very low at present and which will have to be increased. According to some educationists it is possible to reduce the incidence of these salaries substantially by introducing suitable reforms such as increasing the number of students per teacher, introducing the part-time system, framing suitable curricula, etc. Increase in the number of students per teacher would alone reduce the cost by about 50 per cent. The League of Nations' Mission of Educational Experts which reported on the reorganization of education in China remarks: "In China as a whole there are 20.3 pupils to one teacher, whereas in many countries of a high standard of education there are 2 to 3 times as many. This should mean that in the same conditions and at the same expense, between 2 and 3 times as many pupils as are actually under instruction could be dealt with by the existing staffs of teachers, and in the present very difficult conditions not less than 50 to 60 pupils per teacher should be taken as basis."[1] But assuming that the present system continues, we calculate the recurring cost of making primary education compulsory to boys and girls between 6 and 11 years of age at an average expenditure per pupil of Rs.15

[1] Quoted by Mr. R. V. Parulekar in *Literacy in India*, page 113.

SECTION 32

(£1 2s. 6d.) in rural areas and Rs.25 (£1 17s. 6d.) in urban areas per annum.¹ The cost works out as follows:

Students in rural areas	44.1 million
Average cost per student per annum	Rs.15 (£1 2s. 6d.)
Total recurring cost per annum	Rs.66 crores (£49½ millions)
Students in urban areas	6.5 million
Average cost per student per annum	Rs.25 (£1 17s. 6d.)
Total recurring cost per annum	Rs.16 crores (£12 millions)
Total recurring cost in urban and rural areas	Rs.82 crores (£61½ millions)

To this, 7½ per cent. of the capital expenditure will have to be added for the maintenance of buildings, which would amount to Rs.6 crores (£4½ millions) per annum.

32. *Adult Literacy*

Adult education should aim at literacy for all those who have passed the primary school leaving age of 11 years but have not passed 50 and who have not become literate. It will consist of a short course, mainly part-time, of about 3 to 6 months' duration. It is general experience that adults acquire literacy much more quickly than children if they are given proper instruction. On the basis of experiments made after the inauguration of Provincial Autonomy, the cost of making an adult

---

[1] The average cost per student of primary, middle school and high school education which we have assumed in this memorandum is generally on the low side as compared with that adopted by Mr. Sargent in his report. The figures we have assumed for primary education are, however, 75 per cent. above the pre-war average.

SECTION 33

literate, *i.e.* able to read and write, roughly works out to Rs.4 (6s.) per adult. Theoretically, the total number of illiterate adults on the basis of the 1941 census, which a scheme of adult education will have to tackle, would be about 200 million. In actual practice, however, the number would be smaller, as a large proportion of the adults will pass out of the 11-50 age range and some others may die before it is possible to provide them with the necessary facilities for acquiring literacy. These two factors will bring down the number of adults to be made literate to about 165 million if the programme is spread over 15 years. At the rate of Rs.4 (6s.) per adult, the cost of liquidating the illiteracy of our adult population will therefore amount to about Rs.66 crores (£49½ millions). This, however, will not be a recurring cost, since once the existing illiterate adults are made literate, further efforts in this direction would not be necessary. Adult education classes, which will have to be generally morning or evening classes, can be conducted in buildings provided for primary, secondary or higher education or at the places where the persons are working and would not, therefore, require any expenditure on buildings. The total cost of making the whole of our present population literate would thus amount to:

Primary education—	
Non-recurring cost	Rs.86 crores (£64½ millions)
Recurring ,, ...	Rs.88 crores (£66 millions)
Adult education ,, ...	Rs.66 crores (£49½ millions)

33. *Minimum Cost of Living*

The aggregate amount of income required to meet the barest requirements of human life, as set out in the

SECTION 34

foregoing paragraphs (which, however, exclude a number of small items such as fuel, etc.), would be as follows:

	Income required to be spent— round figures (Rs. crores)	
Cost of food	2,100	(£1,575 millions)
Cost of clothing	260	(£195 millions)
Recurring expenditure on housing	260	(£195 millions)
Recurring expenditure on health and medicine	190	(£142½ millions)
Recurring expenditure on primary education	90	(£67½ millions)
Total	2,900	(£2,175 millions)

34. *Income Below Minimum*

This means that, in order to secure a minimum standard of living, a *per capita* income of Rs.74 (£5 11s.) at pre-war prices is essential. That we are much below this minimum at present is indicated by the fact that according to the latest available estimate[1] of the national income of British India, which relates to the year 1931-32, our *per capita* income does not exceed Rs.65 (£4 17s. 6d.). The figure for 1939 will be lower still if we make allowance for the large increase in the population of British India, 5 million per annum since 1931, which is not accompanied by any significant increase in the total national dividend. It is, therefore, necessary to increase our national income above the present level by a substantial margin even if we aim at nothing more than to secure for our people their bare requirements as human beings.

[1] The estimate of national income and its distribution for British India which has been used in this memorandum is that made by Dr. V. K. R. V. Rao and published in *The National Income of British India*, 1931-32.

APPENDICES

SECTION 35

III
ECONOMIC PLAN EXPLAINED

35. *Low National Income*

The preceding discussion has shown that our present national income is not sufficient to support even a minimum standard of living. But if we are going to develop our resources according to a prearranged plan, we should certainly not be satisfied merely by providing for every person the minimum requirements of life. A planned economy must aim at raising the national income to such a level that after meeting the minimum requirements every individual would be left with enough resources for enjoyment of life and for cultural activities. Our present information, inadequate as it is, regarding the potential resources of the country in respect of raw materials, power and labour leads us to believe that given a systematic plan and adequate organization it is possible to raise our national income within a short time to a level considerably above that required for meeting the minimum needs of life. Comparative figures of *per capita* national income in 1931 for certain countries of the world are given below to indicate the disparity between India and other countries:

ANNUAL PER CAPITA INCOME IN Rs.[1]

U.S.A.	1,406	France	621
	(£105 9s.)		(£46 11s. 6d.)
Canada	1,038	Germany	603
	(£77 17s.)		(£40 4s. 6d.)
U.K.	980	Japan	218
	(£73 10s.)		(£16 7s. 0d.)
Australia	792	Br. India	65
	(£59 8s.)		(£4 17s. 6d.)

[1] The figures except that for India are from *The Conference Board Economic Record*, August 3, 1939. The original dollar figures are converted at 1 $ = Rs.2.289.

SECTIONS 36, 37

36. *Aim of Plan*

The objective we propose for a plan of economic development for India may be stated as follows. There should be a threefold increase in the total national dividend within a period of 15 years from the time the plan is put into execution. The aggregate income of British India as estimated in 1931-32 is Rs.1,766 crores (£1,324½ millions). This should be raised in 15 years to about Rs.5,300 crores (£3,975 millions). Assuming that the figure of *per capita* income calculated for British India is also applicable to the States, the range of increase in the total national dividend would be from Rs.2,200 crores (£1,650 millions) to Rs.6,600 crores (£4,950 millions).

37. *Increase in Per Capita Income*

A threefold increase in the total national dividend will result in an equivalent increase in the *per capita* income only on the assumption that our population over the planning period remains stationary. This assumption is, however, not likely to hold good. In the absence of adequate reliable data regarding fertility, it is extremely difficult to make any forecast about the future growth of our population over a period of years. But after balancing the various factors, we are inclined to believe that the rate of increase recorded during the last decade will generally hold good for the period of our plan. With the progress of the plan, both our birth rate and death rate would decline, but the balance of births over deaths is not likely to show any marked change. At the rate of 5 million per annum the population of India at the end of 1960, assuming the plan to start in 1945, will, therefore, be 489 million and a threefold increase in our total national dividend would in effect mean a *per capita* income of Rs.135 (£10 2s. 6d.) representing a doubling of the 1931-32 figure.

38. *A Modest Goal*

This might appear to be too modest a goal for a planned economy to achieve, especially in view of the fact that in the U.S.S.R., within a short period of 12 years since the beginning of the first Five-Year Plan, the national income is reported to have increased from 25 billion roubles to 125 billion roubles, *i.e.* fivefold. As our national resources are not as extensive and varied as those of the U.S.S.R., and as we are anxious to avoid the heavy cost in terms of human suffering which the U.S.S.R. had to pay to achieve this spectacular result, we must necessarily fix our objective at a lower figure.

39. *Balanced Economy*

The proposed threefold increase in India's total national dividend will be brought about in such a way that the present overwhelming predominance of agriculture would be reduced and a more balanced economy established. According to the national income figures for 1931–32, the contribution of industry, agriculture and services to the total national dividend of British India is estimated at 17, 53 and 22 per cent. respectively.[1] (About 8 per cent. of the income has not been classified under any of these categories.) We propose a plan of development under which the respective percentages might be changed roughly to 35, 40 and 20 for the whole of India. On the basis of these percentages, the threefold increase in the national income which is aimed at would involve the following increments in the net

---

[1] As agricultural prices in 1931 were very low on account of the general economic depression, these proportions would be different in normal times. The proportion of income from agriculture would be higher and that from industry and services would be lower.

SECTION 40

income from industry, agriculture and services:

	Net income in 1931–32 (Rs. crores)	Net income expected after 15 years (Rs. crores)	Percentage increase
Industry..	374 (£280½ millions)	2,240 (£1,680 millions)	500
Agriculture	1,166 (£874½ millions)	2,670[1] (£2,002½ millions)	130
Services..	484 (£363 millions)	1,450 (£1,087½ millions)	200

40. *Agricultural Character Unchanged*

At first sight the percentage increase in industrial income which this plan involves might appear to be disproportionately large as compared with the increase in agricultural income. But it has to be borne in mind that our industrial potentialities have to a great extent remained unexploited so far and adequate provision to make up this lag in industrial development would naturally mean a large percentage increase over the present level. On the other hand, as the demand for food crops which form the bulk of our agricultural products is comparatively inelastic, even after taking into account the probable increase in population and the higher level of income which the plan will bring about and the larger demand for industrial raw materials, it is not likely that more than a 130 per cent. increase will be absorbed within the country. It is, however, necessary to mention that, although ultimately the contribution of agriculture to our national dividend will be only 40 per cent. as compared with 53 per cent. in 1931–32, it will not change the essentially agricultural character of

---

[1] It is necessary to point out that this figure is calculated on the basis of Dr. Rao's estimate for 1931–32, which mainly takes into account harvest prices, while the value of minimum food requirements which we have estimated in paragraph 11 is based on retail prices.

our economy. From the point of view of employment, agriculture will continue to employ the greater part of our population. Even the U.S.S.R., in spite of the tremendous development of industries which she has achieved since the inauguration of the first Five-Year Plan in 1928, has not been able to reduce to any marked degree the percentage of population employed in her agriculture.

41. *Industries Classified*

The industries which an economic plan for India would seek to develop may be classified into two principal categories: (*i*) basic industries; and (*ii*) consumption goods industries.

42. *Basic Industries*

Basic industries, which would get priority over the other type of industries in the earlier years, would include among others the following principal groups:

Power—electricity.

Mining and metallurgy—iron and steel, aluminium, manganese, etc.

Engineering—machinery of all kinds, machine tools, etc.

Chemicals—heavy chemicals, fertilizers, dyes, plastics, pharmaceuticals, etc.

Armaments.

Transport—railway engines and wagons, shipbuilding, automobiles, aircraft, etc.

Cement.

43. *Importance of Basic Industries*

These industries are the basis on which the economic superstructure envisaged in the plan will have to be erected. It is obvious that in modern times no industry

SECTION 44

can be established without power, machinery, chemicals, etc. Similarly, without fertilizers it is difficult to imagine any progress in agriculture. In the absence of adequate shipping and other forms of transport, economic life especially in a country of the dimensions of India will remain stagnant. But for the lack of most of these industries, India would not have been left so far behind other countries of the British Empire such as Canada and Australia in the matter of industrial development in response to war conditions. We consider it essential for the success of our economic plan that the basic industries, on which ultimately the whole economic development of the country depends, should be developed as rapidly as possible.

44. *Production of Power*

We have deliberately placed the production of power first in the list of basic industries because we believe that the development of our industries, both large- and small-scale, as also of agriculture and transport, will be determined to a large extent by the development of electricity. The rapid economic development of the U.S.S.R. and Japan during the pre-war period and of Canada during the present war can ultimately be traced to the development of electricity in these countries. In fact in the U.S.S.R. a fifteen-year plan for the electrification of the country, the *Goelro*, was drafted as far back as in 1920, and it was only when the success of this plan was established beyond doubt that the ambitious five-year plans were put into execution. The scope for the development of hydro-electric energy in particular is very large in India. Its potential reserves have been estimated at about 27 million kilowatts, out of which only half a million kilowatts have been developed so far.

45. Consumption Goods Industries

Some of the principal consumption goods industries which should be further developed in India are:
Textiles—cotton, silk and wool.
Glass industry.
Leather goods industry.
Paper industry.
Tobacco industry.
Oil industry, etc.

46. Consumer's Choice

The list of consumption goods industries given above is only illustrative. The nature and kind of consumption goods industries to be developed will ultimately be dependent upon the income of the people. As income increases, the percentage of expenditure on different classes of consumption goods will show marked variations. For example, demand for articles of consumption like furniture, books, artware, etc., which will be relatively small at a low income level, will increase as the general level of income rises. What classes of consumption goods industries should be developed will naturally be decided from time to time, as the plan progresses, in the light of variations in the demands of consumers. As far as is consistent with planning, the free choice of consumers in respect of consumption goods should suffer no restriction.

47. Scope for Small Industries

It is an essential part of our plan for the organization of industries that adequate scope should be provided for small-scale and cottage industries along with large-scale industries. This is important not merely as a means of affording employment but also of reducing the need for capital, particularly of external capital, in the early

SECTIONS 48, 49

stages of the plan. It is difficult to define the considerations on which the choice between large- and small-scale industries and cottage industries should be determined. The factors involved in the choice are numerous and often conflicting. But generally it may be stated that while in basic industries there is little scope for small industrial units, they have an important and useful place in consumption goods industries where their function is in many cases complementary to that of large units.

48. *Capital for Industries*

It is extremely difficult to make an estimate of the amount of capital which India would require to carry out the programme of industrial development outlined above. A large number of the industries proposed would be new to the country and the proportion of capital required by each of them to the net product which it is likely to contribute would show marked variations. It may be explained that by the "net product" of an industry in this context is meant its gross production less the cost of raw materials and power consumed by it. And "capital" includes not merely paid-up capital but also general reserves and borrowed funds. In the nature of things some industries like the hydro-electric industry are bound to require in proportion to their net product a much higher proportion of capital than, say, textiles. The proportion of capital employed will also vary according to the extent to which capitalistic methods of production are employed and technological advances are made use of.

49. *Wide Variations in the Ratio*

No figure either of valuation of capital employed in existing industries in the country or of their net product are available. But the ratios of capital employed to net product worked out on the basis of information given in the balance sheets for the Bombay cotton textile industry, the Associated Cement Companies and the Tata hydro-electric group are as follows:—

	Cotton textile	Cement	Hydro-electricity
1937	2.13	3.12	9.19
1938	2.62	2.11	7.80
1939	3.73	2.53	8.23

50. *A Low Ratio Assumed*

Taking into account the fact that while India has plenty of labour, her capital resources are comparatively small, we think that industries should be organized in such a way that over the whole planning period the ratio of capital including land and buildings to net product would not be too high. Provision for small-scale and cottage industries in the industrial organization of the future has been suggested by us partly with this object in view. Assuming a ratio of 2.4, which as compared with similar ratios in other countries is a low proportion, the total amount of capital required to increase our net industrial output to Rs.2,240 crores (£1,680 millions) as visualised in the plan would be in the neighbourhood of Rs.4,480 crores (£3,360 millions).. In this connection it may be mentioned that the amount of capital invested in our industries, excluding railways and other forms of transport, in the pre-war period has been estimated at about Rs.700 crores (£525 millions).

51. *Agricultural Development*

In the proposed plan we have aimed at increasing our agricultural production by 130 per cent. The target has deliberately been fixed low. Our idea is that in respect of agricultural commodities India should as far as possible aim at feeding her own population adequately and should not aspire in the initial years of planning to export to foreign markets. Our plan for

SECTION 52

agricultural development aims not merely at increasing production generally but also at increasing the production of those crops which are necessary for feeding the population. This would necessarily involve a readjustment of the areas under cultivation of different crops. Areas under commercial crops like jute, tea, cotton, oilseeds, etc., the fortunes of which are to a substantial extent dependent on foreign trade and which have introduced a serious element of uncertainty in our economic life, would have to be adjusted to the conditions of international trade that might prevail in the post-war period. The substitution of a large proportion of the existing short staple cotton by long staple varieties and the development of cotton textile and oil-crushing industries within the country would, however, reduce the dependence of these crops on foreign markets. In respect of food crops it is not only desirable that their production should be increased but the proportion of areas under cereals, pulses, vegetables, fruit, etc., would have to be fixed in relation to the requirements of a nutritive diet.

52. *Reforms Proposed*

Increase in agricultural production, however, presupposes certain fundamental reforms. The most important question to be solved is that of the size of agricultural holdings. The average holding at present is not more than three acres scattered over the village in tiny fragments. Although there may be definite limits to the advantages arising out of consolidation of holdings and increase in their size, it is one of the main reforms which would be necessary for the adoption of intensive farming. To bring it about, co-operative farming appears to present less difficulties than any other method that may be suggested. It increases the size of the holding for purposes of cultivation without depriving the cultivators of their right to the ownership of their existing holdings. In order that co-operative farming should come into vogue as early as possible, some measure of compulsion appears desirable.

53. *Rural Indebtedness*

It is also necessary to liquidate the burden of agricultural indebtedness. The debt which was estimated at Rs.1,200 crores (£900 millions) before the war has since been probably reduced to a considerably smaller figure as a result of the favourable prices realized by agriculturists during the last two years. It is perhaps possible to reduce this further by means of conciliation. The liquidation of debt should be arranged principally through co-operative societies, which would require to be suitably organized for the purpose and provided with sufficient long-term finance. It may be pointed out that the finance required for this is not included in our estimate of capital expenditure since the debt of the agriculturist represents the savings of another class and these savings would themselves be available directly or indirectly for financing co-operative societies.

54. *Soil Erosion*

In addition to the size of holdings and rural indebtedness, there is a third problem the seriousness of which has not yet been fully realized but which will need attention if our agriculture is to be improved. This is the problem of soil erosion. Every year large quantities of valuable top soil are washed away by rain never to come back. If this process goes on, millions of acres of land will be permanently lost for cultivation. It is essential to check this evil in time by terracing arable lands, launching schemes of afforestation and adopting other measures suitable to conditions in different tracts. For soil conservation and other permanent improvements

SECTIONS 55, 56, 57

to land, a sum of about Rs.200 crores (£150 millions) should be provided as capital outlay and Rs.10 crores (£7½ millions) as recurring expenditure.

55. *Ways of Increasing Output*

When these three fundamental questions, **viz.**, the size of holdings, indebtedness, and soil erosion, have been tackled, agricultural production in India can be increased by (*i*) extending the area under cultivation or by (*ii*) improving the yield per acre or by (*iii*) a combination of both. Although at present 18 per cent. of the area in British India, 94 million acres, is classified as cultivable waste, it is extremely doubtful whether much of it is really cultivable. The question deserves to be thoroughly investigated.

56. *Yield per Acre*

Improvement in yield, on the other hand, appears to have great possibilities. The following comparative figures are significant:

YIELD PER ACRE IN TONS—1939–40

	Rice	Wheat	Sugar cane	Cotton
U.S.A.	1.01	0.37	20.06	0.11
Canada	—	0.52	—	—
Australia	—	0.42	—	—
Japan	1.61	—	—	—
Egypt	—	—	—	0.23
Java	—	—	54.91	—
India	0.35	0.32	12.66	0.04

57. *Irrigation*

Improvement in the yield per acre can only be brought about by better methods of farming which would include irrigation, better rotation of crops, use of better varieties of seeds, manure, improved types of implements, etc. Of the total area of 209 million acres

APPENDICES

SECTION 58

under cultivation in British India in 1938-39, only 54 million acres were irrigated—28 million acres by canals, 6 million by tanks, 13 million by wells and 7 million by other sources. It is necessary to increase the area under irrigation substantially if the yield of our crops is to be improved. We estimate the increase required at 200 per cent. in the area irrigated by canals and by all the other means combined. The total capital outlay on the existing canals amounted to Rs.153 crores (£114¾ millions) in 1938-39 and the annual working expenses were in the neighbourhood of Rs.5 crores (£3¾ millions) On this basis the capital cost of the additional canals would work out to Rs.303 crores (£227¼ millions) and their maintenance would require a sum not exceeding 10 crores of rupees (£7½ millions) per annum. Construction of new canals to this extent will, however, involve the erection of expensive dams for impounding water. In view of this, the amount of capital required for the construction of canals may be increased to Rs.400 crores (£300 millions). It may be mentioned incidentally that in constructing new canals the possibility of their being used for the production of hydro-electric power should not be lost sight of. The cost of constructing tanks, wells, etc., to irrigate another 48 million acres may be roughly estimated at about Rs.50 crores (£37½ millions). Maintenance charges for this form of irrigation would be relatively small.

58. *Model Farms*

In order to popularize improved methods of cultivation and dairy farming and to educate the cultivator in their use, a large extension of model farms would be necessary. On the basis of one farm for 10 villages,. the number of farms required would be about 65,000. Besides educating the cultivator in the use of improved methods of farming, these farms would be expected

SECTIONS 59, 60

to provide improved varieties of seed and manure, agricultural implements, bullocks, etc., and generally to help agriculturists. As improvement in the yield of agriculture will largely depend on the introduction of fertilizers, both organic and inorganic, it will be an important responsibility of the model farm to give proper instruction to the farmer regarding their use. Each of these farms should also be provided with a veterinary branch. The cost of a farm established on these lines may be estimated at Rs.50,000 (£3,750)—Rs.30,000 (£2,250) on account of capital and Rs.20,000 (£1,500) on account of working expenses.

59. *Working Capital*

In addition to the amounts indicated above, it is necessary to provide for the working capital required to finance current agricultural operations. We estimate that a sum of Rs.250 crores (£187½ millions) would be sufficient to finance the increase in agricultural output expected under our scheme.

60. *Capital for Agriculture*

The total amount of capital required for increasing agricultural production to the target figure is shown below:

	Non-recurring expenditure (Rs. crores)	Recurring expenditure (Rs. crores)
Soil conservation, etc.	200 (£150 millions)	10 (£7½ millions)
Working capital	—	250 (£187½ millions)
Irrigation—		
Canals	400 (£300 millions)	10 (£7½ millions)
Wells	50 (£37½ millions)	—
Model farms	195 (£146¼ millions)	130 (£97½ millions)
	845 (£633¾ millions)	400 (£300 millions)

61. *Transport and Communications*

An increase in the volume of industrial and agricultural production as envisaged in the previous paragraphs will result in a large movement of goods and services within the country. The increase in the net income from trade and services which we anticipate is about 200 per cent. Internal trade may well be expected to increase to an extent which would necessitate a large expansion of the means of communication, particularly railways, roads, shipping and civil aviation. In all these spheres India is seriously deficient. India with an area of approximately 1,580,000 square miles has about 41,000 miles of railway, while Europe, excepting the U.S.S.R., with an area of 1,660,000 square miles has 190,000 miles of railway. Similarly, in British India the proportion of road mileage to area works out at 35 miles per 100 square miles. The corresponding figure for the U.S.A. is 100 and for the U.K. 200. Coastal shipping has been even more seriously neglected. Taking into account the fact that railways have received comparatively more attention in India and that in future the necessity of developing communications in rural areas would be more urgent, we should aim at an increase of 21,000 miles in railways and 300,000 miles in roads. This would mean an increase of 50 per cent. over the existing railway mileage and an increase of 100 per cent. in the mileage of roads in British India alone. For the development of shipping, our aim should be to improve the small natural harbours that are scattered along India's extensive coast-line and to provide them with loading and unloading facilities. As regards civil aviation, since the expenditure likely to be incurred at the present stage will be relatively small, we have included no specific proposals regarding it.

62. *Railways*

The total route mileage of railways in India was

SECTION 63

41,000 miles in 1938-39 and the total capital at charge was Rs.848 crores (£636 millions). Assuming that the ratio of capital to route mileage remains the same, the capital cost of adding about 21,000 miles of new railway line in this country would roughly amount to Rs.434 crores (£325½ millions). Maintenance charges at the rate of about 2 per cent. would work out to Rs.9 crores (£6¾ millions) per annum.

63. Roads

The length of existing roads in British India is in the neighbourhood of 300,000 miles. Of these 74,000 miles are metalled and 226,000 miles are unmetalled. The programme of doubling this mileage in 15 years is intended to cover mainly village roads and the humbler district roads. Our idea is that all important villages should be connected with the main highways of trade so that "no village with a population of 1,000 and over should be more than, say, a mile or half a mile from a public road."[1] If side by side with this road development the bullock cart, which is bound to remain the principal means of vehicular traffic in rural areas, is also improved, especially by making the use of pneumatic tyres universal, it would go a long way towards reducing the cost of maintenance. As villages are not likely to have heavy traffic, we suggest that the roads connecting them with traffic roads or trunk roads should be ordinary metalled roads. The use of pneumatic tyres for bullock carts should make them quite suitable for such roads. On an average the cost of a metalled road, 18 feet wide, is estimated at Rs.10,000 (£750) per mile. On this basis the cost of constructing 300,000 miles of additional road mileage in India would amount to Rs.300 crores (£225 millions). The cost of maintenance would be Rs.35 crores (£26¼ millions).

[1] Presidential address of Sir Kenneth Mitchell to the eighth session of the Indian Roads Congress, 1943.

APPENDICES

SECTIONS 64, 65, 66

64. *Reconstruction of Existing Roads*

If India is to have an adequate road system in future it is necessary, in addition to constructing this new mileage of roads, to metal the 226,000 miles of ordinary earth roads that are being used for vehicular traffic at present. The cost of reconstructing these roads at the rate of, say, Rs.5,000 (£375) per mile would amount to Rs.113 crores (£84¾ millions). If they are reconstructed, the cost of their maintenance will be less than what is incurred at present.

65. *Shipping*

For a long time past, very few ports in India except Bombay, Calcutta, Madras and Karachi have had adequate shipping facilities. In recent times several smaller ports, principally in Indian States, have been developed, but still the number of ports suitable for shipping is very small. If shipping is to occupy its legitimate place in the transport system of the future, it is necessary to provide more harbours suitable for small ships. A capital expenditure of about Rs.50 crores (£37½ millions) may be estimated for the purpose. At 10 per cent. the maintenance charges would amount to Rs.5 crores (£3¾ millions) per annum.

66. *Cost of Transport*

The total cost of increasing rail and road mileage and improving ports would thus be:

	Non-recurring expenditure (Rs. crores)	Recurring expenditure (Rs. crores)
Railways	434 (£325½ millions)	9 (£6¾ millions)
Roads—		
New construction	300 (£225 millions)	35 (£26¼ millions)
Reconstruction	113 (£84¾ millions)	—
Ports	50 (£37½ millions)	5 (£3¾ millions)
Total	897 (£672¾ millions)	49 (£36¾ millions)

271

SECTIONS 67

67 Co-operation of the People

In the execution of a comprehensive plan of economic development, it is essential that we should be able to count on the willing co-operation of the people. This will be possible only if the masses are able to read and write and are in a position to understand for themselves the broad implications of the developments embodied in the plan. The execution of a plan which aims at an all-round development will also require a huge personnel trained for technical posts in agriculture, industry and trade and for general administration. Provision of primary education, which has been mentioned as one of the essential requirements of a reasonable standard of living, would under Mr. Sargent's scheme require about 1,800,000 teachers in British India alone. Provision of adequate medical help would need a large number of doctors and nurses. As our natural resources such as minerals, hydro-electric power, soil, etc., are not yet properly surveyed, extensive surveys[1] will have to be undertaken to ascertain their quantity, quality and distribution and a large number of research stations will be required to carry out investigations. Some idea of the personnel required for large-scale economic planning may be gathered from the following statement relating to Soviet Russia in 1939:[2]

---

[1] Sir Cyril Fox states: As a result of 97 years' work carried out by officers of the Geological Survey of India, it has been found that an average of 500 square miles can be accurately surveyed each year, and that the average service in the field is about 10 years per geologist. Roughly, 100 geologists in all have been so employed since 1846, so that theoretically only 500,000 square miles could have been examined in any detail in the time, and there remain over a million square miles still to scrutinise.

[2] E. Strauss: *Soviet Russia*, page 317.

Managing staff of Soviet economy—	
Heads of administration, etc.	450,000
Managers of State industry ..	350,000
Managers of State and collective farms	582,000
Others ..	369,000
Engineers, architects	330,000
Technicians ..	906,000
Teachers, research workers ..	1,049,000
Accountants, economists, statisticians	2,439,000
Others ..	3,116,000
Total Soviet intelligentsia	9,591,000
Total Soviet population ..	170,000,000

68. *Programme of Education*

To achieve mass literacy and to secure a sufficient number of educated administrators and trained technicians, a comprehensive programme of education is necessary. This should cover the following main aspects:

Primary education.
Adult education.
Secondary and vocational education.
University education.
Scientific education and research.

69. *Adult Education*

The expenditure necessary to provide universal primary education and to secure literacy for adults has already been indicated in paragraph 32. As regards adult education, something more is necessary under a plan of development than the minimum provision suggested in that paragraph. The content of adult education should be widened so that it will make "every possible member of a state an effective citizen and thus give reality to the ideal of democracy." To achieve this, a scheme of adult education must also provide for cultural and vocational

SECTION 70

education besides the teaching of the three R's. We estimate the cost of this per adult roughly at Rs.2[1] (3s.) and the total at Rs.33 crores (£24¾ millions). This will bring the aggregate cost of adult education, including the provision made in paragraph 32, to Rs.99 crores (£74¼ millions).

70. *Secondary Education*

It is necessary to split up secondary education into two parts: middle school and high school education. The former is considered as important as primary education. "There is little hope of permanently improving the conditions of village life and of making the rural population responsive to fruitful ideas unless the younger generation is educated beyond the primary stage up to an age when boys and girls realize that they are becoming social and economic assets to the community."[2] All primary school students should, therefore, be given a course of middle school education for three years in order to make them useful citizens. Approximately, the expenditure on accommodation for middle schools will be half that for primary schools. For high schools, the accommodation required would be mainly in the bigger villages and urban areas and its cost may be calculated on the basis of building costs in urban areas. Mr. Sargent suggests that "roughly one child in every five will be able with profit to enter the high school stage." The likely number of high school students on this basis would be round about 10 million. An approximate estimate of recurring expenditure on secondary education may be made by applying the average cost per student in middle schools and high schools in the country during the pre-war period. The

[1] Figure based on Mr. Sargent's estimate.
[2] *Report on Vocational Education in India*, page 13.

SECTION 70

total expenditure on middle school and high school education would then be as follows:

Middle schools in rural areas—buildings and equipment ..	Rs.34 crores (£25½ millions)
Middle school students in rural areas	22 million
Average cost per student per annum	Rs.22 (£1 13s.)
Cost of middle school education in rural areas	Rs.49 crores (£36¾ millions)
Middle schools in urban areas—buildings and equipment ..	Rs.11 crores (£8¼ millions)
Middle school students in urban areas	3.3 million
Average cost per student per annum	Rs.31 (£2 6s. 6d.)
Cost of middle school education in urban areas	Rs.10 crores (£7½ millions)
High schools—buildings and equipment	Rs.33 crores (£24¾ millions)
Number of high school students	10 million
Average cost per student per annum	Rs.64 (£4 16s.)
Cost of high school education ..	Rs.64 crores (£48 millions)
Cost of maintenance of middle school and high school buildings at 7½ per cent. of capital expenditure	Rs.6 crores (£4½ millions)

SECTIONS 71, 72

71. *University and Technical Education*

For vocational education,[1] university education and scientific education and reasearch, the data necessary for a detailed calculation are lacking. We propose, therefore, to take roughly 5/1000ths of the national income per year as a comprehensive measure of the expenditure which would be required. This would amount roughly to Rs.10 crores (£7½ millions) in the first year of the plan and to Rs.30 crores (£22½ millions) in the last year. It may be mentioned that the total expenditure on scientific education and research amounts to 1/1000th of the national income in the U.K., 6/1000ths of the national income in the U.S.A. and 10/1000ths of the national income in the U.S.S.R. All told, the amount of expenditure on education would be:

	Non-recurring expenditure (Rs. crores)	Recurring expenditure (Rs. crores)
Primary education	86 (£64½ millions)	88 (£66 millions)
Adult education	99 (£74¼ millions)	—
Secondary education	82 (£61½ millions)	129 (£96¾ millions)
University education, scientific education and research	—	average 20 (£15 millions)
Total	267 (£200¼ millions)	237 (£177¾ millions)

72. *Public Health*

The expenditure necessary under public health has been indicated in paragraph 28. No further provision is necessary under a 15-year plan.

[1] The average cost per pupil per annum in the technical and industrial schools in the U.P. in 1937 ranged from Rs.155 (£11 12s. 6d.) to Rs.869 (£65 3s. 6d.), although there was a good deal of concentration between Rs.200 (£15) and Rs.300 (£22 10s.). The Industrial Commission, 1916-18, estimated that the average cost per pupil in industrial schools would be about Rs.200 (£15) and that they could be established with a capital of Rs.500 (£37 10s.) per student.

SECTIONS 73, 74, 75

73. *Allowance for Increase in Population*

In estimating the capital outlay on education and public health, we have not taken into account the probable increase in population during the period of the plan. This is because we have not made any allowance in our estimate for the expenditure which has already been incurred on education and public health up to now, and we assume that this amount would be sufficient to cover the expenditure due to increase in population.

74. *Cost of Additional Housing*

In the case of housing, however, there is no such reserve in the estimate given in paragraph 15 out of which provision may be made for an increase in population. In estimating the capital expenditure on house construction during the period of the plan, we must, therefore, take into account the additional housing necessary for increase in population. A capital outlay of about Rs.800 crores (£600 millions) would be required for this purpose. The total amount of capital required for bringing existing housing up to the minimum standard we have laid down and for providing new houses to meet an increase in population would, therefore, amount to Rs.2,200 crores (£1,650 millions). At $7\frac{1}{2}$ per cent. of the total capital expenditure, including the value of existing housing, the cost of maintenance would be Rs.318 crores (£238½ millions.)

75. *Miscellaneous Capital Expenditure*

For miscellaneous capital expenses which have not been specifically mentioned, a sum of Rs.200 crores (£150 millions) might be provided. No separate figure for maintenance charges under this head seems necessary.

SECTIONS 76, 77

76. Cost Classified

The total expenditure which the plan is likely to involve is summarized below:

	Non-recurring expenditure (Rs. crores)	Recurring expenditure (Rs. crores)
Industry	4,480[1] (£3,360 millions)	—
Agriculture	845 (£633¾ millions)	400 (£300 millions)
Communications	897 (£672¾ millions)	49 (£36¾ millions)
Education	267 (£200¼ millions)	237 (£177¾ millions)
Health	281 (£210¾ millions)	185 (£138¾ millions)
Housing	2,200 (£1,650 millions)	318 (£238½ millions)
Miscellaneous	200 (£150 millions)	—
Total	9,170 (£6,877½ millions)	1,189 (£891¾ millions)

77. Total Capital Required

Throughout this section we have shown recurring and non-recurring expenditure separately. We have made this distinction with the object of indicating how the capital expenditure is distributed and how it has been arrived at. In view of the fact that income from agriculture and industry and the revenue required for such services as education, health and communications may not be available in sufficient amount in the initial years, we have thought it desirable to include in our estimate of the total amount of capital which the plan is likely to require, the recurring charges for one year in respect of the completed plan. On this basis the total capital requirements of the plan we have outlined would amount to about Rs.10,000 crores (£7,500 millions) distributed as follows:

[1] The ratio of 2.4 which we have assumed for estimating the total amount of capital required for industrial development includes both fixed capital and working capital. The figure of working capital is not therefore separately calculated.

SECTION 78

		(Rs. crores)	
Industry	..	4,480	(£3,360 millions)
Agriculture	..	1,240	(£930 millions)
Communications	..	940	(£705 millions)
Education	..	490	(£367½ millions)
Health..	..	450	(£337½ millions)
Housing	..	2,200	(£1,650 millions)
Miscellaneous	..	200	(£150 millions)
Total	..	10,000	(£7,500 millions)

IV

SOURCES OF FINANCE

78. *External and Internal Finance*

In examining the sources from which the finance required for the plan may be obtained, it is important to distinguish between external finance and internal finance. External finance is the finance available for payment to foreign countries for goods and services imported from them, while internal finance is that required within the country for the mobilization of our resources. In the initial years of planning, India will be dependent almost entirely on foreign countries for the machinery and technical skill necessary for the establishment of both basic and other industries. As the plan develops, our dependence on foreign countries in this matter should steadily decline. The imports of machinery and technical skill inevitable in the initial years of planning would require a large amount of external finance, the raising of which constitutes an important problem in a plan of economic development. Internal finance on the scale which we consider necessary will also raise serious difficulties, but in a planned economy these would not be insurmountable. The sources of external and internal finance which would be available to us are:

SECTIONS 79, 80

External finance:
> The hoarded wealth of the country, mainly gold.
> Our short-term loans to the U.K.—sterling securities held by the Reserve Bank of India.
> Our favourable balance of trade.
> Foreign borrowing.

Internal finance:
> Savings of the people.
> New money created against *ad hoc* securities, *i.e.* on the inherent credit of the government.

79. Hoarded Wealth

The volume of hoarded wealth in India has been estimated at about Rs.1,000 crores (£750 millions) after allowing for the recent exports of "distress" gold. A part of this should become available for capital investment if, as is assumed at the beginning of this memorandum, a national government comes into power in which people have full faith and if suitable means are adopted for attracting hoards from their place of concealment. The amount available from this source may be estimated at not more than Rs.300 crores (£225 millions).

80. Sterling Securities

Our sterling securities in the Banking and Issue Departments of the Reserve Bank of India amount to about Rs.800 crores (£600 millions) at the moment. If the war continues for a year or two and His Majesty's Government continue to make purchases from India on the same scale as they have been making them hitherto, the amount is likely to increase to Rs.1,000 crores (£750 millions). This could be utilized for importing the capital goods required at the beginning of the plan.

SECTIONS 81, 82

81. *Balance of Trade*

As a result of the general policy of directing agricultural production primarily with a view to meeting the internal demand which we advocate in this plan, our export trade is likely to diminish in future. Side by side, the development of consumption goods industries and food crops within the country will bring about a reduction in the volume of imports. Our favourable balance on normal trade account is not, therefore, likely to shrink below Rs.40 crores (£30 millions) per annum which, because of the repatriation of most of our sterling debt, will be available as external finance. The total amount which might be expected from this source in 15 years will, therefore, be about Rs.600 crores (£450 millions).

82. *Foreign Borrowing*

India's credit in foreign capital markets is now very high and she can, therefore, borrow substantial amounts of capital if she so wishes in these markets, especially in America. Such capital, if it is not accompanied by political influence or interference of foreign vested interests, should not be unwelcome. Even if India resorts to "created money" as she is likely to, since this finance is to be employed for promoting an expansionist economy, its effect on her credit in foreign markets would not be so serious as it otherwise would be. By giving priority to basic industries in our programme of development and by using our sterling balances in the initial stages for importing the necessary plant, machinery and technical experts, it is, however, possible to curtail our requirements of external finance. As the plan proceeds, India would be able to satisfy her requirements of heavy machinery and other capital goods from her own industries. We may put the figure of foreign loans at about Rs.700 crores (£525 millions).

SECTIONS 83, 84, 85

83. *Savings in Foreign Countries*

An important source of finance which would assume considerable proportions as national income grows, is the volume of savings within the country. The percentage of savings to national income in some foreign countries is given below:[1]

	U.K.	U.S.A.	Germany	Japan	Russia
1900–10	12.2	14.3	19.1	—	8.2
1919–24	8.1	12.2	—	21.9	—
1925–30	7.6	10.9	7.7	19.8	7.8
1934–37	7.0	5.0	11.8	21.9	14.2

84. *Savings in India*

In India, taking into account the fact that the present standard of living is extremely low and that no provision has been made for the increased taxation which a planned economy would necessitate, we do not assume that more than 6 per cent. of the national income on an average would become available for investment during the period of the plan. On this basis the total amount which could be obtained over the whole period from the savings of the people would be in the neighbourhood of Rs.4,000 crores (£3,000 millions).

85. "*Created Money*"

We have estimated the savings which would be available for investment at a conservative figure. It is possible that a larger percentage of the national income than we have estimated may be forthcoming as savings. If this possibility, however, does not materialize, a large part of the capital required, about Rs.3,400 crores (£2,550 millions) would have to be created by borrowing against *ad hoc* securities from the Reserve Bank. New money to this extent can be created only if people have full

[1] Colin Clark: *The Conditions of Economic Progress*, page 406

confidence in the resources and *bona fides* of the government that creates it. There is nothing unsound in creating this money, because it is meant to increase the productive capacity of the nation and in the long run is of a self-liquidating character. At the end of the period, the general level of prices would in all probability be lower than at the beginning of the plan. During the greater part of the planning period, however, financing of economic development by means of "created money" on this scale is likely to lead to a gap between the volume of purchasing power in the hands of the people and the volume of goods available. How to bridge this gap and to keep prices within limits will be a constant problem which the planning authority will have to tackle. During this period, in order to prevent the inequitable distribution of the burden between different classes which this method of financing will involve, practically every aspect of economic life will have to be so rigorously controlled by government that individual liberty and freedom of enterprise will suffer a temporary eclipse.

86. *Sources of Finance Summarized*

The amount of capital which we expect to get from the various sources mentioned above is summarized below:

External finance:

	(Rs. crores)		
Hoarded wealth	300	(£225 millions)	
Sterling securities	1,000	(£750 millions)	
Balance of trade	600	(£450 millions)	
Foreign borrowing	700	(£525 millions)	
	2,600		(£1,950 millions)

SECTIONS 87, 88, 89

Internal finance:

Savings	4,000	(£3,000 millions)
"Created money"	3,400	(£2,550 millions)
	7,400	(£5,550 millions)
Total	10,000	(£7,500 millions)

87. *Method of Raising Finance*

Our object in this section has been to indicate the sources from which the capital expenditure required for the plan may be met. The precise form in which the capital may be raised, whether by the state in the shape of taxation or government borrowings or by private voluntary investment, is a question which can only be considered, when the plan is ready for execution, in the light of conditions then prevailing. It will depend among other things on the role to be assigned to the state in the future economy of the country and also on the position of the money market after the war.

88. *Finance, only a Camp Follower*

It is necessary to emphasize that in a planned economy we are primarily thinking in terms of commodities and services. Money or finance is therefore completely subservient to the requirements of the economy as a whole and must be treated merely as a means of mobilizing the internal resources of the country in materials and man-power.

V

STAGES OF DEVELOPMENT

89. *Determination of Stages*

In determining the stages by which the plan is to be completed, the following factors should be taken into account: (*i*) the extent to which natural resources, labour, capital goods and managerial ability could be made available; (*ii*) the necessity of giving priority to certain kinds of development over others for the success of the whole plan; and (*iii*) the importance of avoiding too great a strain on the country's economy in the execution of the plan.

90. *Adequacy of Resources*

Regarding (*i*) it may be stated that it will be an essential part of the plan to make a thorough survey of our soils, water-power resources, geological wealth, etc. On the basis of available information, which is admittedly incomplete, it is probable that most of the raw materials required for the plan outlined in this memorandum would be available within the country in requisite quantities. In respect of labour, capital and managerial ability, the situation would be somewhat different in the initial years. We have plenty of unskilled labour in the country, but in addition to this, a large supply of skilled labour and trained technicians will be necessary. This will become available as in Russia and Poland when the schemes for their recruitment and training, which in themselves would be an important part of the plan, are complete and put into operation. But till this supply is forthcoming, India will have to import foreign technicians. The plan will, therefore, have to be arranged in such a way that the schemes undertaken in the earlier years can be carried out with a minimum of skilled labour. For capital goods, mainly machinery, India will have to depend on foreign countries for a longer time and to a larger extent than for labour; our ability to secure these from foreign countries would be determined mainly by the extent of our foreign resources. As to managerial ability, which is an important factor in modern business organization, no serious difficulty need be anticipated in rendering the country self-sufficient within a short period.

SECTIONS 91, 92, 93

91. *Priority for Basic Industries*

In carrying out the stages of development, we shall have to pay special attention to basic industries, such as the manufacture of machinery, chemicals, etc. On these industries will depend the development not only of all other industries but of the whole economic life of the country. Till these industries are developed, we shall naturally be at the mercy of foreign countries. To shorten this period of dependence it is necessary to give priority to basic industries over other industries and thus to speed up development.

92. *Needs of Consumers*

Planning without tears is almost an impossibility. But we can learn some lessons from the Russian experiment and avoid the errors to which planners in their over-enthusiasm are liable. Two features of the Russian Plans which caused misery and hardship to the masses were: (*i*) their over-emphasis on heavy industries and indifference to consumption goods industries, and (*ii*) their enthusiasm for building huge industrial plants which took years to come into operation. It is necessary in India to pay special attention to basic industries, but it should be our aim simultaneously to develop consumption goods industries so as to meet at least our essential requirements. Similarly, we should try, as far as possible, to build our industrial units on a scale which is not larger than is strictly necessary for economical working so that they can come into production within a short time and lend themselves more easily to regional distribution.

93. *Imperfections in Early Stages*

In the light of these considerations, we give in the next paragraph a rough outline of the stages by which the economic plan should be carried out. In the nature

SECTIONS 94, 95

of things, any such programme must be full of imperfections. "In the first years, indeed, only bad plans can be drawn up, since there is no stable basis on which one can rely and all the problems must be solved simultaneously. But as time goes on, the ground is cleared more and more and the number of problems diminishes."[1]

94. Three-Five-Year Plans

For purposes of execution, the plan outlined in this memorandum should be subdivided into three plans, each covering a period of five years. The expenditure to be incurred during each of these plans, as estimated in paragraph 77, is indicated below.

	First plan (Rs. crores)	(£ mills.)	Second plan (Rs. crores)	(£ mills.)	Third plan (Rs. crores)	(£ mills.)	Total (Rs. crores)	(£ mills.)
Industry	[790]	(592½)	[1,530]	(1,147½)	[2,160]	(1,620)	[4,480]	(3,360)
Basic industry	480	(360)	1,200	(900)	1,800	(1,350)	3,480	(2,610)
Consumption goods industry	310	(232½)	330	(247½)	360	(270)	1,000	(750)
Agriculture	200	(150)	400	(300)	640	(480)	1,240	(930)
Communications	110	(82½)	320	(240)	510	(382½)	940	(705)
Education	40	(30)	80	(60)	370	(277½)	490	(367½)
Health	40	(30)	80	(60)	330	(247½)	450	(337½)
Housing	190	(142½)	420	(315)	1,590	(1,192½)	2,200	(1,650)
Miscellaneous	30	(22½)	70	(52½)	100	(75)	200	(150)
Total	1,400	(1,050)	2,900	(2,175)	5,700	(4,275)	10,000	(7,500)

95. Plans Explained

In the initial period the total amount to be spent has been deliberately kept low because the material resources and personnel available at the beginning of the plan would be comparatively small. With the development of the plan, both material resources and personnel

[1] Ferdynand Zweig: *The Planning of Free Societies*, page 125. Also see his following statement: "Every beginning in planning must be bad, and the time needed for its improvement is considerable. This point is extremely important, because the antagonists of planning experiments try to kill them at the start by airily pointing out the failures and defects inevitable during their teething stages."

SECTION 96

would become available in rapidly increasing proportions and the tempo of progress would be accelerated. While the first five-year plan will be handicapped by the fact that there will be no previous preparation in anticipation of its requirements, the second and third plans would have their requirements studied in advance and adequate preparations made for their inauguration. Although the first plan will therefore start almost *in vacuo*, it will lay the foundation for the second plan which in its turn will be the basis for the third one. In allocating the amount of capital expenditure to be incurred during each of the three stages, we are mainly guided by this consideration. To put it briefly, we have planned the expenditure to increase in geometric progression.

96. *Consideration for Consumer*

The developments in the different sections of the plan have been mapped out generally in accordance with the considerations discussed earlier in this part. For instance, it will be seen that even in the first five-year plan, side by side with basic industries, we have provided a comparatively large amount of capital for the development of consumption goods industries also. The importance of this will be understood if we realize that in the first five-year plan a substantial part of this capital will have to be spent in foreign countries for importing the necessary equipment which will not be available in the country. This will mean a reduction in the limited volume of external finance which is available to us and which is essential for the establishment of basic industries. In the succeeding stages the capital equipment required by consumption goods industries would be supplied to an increasing extent by our own industries and the dependence on external finance would be reduced. It is also necessary to emphasize that in the production of consumption goods we presume that small-scale and cottage industries which require a comparatively small amount of capital equipment would play an important part.

97. *Basic Industries and Consumption Goods*

The ratio between the capital outlay on basic industries and consumption goods industries over the whole period is roughly 3.5, which is much smaller than in the case of the U.S.S.R. This brings out the fact that we have given more attention to consumption goods in our plan.

98. *Progress of Basic Industries*

The total expenditure on basic industries over the whole period is estimated at Rs.3,480 crores (£2,610 millions). A large proportion of this will have to be spent on the import of foreign capital equipment. The total amount of external finance which is likely to be available to us is, however, in the neighbourhood of Rs.2,600 crores (£1,950 millions) only. The expenditure on basic industries during the first two plans which amounts to Rs.1,680 crores (£1,260 millions) is well within the limits of our external finance, and we presume that the basic industries which would be developed in the first two plans would be such as would themselves produce a substantial proportion, if not the whole, of the capital equipment needed for the basic and consumption goods industries to be developed in the third period.

99. *Balanced View*

While fixing targets for the development of agriculture, communications, education, health and housing, we have attempted, as far as possible, to strike a balance between the requirements of each stage of development and the resources and personnel available during that stage.

BOMBAY PLAN

MEMORANDUM OUTLINING
A PLAN OF ECONOMIC DEVELOPMENT FOR INDIA
PART II

CONTENTS OF PART TWO

		PAGE
I.	INTRODUCTORY	65
II.	DISTRIBUTION OF THE NATIONAL INCOME	66
III.	THE STATE AND ECONOMIC ORGANIZATION	89
	INDEX	105

NOTE

The Authors regret that Sir Ardeshir Dalal, who was a signatory to Part I of the PLAN, is unable to sign this part, owing to his appointment as Member for Planning and Development in the Government of India. They wish to express their keen appreciation of his valued contribution towards the preparation of this memorandum before his assumption of office in August 1944.

December 1944

I
INTRODUCTORY

1. *Preliminary*

Our first memorandum dealt chiefly with the problem of production. Both logically and as a matter of practical necessity, the question of production must come before that of distribution in a plan of economic development. This is because in a country of comparatively low production such as India, no system of distribution, however meticulously framed, will help to raise the standard of living unless production is vastly increased. But it does not follow that increased production will necessarily remedy the problem of poverty if it is not based on a proper system of distribution. The present memorandum sets out our views regarding distribution and also the allied question of the part to be assigned to the State in a planned economy.

2. *Line of Approach*

Our approach to these problems is twofold. On the one hand, we recognize that the existing economic organization, based on private enterprise and ownership, has failed to bring about a satisfactory distribution of the national income. On the other hand, we feel that in spite of its admitted shortcomings, it possesses certain features which have stood the test of time and have enduring achievements to their credit. While it would be unwise to blind ourselves to the obvious weaknesses of the present system, we think it would be equally a mistake to uproot an organization which has worked with a fair measure of success in several directions.

SECTIONS 3, 4, 5

3. *Twin Foundations of Economic Structure*

Briefly, we plan for change but we also plan for stability and orderly development. It is our firm belief that if the future economic structure of the country is to function effectively, it must be based on these twin foundations. It must provide for free enterprise, but enterprise which is truly enterprising and not a mere cloak for sluggish acquisitiveness. It must ensure at the same time that the fruits of enterprise and labour are fairly apportioned among all who contribute to them and not unjustly withheld by a few from the many.

II

DISTRIBUTION OF THE NATIONAL INCOME

4. *Production and Distribution Closely Related*

The primary object of the plan of economic development outlined in the previous memorandum is to improve the standard of living of the masses. In fact, increased production will be meaningless unless it is directed towards the eradication of poverty. Logically, an improvement in the general standard of living, therefore, involves both increased production and equitable distribution, and although we have dealt with them separately, they are closely interrelated and react on each other.

5. *Disparities of Income*

At present our production is very small and it is not equitably distributed. The average *per capita* income of Rs.65 (£4 : 17 : 6) in 1931-32, to which we have referred in our first memorandum, is an arithmetical average

SECTION 6

which bears little relation to the income realized by the majority of the population, which must be considerably below this figure. The *per capita* average itself varies from Rs.51 (£3 : 16 : 6) to Rs.166 (£12 : 9s.) in rural and urban areas respectively. In 1931-32 one-half of the total urban income was in the hands of less than 10 per cent of urban workers and " even among the comparatively well-to-do class, whose annual incomes exceed Rs.2000 (£150) a year, 38 per cent of their number could claim only 17 per cent of their total income, while a little more than 1 per cent were in possession of as much as 10 per cent of their total income ". In rural areas, the income of the majority of the people must have been less than the average of Rs.51 (£3 : 16 : 6). This is because farmers holding less than 2 acres of land form a large proportion of the cultivating class. Moreover, the agricultural labourer, whose wage is sometimes as low as 2 to 3 annas (2d. to 3d.) a day, and the cultivator, are generally without any work for 3 to 6 months in the year. The increase in population since 1931 must have considerably increased the pressure on this class.

6. *Equitable Distribution*

In so far as the volume and nature of production are ultimately determined by the consumer demand, gross inequalities in income tend to retard the development of a country's economic resources. They prevent the needs of the vast majority of the population from exercising any influence on the volume of production, which has naturally to be restricted, and lead to social cleavages and disharmony. Productive resources under these conditions tend to be devoted to satisfying the demands of the well-to-do classes while large numbers of people remain inadequately fed, clothed, housed, educated and

SECTION 7

medically cared for. The large increase in production which is postulated in the plan will be difficult to achieve if the present disparities in income are allowed to persist. To this extent, therefore, equitable distribution is necessarily implied in a plan for increased production. A policy which specifically aims at securing this object should have a double purpose : i) to secure to everybody a minimum income essential for a reasonable standard of living and (ii) to prevent gross inequalities in the incomes of different classes and individuals.

7. *Ownership of the Means of Production*

Concentration of the means of production in the hands of a small group of people has been considered one of the potent causes of the inequalities of income which prevail in the world at present, as it is also to some extent an incidental result of such inequalities. In the U.K., for example, it is estimated that 1 per cent of the persons above twenty-five derive from their property rights about 20 per cent of the total income of the country. " Unequal distribution of incomes from property makes for unequal distribution of incomes as a whole, not only directly through its existence, but also indirectly through its effect on other incomes." To secure an equitable distribution of income, it is therefore necessary gradually to reduce the existing inequalities of wealth and property and to decentralize the ownership of the means of production. Imposition of death duties and other similar levies, if undertaken in pursuance of well-defined social objectives, by a government fully responsible to the people, would contribute towards achieving the first object. Reform of the system of land tenures which we suggest would further help progress in the same direction. In the sphere of industry, we have

SECTION 8

already indicated in our previous memorandum that the fullest possible scope should be provided for small-scale and cottage industries, particularly in the production of consumption goods. The process of decentralization would be further advanced by encouraging the widespread distribution of shares in joint-stock companies, by regional distribution of industries and through the development of cooperative enterprises. Control by the State, accompanied in appropriate cases by State ownership or management of public utilities, basic industries, etc., will also tend to diminish inequalities of income.

8. *Total Abolition of Inequalities Undesirable*

It is necessary, however, to make clear that although gross inequalities are undesirable, total abolition of inequalities, even if feasible, would not be in the interest of the country. Subject to the provision of a basic minimum, it is desirable to leave enough scope for variations in income according to ability and productivity. This will provide the necessary incentive for improvement in efficiency which is an important factor in the progress of a planned economy. Even in Soviet Russia, after the first flush of enthusiasm for the equalitarian ideal had passed, variations in industrial incomes have been allowed as an important motivating factor making for efficiency. The encouragement given to *Stakhanovism* is an indication of the change that is rapidly coming about. There is much force in what Lord Keynes says on the point : " I believe that there is social and psychological justification for significant inequalities of incomes and wealth, but not for such large disparities as exist to-day. There are valuable human activities which require the motive of money-making and the environment of private wealth ownership

SECTIONS 9, 10

for their full fruition. Moreover, dangerous human proclivities can be canalized into comparatively harmless channels by the existence of opportunities for money-making and private wealth, which, if they cannot be satisfied in this way, may find their outlet in cruelty, the reckless pursuit of personal power and authority, and other forms of self-aggrandisement." [1]

9. *Rewards to Factors of Production*

Side by side with the decentralization of production and control, ownership or management of public utilities and basic industries by the State, it is also necessary to adjust the rewards of the various factors of production so as to further the reduction of gross inequalities. As a general rule, these rewards, *viz.* wages, interest and profits, should continue to be determined on the basis of demand and efficiency as at present, subject to the overriding consideration that wages should not fall below a certain minimum and that interest rates should be controlled with a view to maintaining full employment. Profits should be kept within limits through fixation of prices, restriction of dividends, taxation, etc. But care should be taken to leave sufficient incentive for improvement in efficiency and expansion of production.

10. *Measures to Secure a Minimum Standard*

To secure a minimum standard of living we propose two classes of measures : (i) those that would raise the general level of income and (ii) those that would reduce

[1] *The General Theory of Employment : Interest and Money*, p. 374.

the burden of individual expenditure on consumption goods and services, *i.e.* the cost of living.

11. *Income Level*

The measures which we have in view for increasing the general level of income and which we explain in more detail in the paragraphs that follow are :

(1) provision of full employment ;
(2) increase in efficiency ;
(3) improvement in urban and rural wages ;
(4) security of agricultural prices and development of multi-purpose cooperative societies, and
(5) reform of the land system.

12. *Full Employment*

Of all the measures that we suggest for raising the general level of income in India, provision of fuller scope for employment is the most important. Although no reliable information regarding the extent of unemployment or under-employment in India is available, it is recognized that lack of employment is one of the major causes of the poverty of our people. Provision of full employment for the working part of the population would no doubt present formidable difficulties, but without it the establishment of a decent standard of living would remain merely a pious hope. " If the giant Idleness can be destroyed, all the other aims of reconstruction come within reach. If not, they are out of reach in any serious sense and their formal achievement is futile." [1] In general terms, provision of full employment means ensuring for every grown-up person suitable opportunities for earning his or her livelihood, that is, a recognition of the individual's right to work, increased mobility of

[1] Sir William Beveridge, *Pillars of Security*, p. 43.

SECTION 13

labour being an essential condition for achieving this object.

13. *Employment in Industry*

We expect that the industrial expansion which we have suggested in our previous memorandum will absorb a part of the working population when the plan is completed. In order that the new industries which would be established in the country should provide the maximum volume of employment, we have suggested a comparatively low ratio of capital intensification, *i.e.* a smaller proportion of capital per worker than is usually met with in industrialized countries, and the fullest possible development of small-scale and cottage industries. In this respect India will do well to take a leaf from the experience of Japan, where, as in India, labour is comparatively plentiful and capital scarce. Statistical investigations show that about one-half of the persons employed in the manufacturing industry of Japan in 1930 were in workplaces employing under 5 persons each and about 70 per cent were in workplaces employing under 50 persons. According to the information compiled by the Ministry of Commerce and Industry, workplaces employing between 5 and 30 workers accounted for 29 per cent of the employment and 19 per cent of the output in manufacturing industry. The industrial cooperatives which have been recently developed in China might also prove a useful guide to India in this respect. Besides employment in industries, a large part of the population will be absorbed in trade and other services, which will necessarily increase in the wake of increased production and rising standards of living. And yet this will barely touch the problem of " disguised unemployment " in agriculture, which is the crux of the situation.

SECTIONS 14, 15

14. *Seasonal Unemployment in Agriculture*

The agriculturist and the agricultural labourer are generally without work for periods extending from 3 to 6 months in the year at present. This unemployment occurs at intervals and is of a seasonal character. Provision of work during these periods of seasonal unemployment is of importance if a policy of full employment is to be successful. The steps which we contemplate for achieving this object are : (i) introduction of mixed farming, *i.e.* cultivation accompanied by dairy farming, market gardening, etc., (ii) cultivation of more than one crop in a year with the help of better irrigation facilities and increased use of manures, and (iii) provision of subsidiary industries which the cultivator can take up when he has no work on the farm. Among such subsidiary industries may be mentioned the following : spinning and weaving, shoe making, paper making, tanning, gur making, soap making, oil crushing, fruit preserving, basket weaving, flour and starch making, etc.

15. *Occupational Distribution*

The pattern of occupational distribution when the plan is completed would naturally be different from what it is to-day. Even where complete statistical data regarding existing occupational distribution and future demographic trends are available, it is difficult to forecast with reasonable accuracy the nature of the occupational pattern that might develop after a period of fifteen to twenty years. For India this is specially difficult because the occupational tables for the 1941 census are not yet published. Some indication, however, of the occupational pattern that will result when the plan is completed may be attempted on certain broad assumptions. We assume that the proportion of population engaged in different

SECTION 15

occupations when the plan begins to operate will be the same as in 1931 and that our population may continue to increase at the rate of 5 millions per annum, which is the average rate of increase for the decade covered by the 1941 census. The volume of employment in industry which the investment programme envisaged in the plan would provide, is calculated on the basis of a capital equipment of Rs.1500 (£112 : 10s.) per worker and is added to the number of persons employed in industry in 1947 when the plan might come into operation. The ratio of capital equipment per worker seems reasonable if allowance is made for the fact that small-scale industries would have an important scope in the economic development of the country and that adoption of shift working would be necessary with a view to economizing capital and providing as much employment as possible. According to the 1931 census, the number of persons employed in services such as public administration, trade, transport, professions, etc., was 80 per cent of that in industry. The development of social services like education and public health on the scale suggested in the plan and the needs of general administration and defence would, on the completion of the plan, absorb a much larger number of people in services than at present. The general economic development of the country would also lead to a substantial increase in trade and transport. However, since the development in services which we have postulated in our previous memorandum is proportionately much less than in industries, it is reasonable to assume that the total employment in services when the plan is complete would be about 60 per cent of that in industry. The rest of the population would be dependent on agriculture. On these assumptions, the distribution of working population according to the principal occupations in 1962, that is, in the year

SECTION 16

following the completion of the plan, would be somewhat as follows, as compared with that in 1931 :

OCCUPATIONAL DISTRIBUTION IN 1931 AND 1962

	1931 Millions	1931 Per cent	1962 Millions	1962 Per cent
Agriculture	106·3	72	129·7	58
Industry	22·1	15	57·9	26
Services*	19·2	13	34·7	16
Total working population	147·6	100	222·2	100
Total population	338·1	..	494·0	..

16. *Temporary Unemployment*

It should not be forgotten that a policy of full employment, even if successfully carried out, does not necessarily imply in practice that every person willing to work is always employed. In the first place, owing to the inherent imperfections in the working of a social policy, which has to take into account a number of incalculable factors, a small percentage of population would always be without work. Secondly, certain trades like the building trade, being seasonal in character, give rise to seasonal unemployment. Finally, owing to constant changes in the technique of production and to variations in demand, large numbers of employed workers are constantly being displaced. The number of persons who would be without work at any particular time owing to these causes could, however, be reduced to manageable dimensions if a well-thought-out policy of employment was in existence. When the plan is sufficiently advanced

---

* This category includes trade, transport, government administration, professions and domestic service. Persons living on their own incomes or engaged in unproductive occupations, whose number was 1·8 millions in 1931, are also added to this category for the sake of convenience.

SECTIONS 17, 18

and economic conditions are to a certain extent stabilized, it ought to be possible to devise schemes of relief such as unemployment insurance for workers subject to unexpected and prolonged periods of unemployment. Government's public works programme, in respect of both new construction and repairs, should be regulated with a view to reducing the volume of seasonal and temporary unemployment. For those who are unemployed because of technological changes, suitable courses of training to fit them for new jobs should be framed. We believe that during the progress of the plan the amount of construction work, which the investment programme would involve, would itself provide a very substantial increase in the scope for employment.

17. *Increase in Efficiency*

As a result of the spread of general and technical education among workers, better organization of industries, especially small-scale and cottage industries, better organization of agriculture and trade, fuller use of cattle power, provision of cheap electricity, improved tools and appliances and fertilizers, etc., the general efficiency of production is bound to record a marked improvement at the end of the planning period. Under a system of decentralized production, the benefits of higher efficiency will be increasingly available to the smaller producer and the worker in the form of a corresponding increase in their incomes. Since a higher standard of living arises largely from increased productivity of labour, improvement in efficiency of production is a material factor in raising the general level of well-being.

18. *Urban and Rural Wages*

If every person is to be assured a minimum standard of living, it automatically follows that the general level of wages must increase and that the wage rates of industrial and agricultural labour must be gradually adjusted so that the present disparity between them is reduced. The process of improvement must necessarily begin with the wages of agricultural labourers, whose number was 30 millions in 1931. It must be borne in mind that industrial wages, and with them the living standards of industrial workers, cannot be advanced beyond a certain limit unless at the same time the standard of living of the rural population is also substantially improved. Generally speaking, the daily wages of agricultural labour under pre-war conditions may be said to range from 2 to 5 annas (2d. to 5d.) a day for men, $1\frac{1}{2}$ to 4 annas ($1\frac{1}{2}$d. to 4d.) for women, and 1 to 2 annas (1d. to 2d.) for children. The average wage of unskilled agricultural labour in 1939 was 5 annas (5d.) per day in the Bombay province and 2 annas 9 pies ($2\frac{3}{4}$d.) per day in the U.P. Even at these low rates the agricultural labourer hardly found employment all the year round. Obviously, a number of these workers exist below the subsistence level, always an easy prey to epidemics and famines. When the developments in agriculture which we have broadly indicated in our previous memorandum have taken place and the reforms in the land system which we suggest elsewhere in this memorandum have been carried out, it will be necessary to fix minimum rates of wages for agricultural labour on a regional or local basis. With the development of cooperative farming, the enforcement of a minimum agricultural wage, which otherwise might present formidable obstacles, would become less difficult.

19. *A Minimum Wage*

Although the establishment of a basic minimum wage for all occupations cannot be considered at this stage, a beginning may be made in certain well-established

SECTION 20

industries like cotton textiles, sugar, cement, engineering, jute, mining, etc. In the initial stages, the minimum below which wages should not be allowed to fall should be related to the normal wage-level prevailing in each industry. The minimum should be revised from time to time till it corresponds with a reasonable standard of living. The fixation of a minimum wage and its subsequent revision should be entrusted to a Standing Committee constituted for each industry, consisting of representatives of employers and workers and a few independent persons.

20. *Agricultural Prices*

Large fluctuations in the prices of agricultural commodities have been among the most important factors which have prevented agriculturists from making more sustained efforts to improve the yield of the land. To check these fluctuations in future and to assure to the cultivator a measure of security in respect of the prices of his crop, we suggest that for the principal agricultural crops, the government should adopt a policy of fixing fair prices. In fixing a fair price, account should be taken of the cost of living in the area concerned as well as the cost of production. It would be necessary for enforcing these prices to build up adequate commodity reserves which could be utilized to check violent fluctuations. To prevent a depression in the prices of specific agricultural commodities as a result of foreign imports, the volume of imports should be regulated by means of tariffs or by fixing quotas. It is possible that a large variety of agricultural crops may in future be subject to international agreements. Such agreements, provided in respect of them India is accorded representation on an independent footing, may be expected to lead to a fair measure of stability at a reasonable level in the prices of some of our staple crops.

SECTION 21

21. *Cooperative Societies*

Another factor which prevents the cultivator from improving his output and consequently his income is that, because of the handicaps which he suffers in respect of the marketing of his crop, his realizations fall considerably short of the prices which he might otherwise secure. There are several reasons for the large differences observed in respect of most of our agricultural crops between the price paid by the consumer or exporter and the price realized by the cultivator. As the holding power of the cultivator is generally small, he has to part with his crop almost immediately it is harvested, and it is well known that prices during harvest-time are at their lowest, except of course in times of abnormal demand. Very often the purchaser is the money-lender himself, to whom the crop is sold under a tacit understanding, previously entered into, at what is generally an uneconomic rate for the cultivator. Only a small proportion of the cultivators take their produce to the marketing centres for sale. In most cases, for lack of adequate facilities for storage and finance, it is sold in the village itself, which prevents the cultivator from securing a better price. If multipurpose cooperative societies are established, the difficulties which the cultivator is experiencing at present in marketing his crop, particularly in the matter of adequate finance and storage facilities, would be removed, and his share in the price paid by the final consumer increased. Special attention should, therefore, be devoted to this type of society, which so far appears to have found little encouragement in the Indian cooperative movement. Development of communications, standardization of weights and measures, regulation of markets, spread of commercial intelligence, etc., would further help the primary producer to realize his due share of the price.

SECTION 22

22. Land Tenures

Along with the development of cooperative farming and irrigation, prevention of soil erosion and waterlogging, afforestation, etc., a fundamental reform which is necessary, if the target for agricultural production which we have laid down is to be reached and if the income of the cultivator is to be raised, is the reform of the land system. Ownership of the land and its taxation, that is, land tenure and land revenue, are the two principal problems which require to be tackled in this connection. As regards ownership, the systems of land tenure which prevail in India to-day can be roughly classified under three categories, viz. : (i) the Ryotwari system under which land is held directly under the government by individual cultivators who are responsible for the payment of land revenue, (ii) the Mahalwari or joint village system under which village estates are held by co-sharing bodies, the members of which are treated as jointly and severally liable for the land revenue, and (iii) the Zamindari system under which one person or a few joint owners hold the land and are responsible for the payment of land revenue on the whole estate. The last two categories are essentially similar in character. According to whether the revenue is fixed permanently or is amenable to periodic revisions, the land tenure system is also classified as Permanent and Temporary, but that is not relevant from our point of view. The area under the Ryotwari and the Zamindari and Mahalwari systems in British India is shown below :

(Area in thousand acres)

Ryotwari	183,034	36 per cent
Zamindari and Mahalwari	326,998	64 ,,
Total	510,032	100 ,,

Farming in India is predominantly tenancy farming.

SECTION 23

Most of the cultivators are tenant farmers who acquire land on lease from the Zamindars or bigger ryots on payment of rent. In this connection it is necessary to realize that all the land held under the Zamindari system is not, as is sometimes contended, let out for cultivation to tenant farmers, nor is all the land held under the Ryotwari system cultivated by peasant proprietors. In the United Provinces for instance, which is a Zamindari province, as much as one-fifth of the total cultivated area of 35 million acres is cultivated by the landowners themselves. On the other hand, in the Punjab, which is mainly a land of peasant proprietors, the western part of the province is the stronghold of the landlord and the landlord is too often an absentee. Contrary to the common belief the actual cultivator under the Zamindari system, who in the large majority of cases is the occupancy tenant, is for all practical purposes the proprietor of the land he cultivates. His rent is fixed save to the very limited extent to which enhancement is possible under certain conditions; his holding is both heritable and transferable. The various Tenancy Acts have in effect deprived the Zamindar of a considerable part of his proprietary right over the soil and rendered him to that extent a mere collector of rent. Similarly, the incidence of rent under the Zamindari system often compares favourably with rents prevailing in the Ryotwari areas.

23. *Ryotwari System*

As a general proposition it is nevertheless true tha under the Zamindari system the landlord has largely become a mere rentier and that the system as such has ceased to serve any national interest. Nowhere in India has the system created, as was expected of it, a class of landlords willing to supply capital for the improvement of the land and the extension of cultivation.

APPENDICES

SECTION 24

Although the Ryotwari system is not altogether free from the evils commonly associated with the Zamindari system, it has the great advantage of bringing the actual cultivator directly in contact with the State. This gives to the cultivator a better status and awakens the State to its responsibilities in the matter of cooperative farming, irrigation, prevention of soil erosion, etc., without which even under a Ryotwari system no agricultural improvement would be possible. The Floud Commission which recently reported on the land revenue system of Bengal has, after a thorough examination of the question, recommended the introduction of the Ryotwari system in the place of the existing Zamindari tenures. We suggest the gradual application of this recommendation to the Zamindari areas in the whole of India where the landlord is not directly interested in the cultivation of the land he owns. As a first step, " the State should take over the landlord's functions and pay the landlord a fair rent for the land, deducting therefrom the expenses incidental to the discharge of these duties. Later on, when the State is in a better position, this may be commuted into a lump-sum payment and the landlord's claim thus finally extinguished. For the immediate present, the link between the landlord and the tenant should be broken."[1] Side by side it would also be necessary to check the transfer of land from cultivators to non-cultivators and to control rents with a view to reducing the attractiveness of land to speculative investors.

24. *Land Revenue*

Along with the establishment of a class of peasant proprietors an urgent reform of the system of land

[1] Sir Manilal B. Nanavati and J. J. Anjaria, *The Indian Rural Problem*, p. 349.

revenue is also called for. At present the assessment of land revenue is not based on a uniform system. In certain areas the basis of assessment is rent while in others it is the net produce. There is also no provision for introducing variations in assessment according to price changes, while at the same time the Settlement Officers who assess the revenue have the discretion to modify the basic principles by introducing a number of miscellaneous considerations. As a result, the incidence of land revenue shows marked variations in different areas. It is also fairly heavy. The reform of the present system would therefore lie mainly in the direction of making the basis of assessment uniform all over the country so as to secure equality in the incidence of revenue, while retaining a certain measure of elasticity by a provision to vary the assessment from time to time in accordance with the trend of prices. The pitch of assessment should also be lowered. The general trend in other countries is to treat agricultural incomes in the same fashion as other incomes and to apply to them the principles of income tax—an exemption limit and a graduated scale of taxation. It is hardly possible at the present stage to determine how far it would be practicable in the exigencies of public finance to fix an exemption limit for agricultural income. But we consider that agricultural income above a certain level must be subject to income tax like other incomes. This has already been done in Bihar and Bengal.

25. *Income Distribution in 1962*

As a result of the measures indicated above, the lower incomes would record a steady improvement and consequently the income structure of the country would be more broad-based. For individual earners this improvement would arise from increased output as well as better prices. The cumulative effect of the measures proposed

SECTIONS 26, 27

on the incomes of the different occupational classes is roughly indicated in the table given below. The table is based on the occupational pattern given in paragraph 15 and on the estimated income from agriculture, industry and services at the end of the plan. It is assumed that persons following agriculture as their principal occupation would also secure through subsidiary occupations 5 per cent of the income from industry and services.

AVERAGE INCOME PER OCCUPIED PERSON

	1931	1962	Percentage Increase in 1962
Agriculture	Rs. 114 (£8 : 11s.)	Rs. 220 (£16 : 10s.)	93
Industry	161 (£12 : 1 : 6)	368 (£27 : 12s.)	129
Services	264 (£19 : 16s.)	397 (£29 : 15 : 6)	50

26. *Cost of Living*

The suggestions made so far are calculated to increase the incomes of those who are at present below the subsistence level. The measures which we propose for reducing the cost of living fall into two categories :

(i) provision of free social services, *e.g.* primary and middle school education, adult education and medical treatment, and

(ii) provision of essential utility services, *e.g.* electricity and transport, etc., at low cost.

27. *Free Social Services*

In our previous memorandum we have proposed a comprehensive scheme of education and medical relief. In order that every person, whatever his means, should be able to secure the benefits of education and medical relief, we have suggested that primary, middle school and adult education and medical treatment both in rural dispensaries and in hospitals should be provided free of charge. This would mean a considerable relief in the cost of living.

28. *Utility Services*

At present essential utility services such as electricity, gas, transport, etc., are supplied on a comparatively limited scale and for the majority of people at a cost which they cannot afford. We have proposed a large increase in the supply of these services and it is an essential part of our plan that their cost to the consumer both for domestic use and for cottage and rural industries should be as low as possible and within the means of the bulk of the population. In order to achieve this object, we propose that these services should be subsidized by the State to such extent as may be necessary and the margin of profits in such services should be subjected to control.

29. *National Relief Fund*

It is possible that in spite of these measures, owing to unforeseen causes such as a failure of the monsoon or any other natural calamity, conditions of living for large sections of the population may suffer a serious setback. To meet such emergencies we suggest the creation of a National Relief Fund on the lines of the present Famine Relief Fund, but larger in resources and in scope, to be utilized as and when the need arises. A part of this fund should be held in the form of consumption goods which could be mobilized for instantaneous relief in times of emergency.

SECTIONS 30, 31

30. *Social Security*

We are aware that our proposals do not constitute a complete scheme for providing security of income or freedom from want, which must be the ultimate objective of economic planning. There are several contingencies such as sickness, old age, technological unemployment, etc., which are not specifically covered by these proposals. These contingencies cannot be met except by a comprehensive scheme of social insurance. Although the need for such a scheme is urgently felt in India, we do not think that it will be possible to introduce it (i) until a policy of full employment has had time to work itself out, and some approximation is made to a position of stable employment for the greater part of the population, *i.e.* until the risks insurable are reduced to manageable proportions, and (ii) until the average individual income has risen sufficiently high to meet the contributions necessary under a scheme of insurance. We, however, suggest that as in the case of fixing a minimum wage, a beginning in the direction of social insurance may be made by introducing sickness insurance and holidays with pay for workers in organized industries. The scope of the existing legislation in respect of maternity benefits should also be widened by making it applicable to all industrial establishments coming under the Factories Act in the whole of India.

31. *Taxation of Income*

The policy we have outlined so far is mainly intended to secure the first objective of an equitable distribution of national income, *viz.* to assure to every person a minimum standard of living. To a considerable extent it will also help to reduce gross inequalities of income, which is the second objective. The most important method, however, of preventing gross inequalities is

SECTION 32

direct taxation, which in effect transfers income from the comparatively richer classes of society to the poorer. A steeply graduated income tax which would keep personal incomes within limits would obviously be the most important weapon for this purpose in the fiscal armoury of the country. But in any such scheme of taxation, consistently with the development programme envisaged in the plan, it is necessary to emphasize that adequate remission should be granted in respect of the depreciation of the assets employed in production, and that incomes ploughed back for increasing industrial or agricultural production should also be granted similar remission. Further, in the taxation of personal incomes, distinction should be made between earned and unearned income, so as to make the latter taxable at a higher rate. As a means of correcting the existing inequalities of wealth, the device of death duties, which has been successfully utilized in other countries, might also be adopted. The advisability of taxing inherited estates more severely at the second and later transfers than at the first would be a further step in the same direction. It is obvious that India's fiscal system will have to place more and more reliance on direct taxation in future if the increase in the cost of administration which planning will involve is to be met and if provision is to be made for free social services like education, medical treatment, etc., and subsidies for essential utility services.

32. *Regional Development*

Throughout our investigations we have assumed that a programme of economic development of the kind we envisage should include the whole of India—the States as well as British India—in its scope. A territorially unbalanced economy will result in an imperfect utilization

SECTION 32

of the country's resources and also prevent its purchasing power from developing *pari passu* with the estimated increase in production. Not merely in the matter of industrialization but in almost every other line of development covered by our plan, the States, with certain notable exceptions, have tended to lag behind most parts of British India. We consider it a matter of the greatest importance for the future of India that economic progress should be so planned that, as far as circumstances permit, the targets as well as the pace fixed for the plan should have uniform application to British India and to the States. The objectives we have outlined are of equal importance to both, and, further, the development of each is to a large extent conditioned by that of the other. It follows therefore that if a plan of economic development for India is to achieve its aim to any tangible extent, it should proceed on the principle that in the results it seeks to achieve and consequently in the sacrifices it demands, British India and the States should share alike. Although the States represent two-fifths of the territory and one-fourth of the population of India, it must be recognized that industrial investment in the States, as also in backward areas in British India, remains disproportionately low. It is clear therefore that there is much leeway to be made up. Unless this disparity is remedied, a proper regional distribution of economic development will be difficult to secure. Meanwhile any unequal distribution of financial burdens between manufacturing concerns in British India and the States will operate to prevent a healthy all-round industrial development, since natural advantages under such circumstances will be swamped by the adventitious benefits resulting from differences in local measures of taxation.

33. Conditions for Heavy Taxation

Taxation on the scale we have proposed will place a very heavy burden on the country and will be justified only if its utilization for the purposes for which it is intended is fully guaranteed by a national government responsible to the people of the country. It is necessary to emphasize this fact because, as experience has often shown in the past, it is a dangerous thing to vest large powers of taxation in a foreign government bred in traditions of imperialistic exploitation. Both our plan of development and our proposals for meeting its cost imply the existence of a responsible national government as an essential condition. Unless this condition is satisfied, there can be no assurance that planning will be directed either along right lines or towards right ends, or that the resources released for the purpose will be wisely and fruitfully expended.

III

THE STATE AND ECONOMIC ORGANIZATION

34. Choice of Economic Organization

The nature and scope of the measures necessary to secure an equitable distribution of the national income depend to a large extent on the lines on which production is organized. This in its turn is influenced by the principles on which the economic system of the country as a whole is based. It is therefore necessary to indicate the type of economic organization which, having regard to the circumstances of India, would be appropriate to the plan we have outlined. This is a subject on which it is possible to hold widely different opinions and which in the past has lent itself to acute controversy. In con-

APPENDICES

SECTION 35

sidering it we should therefore eschew preconceived notions and approach the question from a detached point of view. Since planning is primarily a matter of organizing the human and material resources of a country, our aim should be to devise a system which would help to utilize them to the maximum advantage. The plan must fit in with the general outlook and traditions of our people and the cost of efficiency in terms of human suffering and loss of individual freedom must not be unduly heavy.

35. *State Intervention Inherent in Planning*

It is a rather widely-held assumption that a planned economy can only function within the political framework of a totalitarian government. This assumption is natural since in the two countries which have witnessed the most impressive experiments in economic planning undertaken in recent years, namely Soviet Russia and Germany, the State has exerted over the activities of its citizens in every sphere of life a degree of authority which provides little scope for the exercise of individual freedom. It is inevitable that in executing a comprehensive plan of economic development, especially in a country where the beginnings of such development have yet to be laid, the State should exercise in the interests of the community a considerable measure of intervention and control. That this would be an indispensable feature of planning was recognized by us in our first memorandum. We have, for instance, indicated in that memorandum that no economic development of the kind proposed by us would be feasible except on the basis of a central directing authority, and further that in the initial stages of the plan rigorous measures of State control would be required to prevent an inequitable distribution of the financial burdens involved in it. An enlargement of the

SECTION 36

positive as well as preventive functions of the State is essential to any large-scale economic planning. This is inherent in the idea of planning and its implications must be fully admitted.

36. *Planning and Democracy*

This, however, is not to concede that no society can undertake a comprehensive and integrated plan of economic development except by discarding the fundamental postulates of democratic government. There is no warrant in logic or history for such an assumption. If democracies can successfully plan and organize their resources for waging wars, it stands to reason that they can do so equally for fighting social evils such as poverty, disease and ignorance. Democracy rests on the belief that the freedom of the individual to give full expression to his personality is one of the supreme values of life and among its basic needs ; the State cannot demand a surrender of that freedom except for well-defined ends and except with the assent of the community freely expressed through constitutional channels and with opportunities for the free functioning of parties holding divergent views. If a planned economy involves, as it necessarily must, the restriction of individual freedom in varying degrees, such restriction under a democratic government will be of limited duration and confined to specific purposes. Whereas in a totalitarian society the individual is merged in the State and belongs to it, having no rights except those which the State chooses to confer, in a democracy the State belongs to the people and is but a means of securing the fulfilment of the individual's rights, and therefore any restriction which it imposes on his freedom must be justified by that test. We believe that planning is not inconsistent with a democratic organization of society. On the contrary, we consider

SECTION 37

that its objects will be served more effectively if the controls inherent in it are voluntarily accepted by the community and only enforced with its consent.

37. Basic Principles

In discussing different types of economic organization from the point of view of planning it is perhaps worth while pointing out that the distinction which is generally drawn between capitalism and socialism is somewhat overdone. The principle of *laissez faire*, which is regarded as the dominant note of capitalism, has during the last hundred years been so largely modified in the direction of State intervention in various spheres of economic activity that in many of its characteristic aspects capitalism has been transformed almost beyond recognition. Similarly, countries which in recent years set out to organize their economic life on orthodox socialist lines have found it necessary in several important respects to accept capitalistic ideas in their effort to evolve a workable form of society. As a result of these developments, the distinction between capitalism and socialism has lost much of its significance from a practical standpoint. In many respects there is now a large ground common to both and the gulf between the two is being steadily narrowed further as each shows signs of modifying itself in the direction of the other. In our view, no economic organization can function effectively or possess lasting qualities unless it accepts as its basis a judicious combination of the principles associated with each school of thought. These principles may be summed up as follows: first, that there should be sufficient scope for the play of individual initiative and enterprise ; secondly, that the interests of the community should be safeguarded by the institution of adequate sanctions against the abuse of individual freedom ; and thirdly, that the State should play a positive role in the direction of economic policy and the development of economic resources. It is from this angle that we approach the problem of determining the place of the State in a planned economy in India. We believe that capitalism, in so far as it affords scope for individual enterprise and the exercise of individual initiative, has a very important contribution to make to the economic development of India. We believe at the same time that unless the community is endowed with powers for restraining the activities of individuals seeking their own aggrandizement regardless of public welfare and for promoting the main objectives of economic progress, no plan of economic development will succeed in raising the general standard of living or promoting the common good. " The problem of this century is to find the most fruitful method of combining planning —the right kind and degree of planning—with freedom. Competition and central direction may, indeed, be so applied that they spend all their energies merely in frustrating each other. But if . . . they are sorted out and each applied by itself to the problems for which it is appropriate, there is no inherent reason to doubt that an economy based on both planning and free enterprise would be superior to either of the extremes." [1]

38. *Role of the State*

In dealing with the relation of the State to economic activity it is necessary to make a distinction between the role which the State may generally be expected to play in future when a planned economy has come into normal operation, and its part during the interim period when the plan is in process of being carried out. As the role to be assigned to the State in normal times is of more fundamental importance, we deal with it first.

[1] *The Economist*, May 13, 1944, p. 639.

SECTIONS 39, 40

39. *Methods of Intervention*

Coordination of general economic activity, management of currency and public finance, collection of statistical and other information, adoption of legislation to safeguard the interest of economically weak classes, are some of the more important functions which have now been universally recognized as legitimate duties of the State in the economic sphere. We have, however, to deal here with another and a more specific set of functions which are being advocated by important sections of enlightened opinion both in this country and outside. These functions centre round (i) ownership, (ii) control and (iii) management of economic enterprises. A widening of the economic functions of the State in these directions is advocated on the ground that unrestricted private enterprise under the capitalistic system of production has not served the interests of consumers and of the community generally as satisfactorily as it should have. We have therefore to determine the nature and scope of State activity in terms of these three factors in the economy which we visualize.

40. *Control More Important*

Of the three factors mentioned above, from the point of view of maximum social welfare State control appears to be more important than ownership or management. Mobilization of all the available means of production and their direction towards socially desirable ends is essential for achieving the maximum amount of social welfare. Over a wide field it is not necessary for the State to secure ownership or management of economic activity for this purpose. Well-directed and effective State control should be fully adequate. State control of this character is, however, bound to put important limitations on the freedom of private enterprise as it

SECTION 41

is understood at present. Legal ownership would lose some of the essential attributes which are attached to it at present, especially in respect of the use and disposal of economic resources. Monopolies, for example, would not be allowed to limit their output with a view to increasing their profits by raising prices. Scarce natural resources would not be allowed to be exploited without consideration for the future requirements of the country. The rights attaching to private property would naturally be greatly circumscribed. In the light of these considerations we indicate below in general terms the sectors of economic activity which should be owned, controlled and managed by the State.

41. *State Ownership*

State ownership is necessarily involved in all cases where the State finances an enterprise which is important to public welfare or security. State ownership will also arise where in the public interest it is necessary for the State to control an industry, but the circumstances of the industry are such that control is ineffective unless it is based on State ownership. As regards the former class, industries falling within this category may be either entirely new industries or industries new to particular areas, and in both cases may require financial assistance from the State in the initial stages. If later on private finance is prepared to take over these industries, State ownership may be replaced by private ownership, but it is essential in the public interest that the State should retain effective control over them. In the other group of industries in which State ownership exists because it is a necessary means of enforcing State control, ownership by the State will be a more or less permanent feature. In these cases where ordinary methods of State control have to be supplemented by State ownership, it will be

SECTIONS 42, 43

necessary as a rule to place management also in the hands of the State. The manufacture of materials exclusively required for war purposes and the organization of vital communications such as posts and telegraphs are illustrations of this class of industries.

42. *State Control*

Enterprises owned wholly or partially by the State, public utilities, basic industries, monopolies, industries using or producing scarce natural resources and industries receiving State aid should normally be subject to State control. The nature of the control to be exercised will vary from industry to industry and from unit to unit in the same industry according to the specific requirements of each case. The institution of adequate controls which would achieve the object in view without unduly hampering the initiative of the management and the proper enforcement of such controls will present difficult problems. The following are illustrations of the form which control may assume : fixation of prices, limitation of dividends, prescription of conditions of work and wages for labour, nomination of government directors on the board of management, licensing and " efficiency auditing "—a development of cost accounting which will be the watch-dog of public interest rather than of financial interests in the limited sense.

43. *State Management*

Where an enterprise is owned by the State, there is a *prima facie* case for its management by the State. But it does not invariably follow that all enterprises owned by the State should also be managed by it. There are three alternative methods of management open in such cases —by the State, by private enterprise and by *ad hoc* public corporations. To some extent the deciding factor, which determines which of these alternative methods should be adopted in any particular case, is how far the necessary personnel will be forthcoming under each method. But since State ownership generally arises because the industries concerned are of public importance, considerations of efficient management alone cannot be allowed to settle the question. It is necessary to take into account also the wider and more fundamental question of the extent to which public welfare and security will be safeguarded and promoted under each system. It is not possible to lay down a general rule as regards this aspect of the question and each case must be decided on its merits. In the ultimate decision the governing issue will be whether State control is not sufficient to safeguard the public interest, but in addition to it State management should also be provided.

44. *Compromise Formula*

We have set out some of the leading considerations by which the question whether an industry should be left to private enterprise or should be owned and managed by the State is to be determined. The application of these considerations in particular cases is bound to present difficulties and there will necessarily be a wide field in which decision will involve a nice balancing of various factors. It will probably be found in these cases that the arrangement which will best meet the situation is a compromise between the two principles so that while some units of the industry are owned and managed by the State, others are left to private enterprise. Where considerations of efficiency on the one hand, or public welfare on the other, would not permit of a clear-cut decision, it is in the direction of a compromise on these lines between State and private enterprise that a practical

SECTION 45

solution may be sought. Public utilities of a monopolistic character and industries for the products of which the government is the principal customer would among others be the main industries which would fall within this category. Experience of working the same industry partly by State and partly by private enterprise will incidentally afford valuable guidance in shaping public policy in the matter. Moreover, the simultaneous operation of both systems in the same industry will provide a useful incentive and corrective to each system, resulting in all probability in a maximum contribution to the well-being of the community by the industry as a whole. " There is no need to socialise at once all the forms of production it may prove desirable to socialise some time : nor is there any reason why a form of production, socialised at first, should not be handed back, under proper safeguards, to private enterprise if socialisation does not yield good results. Within a single branch of production there may be some parts which it is desirable to socialise, and others which are best left under private ownership and control. The less rigidly the line is drawn, the more room will there be both for diverse experiment and for suiting different types of men and women with jobs in which they have a decent chance of being happy." [1]

45. *Control During Planning Period*

The general propositions regarding State activity in the economic sphere which we have enunciated above will hold good even during the planning period. But during this period in addition to the controls embodied in these propositions the State will have to adopt a number of other controls of a temporary character. Without them a planned economic development will be

[1] G. D. H. Cole, *Great Britain in the Post-War World*, p. 81.

hardly possible. To a large extent the controls to be instituted during the planning period would be similar to those which are in force at present under war conditions and to which the country has become more or less accustomed ; but they will be better coordinated and more systematically administered.

46. *Controls Illustrated*

These controls will operate mainly in the following spheres :
- (1) production,
- (2) distribution,
- (3) consumption,
- (4) investment,
- (5) foreign trade and exchange, and
- (6) wages and working conditions.

Control of production will aim at a proper allocation of resources so as to secure better regional distribution of economic enterprises and to reach the targets set for the different branches of industry. The control will operate chiefly through a system of licences for establishing new units and for extending existing ones. Distribution will be controlled primarily with the object of determining priorities for the release of raw materials, semi-finished materials and capital goods. In the early stages of planning, control will also include rationing and distribution of consumers' goods. The objectives to be kept in view in controlling consumption will be to enforce fair selling prices for essential goods and for goods manufactured by industries receiving State assistance and also to prevent inflation. As regards investment, control will imply that new capital issues should be approved by the State so as to secure a proper distribution of available resources, to prevent inflation, to provide for the orderly development

SECTION 47

of new enterprises, and generally to maintain and promote the interests of Indian nationals. Trade and exchange will be subjected to control to such extent as may be required for conserving foreign exchange and for protecting Indian industries. The control of wages and working conditions will aim at ensuring not merely fair conditions for labour, but also efficiency of management, particularly in public utility concerns and protected industries.

47. *National Government*

The wide powers of direction and control with which the State would be invested for the successful execution of the plan would be exercised through a national government responsible to the people. "The strength of State Authority, not in the physical sense, but in the moral sense of a genuine submission on the part of the great majority of the population, is an important factor in the success of planning."[1] To achieve this moral strength and to ensure harmonious and uninterrupted working during the planning period, the personnel of government should be adequately representative of every considerable body of political thought and sentiment in the country. It is also necessary that while sufficient powers of coordination are vested in the central government, the administration of economic policy should be delegated to provincial and local governments on a basis of wide decentralization. The various controls, both permanent and temporary, which have been indicated will not be effective unless the State has at its disposal a specialized agency possessing the necessary knowledge and experience for handling economic matters. For this purpose a new service—an economic civil service—should be established in the country, composed of persons with

[1] F. Zweig, *The Planning of Free Societies*, p. 255.

SECTION 48

the special education, training and experience appropriate to the economic functions of the State.

48. *Future Economic Organization*

The general shape of the economic organization which will emerge if our proposals are carried out is not unlike the type of society which Professor Pigou foreshadows in his book *Socialism versus Capitalism*. We quote the following passage from it which, *mutatis mutandis*, is applicable to the society we have in view and the role which the State will play in it : " If, then, it were in the writer's power to direct his country's destiny, he would accept, for the time being, the general structure of capitalism ; but he would modify it gradually. He would use the weapon of graduated death duties and graduated income tax, not merely as instruments of revenue, but with the deliberate purpose of diminishing the glaring inequalities of fortune and opportunity which deface our present civilisation. He would take a leaf from the book of Soviet Russia and remember that the most important investment of all is investment in the health, intelligence and character of the people. To advocate ' economy ' in this field would, under his government, be a criminal offence. All industries affected with a public interest, or capable of wielding monopoly power, he would subject at least to public supervision and control. Some of them, certainly the manufacture of armaments, probably the coal industry, possibly the railways, he would nationalise, not, of course, on the pattern of the Post Office, but through public boards or commissions. The Bank of England he would make in name—what it is already in effect—a public institution ; with instructions to use its power to mitigate, so far as may be, violent fluctuations in industry and employment. If all went well, further steps towards nationalisation of

SECTION 48

important industries would be taken by degrees. In controlling and developing these nationalised industries, the central government would inevitably need to ' plan ' an appropriate allocation for a large part of the country's annual investment in new capital. When these things had been accomplished, the writer would consider his period of office at an end, and would surrender the reins of government. In his political testament he would recommend his successor also to follow the path of gradualness—to mould and transform, not violently to uproot ; but he would add, in large capitals, a final sentence, that gradualness implies action, and is not a polite name for standing still."

INDEX TO PART ONE

	Page		Page
Agricultural Capital	40	Finance, How raised	56
,, Character	30	,, Problem of	11
,, Development	35	,, Sources of	55
,, Reforms	36	,, Subservient	56
Aim of Memorandum	7	Five-Year Plans, Three	59
,, Plan	28	Foreign Loans	53
Basic Industries and Consumption Ratio	61	Health, Present State	16
Basic Industries, Priority for	58	,, Standard, Minimum	18
,, ,, Progress of	61	,, see also Public Health	
		Hospitals, General	20
		Housing, Cost of	15
Capital Ratio	34	,, Cost of Additional	49
,, Required	50	,, Needs	15
Clothing, Cost of	14	,, Standard of	16
,, Needs	13		
Communications	41	Imperfections, Early	58
Consumer, Consideration for	60	Income below Minimum	26
Consumer's Choice	33	,, per capita, Increase	28
Consumers' Needs	58	Indebtedness, Rural	37
Consumption Goods Industries	33	Industrial Development	9
Co-operation of People	44	Industries, Basic	31
Cost of Living, Minimum	25	,, Capital for	34
Costs of Plan, Classified	50	,, Classified	31
"Created Money"	54	Irrigation	38
Diet, Balanced	13	Literacy, Adult	24
Difficulties	10	Maternity Hospitals	20
Dispensaries, Cost of	19	Medical Facilities, Lack of	18
,, Village	19	Minimum Standard, Defined	12
Economy, Balanced	29	National Income, Low	27
Education, Adult	45	Nourishment, Cost of	13
,, Minimum Needs	22	Objective of Plan	9
,, Primary, Costs	22	Output, Ways of Increasing	38
,, Programme	45		
,, Secondary	46	Planning Organisation	8
,, Technical	48	Political Assumptions	8
,, University	48	Population, Increase of	49
		Power, Production	32
Farms, Model	39	Preventive Measures, Inadequate	17
Finance, External and Internal	51		

APPENDICES

INDEX

	Page		Page
Public Health, Cost of	22	Small Industries, Scope for	33
,, ,, Expenditure	48	Soil Erosion	37
,, ,, Needs of	17	Specialised Treatment	21
		Stages, Determination of	56
Railways	41	Sterling Securities	52
Resources, Adequacy of	57		
Roads,	42	Trade, Balance of	53
,, Reconstruction of	43	Transport	41
		,, Cost of	43
Sanitation	18		
Savings Abroad	54	Water Supply	18
,, in India	54	Wealth, Hoarded	52
Shipping	43	Yield, Agricultural	38

INDEX TO PART TWO

Agriculture, Unemployment in, 73
Approach, Line of, 65

Capitalism and Socialism, 92
Cooperative Societies, 79
Cost of Living, Reduction of, 84

Democracy, Planning and, 91
Distribution and Production, 65, 66
—, Equitable, 67

Economic Development, Regional Distribution, 87
— Organization, Basic Principles, 92
— —, Choice of, 89
— —, Future, 101
— Structure, Foundations of, 66
Efficiency, Increase of, 76
Employment, Full, 71
—, Industrial, 72
Equalitarianism, Undesirable, 69

Government, National, 100

Income, Disparities, 67, 68, 69
— Distribution, at End of Plan, 83
—, Increased, Measures for securing, 71
Inequalities, Prevention of, 86
Insurance, Social, 86

Keynes, Lord, 69

Land Revenue, 82
— Tenure, Systems of, 80-82

Mahalwari System, 80-82
Means of Production, Ownership of, 68

Minimum Standard, Measures to secure, 70

Occupational Distribution, 73, 74

Pigou, Prof., quoted, 101
Prices, Agricultural, 78
Production and Distribution, 65, 66

Relief Fund, National, 85
Rewards, Determination of, 70
Ryotwari System, 80-82

Social Security, 86
— Services, Free, 84
Socialism and Capitalism, 92
State and Private Enterprise, Balance between, 97
— Control, Field for, 96
— —, Importance of, 94
— Controls, illustrated, 99
— —, in Planning Period, 98
—, Economic Functions, 94
— Intervention, essential to Planning, 90
— Management, 96
— Ownership, 95
—, Role of, 93
States, Development of, 87

Taxation, 86
—, Conditions for, 89

Unemployment, Seasonal, in Agriculture, 73
—, Temporary, 75

Utilities, Essential, 85

Wage, Minimum, 77
Wages, Urban and Rural, 76

Zamindari System, 80-82

ACKNOWLEDGEMENTS

We would like to express our profound gratitude to all the contributors to this volume. We are grateful to Kapish Mehra, Managing Director, Rupa Publications, for readily recognizing the importance of this volume and arranging its early publication. Finally, we wish to record our appreciation for and convey our gratitude to Yamini Chowdhury, Senior Commissioning Editor, for her professionalism and the care with which she helped us put this volume together.

INDEX

Acharya, Shankar, 144
Adult education, 8, 35, 132, 162
Adult literacy, xvi, 162, 208, 210, 220
Adult mass literacy, 167
Advisory Planning Board, 22, 40
Agarwal, Narayan, 76, 120
Agrarian programme, 22
Agricultural development, 48, 161
Agricultural reorganization, 7
Agricultural spending, 36
Ahmedabad Education Society, 24
Akhil Bharatiya Hindu Mahasabha, 53–54
All India Congress Committee (AICC), 154
Ambani, Dhirubhai, 192
Amery, L.S., 39
Amery, Leo, 64

Andhra Valley Power Supply Company, xii, 72
Asian Miracle, 174
Asian Tigers, 174, 205
Associated Cement Companies, xii, 73
Associated Chambers of Commerce & Industry of India (Assocham), xv, 196

Backwardness Model, 200
Bajaj, Rahul, 144
Balance of payments crisis, 143, 218
Balance of Trade, 163, 171
Baru, Sanjaya, vii, xvi, 124, 137–38, 156
Basic industries, importance of, 7
Bengal famine, xi, 3, 113, 171
Benthall, Edward Charles, 80
Beveridge Plan, 175
Bharatiya Jana Sangh, 54–55

Bharatiya Janata Party (BJP), 195
Bhatnagar, Shanti Swaroop, 81
Bihar famine, 201, 210
Birla scheme, 39
Birla, B.M., 138
Birla, G.D. , vii, viii, 2, 12, 23, 25, 29, 41, 44, 55, 76, 97–98, 100, 140, 187, 220
Bolsheviks, 125
Bombay Club, 144, 194
Bose, Subhash Chandra, 125, 175
Bretton Woods Conference, 24, 53
Brown, Michael, 66

Capital distribution, 13
Capital expenditure, 8, 103, 163–64
Capital-intensive growth, 185
Capitalism, 48–50, 98, 107, 118, 120, 136–37, 142, 155, 175–76, 178, 181, 199, 214, 217, 219
Capital-labour ratio, 203, 210
Capital-output ratio, 102
Central Statistical Organization (CSO), 85, 91
Chaebols, xv
Chandavarkar, V.N., 97
Change Management, 166–68
Chhibber, Ajay, xv

Churchill, Winston, 80, 86
Clark, Colin, 176
Communist Party of India (CPI), xiv, 47–51, 53, 183–84
Community development, 36
Companies Act, 172
Compromise formula, 159
Confederation of Indian Industry (CII), xv, 144–45, 196
Constitutional silence, 116
Consumer goods, 40, 43, 102, 174, 202–4, 206–7, 210, 212, 216
Consumption-oriented industries, 37
Cooperative farming, 7, 17, 161, 186–87, 203
Corporate Social Responsibility (CSR), 172
Cost-sharing, 83
Cottage Industries Corporation (CIC), 91
Council for Scientific and Industrial Research (CSIR), 65, 81
Crony capitalism, 141–42
Cropping pattern, 203
Cultural opportunities, 6

Dalal, Ardeshir, vii, xii, 2, 15, 23, 3, 64–65, 67–68, 70–73, 76, 81, 97

INDEX

Decentralization, 214
Defence of India Act, 110
Deficit financing, 104, 157, 164
De-industrialization, 202
Delhi Cloth Mills (DCM), 23
Democratic socialism, 154
Desai, Morarji, 44, 189
Deshmukh, C.D., 186
The Discovery of India, 181
Divide-and-conquer elements, 75
Double cropping, 211
Dutt, R.C., 198

Ease of doing business, 195
Ease of living, 129
East Asian economies, rise of, 132
Eastern Economist, 44
Economic development, ix, xvii, 1, 4, 13–14, 16–18, 22, 25, 28, 42–43, 48, 102, 104, 106–7, 116, 122, 124, 129, 135–36, 138, 148–49, 151–52, 160, 202, 208–9
Economic expansion, 18
Economic freedom, 54–55, 58, 117
Economic growth, 37, 128–29, 146, 152, 193, 199, 203
Economic imperialism, 158
Economic indicators, 129, 218
Economic Programme Committee, 28, 59
Economic reconstruction, 16–17, 83
Economic reforms and liberalization of 1991, 40, 142, 205
Economic regeneration, 177
Economic theory, 151
Economic transformation, 16–18
Economic unity, 13, 130
The Economist, 78
Egalitarian industrial, 198
Electricity Act, 219
Enjoyment of life, 6, 128
Ewing, Ann, 68
Export-led growth, 204–6
External loan, 9

Fabian socialism, 153–54
Family planning, 166
Famine Relief Fund, 113
Farming, 170
Federation of Indian Chambers of Commerce and Industry (FICCI), xiii, xv, 3, 20, 25, 41, 56, 59, 80, 84–85, 89, 117, 144–45, 151, 196
Feldman model, 202, 216
Financial crisis, 219
Financing, 103–4
Five Year Plan, x, xi, 20–21, 30–38, 40–42, 44–47,

50–51, 54, 59–60, 65, 91, 101, 122, 131, 142–43, 172, 184–85, 187–88, 208, 216
Food Corporation of India (FCI), 210
Foreign Direct Investment (FDI), 39, 194, 213
Foreign exchange, 9, 109, 186, 190, 193
Foreign Exchange Regulation Act (FERA), 191
Forum of Free Enterprise, 54, 58
Free Market, 134, 175
Free social services, 115, 162
Fundamental Rights and Economic Policy, 154

Gandhi, Indira, xv, 122, 188–92, 201
Gandhi, Mahatma, viii, 26, 52, 64, 80, 138, 154, 171, 183, 211
Gandhi, Rajiv, 192–93
Gandhian Plan, 76, 121, 127, 131, 173
Gandhian socialism, 155, 171, 192
Garibi Hatao programme, 201
GDP growth, 192, 218, 220
Gerschenkron, Alexander, 200
Ghosh, Ajoy, 183
Ghosh, Atulya, 189

Goal-setting and achievement, 150
Goenka, Badridas, 89
Goods and Services Tax (GST), 130
Gosplan committee, 202
Goswami, Omkar, xiii, 94, 116
Government of India Act, 86
Great depression, 32, 95, 107, 164, 175, 199
Green revolution, 174, 189, 201, 210
Guided capitalism, 199

Harrod-Domar model, 176
Hindu growth rate, 218
Hindu Mahasabha, 54, 58
Hirachand, Walchand, 85, 98
Hoarded wealth, 169–70
Holistic framework approach, 170
Human development approach, 206–9
Human Development Index (HDI), 207

Imperial Bank, 188
Import tariffs, 205
Import-substituting countries, 51
Import-substitution, 204–6
Income inequalities, 158

INDEX

Indian Chamber of Commerce (ICC), 25
Indian Civil Service (ICS), 66–71
Indian Institute of Technology (IIT), 65
Indian National Congress (INC or the Congress), xi, 22, 94, 125, 138–39
Indianization programme, 73
Indraprastha College for Women, 24
Industrial capitalism, 48
Industrial Credit and Investment Corporation of India, 119
Industrial development, 86, 89, 102, 125–26, 160, 163, 181
Industrial Development Bank of India, 119
Industrial Finance Corporation of India, 119
Industrial investment, 37
Industrial Policy Resolution, 38, 50–51, 55, 65, 85, 87–88, 91, 159, 185, 212, 220
Industrial Revolution, 89, 178
Industrialization, 6, 17, 26–27, 29, 39, 42, 44, 89, 101–2, 116, 119, 122, 127, 136, 153–55, 177, 180, 201–3, 204, 208, 213
Industries (Development and Regulation) Act, 122
Inequality, 209–12
Inflation, 190–91
Inflationary financing, 213
Inflationary phase, 12
Inflationary situation, 10
Input-output analysis, 177
Intellectual debt, xi, 21
Internal financing, 163–64
International Monetary Fund (IMF), 75, 143, 192–93
Investment Corporation of India, 24
Investment strategies, 36
IT revolution, 202

J.R.D. Tata, vii, viii, xii, 2, 23, 46, 72, 76, 100, 118, 121, 140, 142, 197, 207, 220
Jana Sangh, 54, 58
Jehangir, Cowasji, 97
JN Tata Endowment, 66
Johnson, Lyndon, 189

Keynes's General Theory, 176
Keynesian style temporary work programmes, 211
Kosambi, D.D., 181
Krishna, V.V., 81
Krishnamachari, T.T., 186
Kuznets, Simon, 176

Lady Shri Ram College, 24

Lalbhai, Kasturbhai, vii, viii, 2, 24, 76
Land reform, 40
Left democratic movement, 49
Leontief, Wasily, 150, 177
Licence-Permit-Control Raj, xvi, 140, 142, 214, 217
Life Insurance Corporation, 188
Living standards, 5
Lokanathan, P.S., vii, x, 1, 151

Macroeconomic implications, 43–44
Mahalanobis strategy, 44, 185
Mahalanobis, P.C., 101
Mahalanobis–Feldman model, 42, 216
Mahatma Gandhi National Rural Employment Guarantee Scheme (MGNREGS), 211
Mahbub-ul-Haq, 207
Managerial and workplace reforms, 23
Marshall Plan, 199
Masani, Minoo, 139–40, 187
Mass education, 8
Maternity leave, 114
Mathai, John, vii, xii, 2, 24, 29, 76, 119, 121
Mehta, Chunilal, 97
Meiji restoration, 178

Minimum living wages, 48
Minimum standard of living, 161, 173
Mixed economy, 134–37
Mixed farming, 211
Modi, Narendra, 129, 147, 175
Mody, Homi, 59, 97
Monetary policy, responsible, 164
Monopolies and Restrictive Trade Practices (MRTP), 219
Montagu Chelmsford reforms, 69
Muslim League, 52
Myint, Hla, 205

Nadar, Kamaraj, 189
Naoroji, Dadabhai, 138, 176, 198
Narayan, Jayaprakash, 127, 187, 191
National Bourgeoisie, xiv, 49, 180–92
National Democratic Alliance (NDA), 194–95, 204
National income, 5–6, 31, 45, 99, 101, 111, 128–29, 152, 164, 176–77
National liberation, 125
National Planning Committee (NPC), 13, 22, 49, 52, 120–21, 125–26, 154, 175, 177, 184

INDEX

National Relief Fund, 113
Nationalism, 79, 87, 124, 180
Nehru era, 41, 46, 49–50, 54, 58, 120
Nehru, Jawaharlal, xiv, 22, 90, 94, 96, 125, 139, 175, 220
Nehruvian Socialism, 152, 154–55, 171, 219
Nehruvian vision of industry-led development, 131
Non-Alignment Movement (NAM), 51
Non-Performing Assets (NPAs), 195

Pant, G.B., 59
Parties of the Right, 53–55
Partition refugees, 184
Patel, Vallabhbhai, 96, 116
Patil, S.K., 189
The People's Plan, 121
Pigou, A.C., 132
Piramal, Gita, xii
Planning Commission, xi, xii, 20–21, 44, 53, 131, 155, 173–74, 184
Populist economic measures, 25
Post-war reconstruction, xii, 3, 15, 18, 29, 65, 79
Poverty and Un-British Rule in India, 138
Power subsidies, 112

Prasad, Rajendra, 96, 116, 138
Prebisch, Raúl, 204
Prebisch-Singer dependency theory, 204
Price control, 12, 199, 201
Princely States, 212
Principal objectives, 4, 152
Private firms, nationalization of, 215
Progressive tax policy, 127
Public enterprises, privatization of, 136
Public policy, x, xiii, 125, 134, 137, 139, 166, 168
Public-Private-Partnership (PPP) models, 172
Purchasing power, 10, 43, 104, 158

Quit India Movement, 26–28, 74, 99, 120, 171

Radical ideas, 112–15
Radical reform of land-tenures, 17
Raisman, Jeremy, 3, 20
Raj Krishna, 217–18
Raj, K.N., 184
Rajagopalachari, C., 96, 139, 187
Ranadive line, 183
Rao, P.V. Narasimha, 136–37, 142

Rao, V.K.R.V., 31, 60, 155, 176
Rao-Singh liberalization, 193
Reconstruction Committees, 82, 84
Recurring expenditure, 8, 163
Reserve Bank of India (RBI), 24, 42, 104, 163
Resources mobilization, 9
Revenue settlements, 130
Right wingers, 96
Roy, M.N., 76, 121, 127, 173
Rupee depreciation, 181
Ryotwari, 48, 130

Saklatwala, Nowroji, xii, 72
Sanyal, Amal, xi, 19, 60, 76, 119
Sarkar, Sumit K., 76
Sarvodaya Plan, 127
Saving rate, 9–10
Schism, 118
Schoettli, Jivanta, 90
Schumpeter, Joseph, 175
Sectoral growth, 32
Sector-wise capital outlay, 33
Sen, Amartya, 128, 207
Sequencing, 105
Serious-minded industrialists, 56
Setalvad, Chimanlal, 97
Seton, Marie, 185
Shah, K.T., 22
Shastri, Lal Bahadur, 188

Shri Ram College of Commerce, 24
Shri Ram Industrial Group, 23
Shri Ram Institute for Industrial Research, 24
Shri Ram, Lala, vii, 23, 26, 117
Shroff, A.D., vii, 2, 53–54, 76
Shroff, D., 24
Singer, Hans, 204
Singh, Manmohan, 21, 46
Singhania, Padampat, 57, 85
Social sectors, 133
Social security, 48, 114, 162–63
Socialism, xiv, 50, 95–100, 107, 116, 118, 134, 140, 152–56, 175–76, 193, 214
Socialistic pattern of society, 122, 139
Soviet growth model, 202, 216
Special community, 89
Spinning revolution, 178
Standard of living, 4, 17, 31, 48, 100–1, 152, 169
State activism, 175
State Bank, 188
State capitalism, 126–37, 139–41
State control, xv, 107–8, 115, 136, 156, 158, 201, 212, 214–15, 218–21

INDEX

State intervention, 107–8, 110, 120, 212
State-owned enterprises, 209, 215, 217, 220
State ownership, 111, 135, 136, 157–58, 201, 212, 215
State planning and state control, 212–15
Statism policy, 54
Stock market scam, 193
Strategic industries, 218
Stress on industrialization, 6
Structural transformation of the economy, 32
Sugar Syndicate, 138
Suit boot ki Sarkar, 175
Swacch Bharat campaign, 166
Swatantra Party, 54, 58, 139–40, 187, 190–91

Taj Mahal Hotel, xii, 73
Target per capita income, 31
Tariff Board, 85
Tata Central Archives (TCA), 67
Tata Chemicals, xii, 73
Tata Oil Mills, xii, 73
Tata, Dorab, xii, 67, 72

Taxation policy, 114
Thakurdas, P., vii, viii, 2, 20, 25–26, 76, 97 98, 119
Theory of Backwardness, 200
Theory of economic growth, 200

Unemployment, 209–12
Unemployment insurance schemes, 162
Unfair Trade Practices Act, 87
United Nation's General Assembly (UNGA), 53
United Nations (UN) vii, 75, 204
Universal literacy, 134, 208

Wardha session, 22
Wavell, Lord, 3, 19, 39
Western pessimism, 184
World Bank, 76, 143, 189, 195
World War I, 69
World War II, xi, 73, 110, 149, 166, 180, 186, 197, 199

Zaibatsu, xv
Zamindari, 48, 130, 162, 211